DEMOCRACY AGAINST THE STATE

DEMOCRACY AGAINST THE STATE

Marx and the Machiavellian Moment

MIGUEL ABENSOUR

Translated by Max Blechman and Martin Breaugh

polity

Polity Press
65 Bridge Street
Cambridge CB2 1UR, UK

Polity Press
350 Main Street
Malden, MA 02148, USA

ISBN-13 978-0-7456-5009-8 (hardback)
ISBN-13 978-0-7456-5010-4 (paperback)

A catalogue record for this book is available from the British Library.

Typeset in 10.5 on 12 pt Sabon
by Servis Filmsetting Ltd, Stockport, Cheshire

For further information on Polity, visit our website: www.politybooks.com

Ouvrage publié avec le concours du Ministère français de la Culture - Centre national du livre

Published with the assistance of the French Ministry of Culture - National Centre for the Book

CONTENTS

TRANSLATOR'S INTRODUCTION "TO THINK EMANCIPATION OTHERWISE"

In a 1976 postscript to his book on William Morris, E. P. Thompson candidly expressed his admiration for the critical acumen of Miguel Abensour, whom he credited for shaking Marxists out of their dogmatic slumber.[1] Thompson was here reporting on Abensour's "remarkable study" on utopian thought in the communist and socialist traditions, and specifically on his break with the self-confirming theses proposed by Marxists in their reception of William Morris's socialist writings.[2] By refusing to explain Morris's thought through the categories of Marxist theory, by emphasizing instead the deliberately open and anti-authoritarian form of Morris's utopian writing, Abensour succeeded in taking the increasingly rhetorical question of how Marxists should criticize Morris over to the more acute question of how Marxism should criticize itself.[3] At stake, then, was not the local issue of the Marxist domestication of Morris. Writing against the gamut of Marxist positivism that reached a pitch with Althusser, Abensour offered a critical diagnosis of the scientific pretensions of Marxism. As with Althusser, the order of the day was to read Marx anew. But rather than place Marx's revolutionary "science" in a position of rupture with the humanist and utopian traditions, Abensour detailed Marx's communism and his critique of utopian socialism from within a multifaceted strain of *utopian self-criticism*. In Abensour's view, Marx did not stand over utopian socialism in judgment as its Owl of Minerva. Rather, Marx intervened in a diverse revolutionary movement that at once included and transcended him. From this perspective, Marx's perspicacious criticisms of utopian socialism helped shape a "new utopian spirit" that sought to resist the conversion of utopia from negativity to positivity – that is, the turn from the indetermination and the multiplication of the fields of revolutionary struggle to the adventitious blueprints of political sectarianism. Far from participating in the genesis of authoritarian regimes, the "new utopian spirit" thus functioned as a salubrious reminder of the dangers involved in rendering emancipation in the terms of a coercively unified knowledge and power. As Abensour later pointed out in an essay on democracy and utopia, the stars of this constellation arguably never ceased to shine in twentieth-century reconfigurations of utopian thought: Pierre Leroux, William Morris, and Gustav Landauer find their vindication in the work of Ernst Bloch, Walter Benjamin, Martin Buber, and Emmanuel Levinas.[4]

An effort to follow the movement of Marx's thought against the current of political orthodoxy equally structures *Democracy Against the State*. As the reader may readily ascertain, a fresh look at Marx here again coheres with a broader, if somewhat occulted, tendency of thought. Of course, the object and the finality of criticism here differs, since Abensour considers Marx's political writings, in particular the 1843 *Critique of Hegel's Philosophy of Right*, as activating a "Machiavellian moment" that reappears in modern theory (Maurice Merleau-Ponty, Claude Lefort, Hannah Arendt). Nonetheless, a common perspective and cluster of concerns guide Abensour's writing, so that different objects of inquiry – from Marx's "true democracy" to Claude Lefort's "savage democracy" – operate as heuristic devices for bringing a heterodox modality of political questioning back into the fray. Just as Abensour's formulation of the "new utopian spirit" placed revolutionary utopianism at equal distance from Marxism and the anti-Marxist platitudes of the *nouveaux philosophes*, a certain conception of democracy is here set against the either/or that would have us choose between Marxist and liberal ideologies. Abensour consistently reveals an excess of politics over political reality, a utopian "more" that makes politics synonymous with permanent critique. It is as though, far from being done with the question of emancipation, as the sycophants of the "end of an illusion" would have it, the debacle of historical Marxism, no less than the contemporary consensus that kneads all thought and practice into the mold of liberal "democracy," were to have the consequence of pushing the most far-reaching theses of Marx's political thinking to the fore. The point, as such, is not to engage on the terrain of the history of ideas in order to recover a "true Marx" hitherto misrepresented, misinterpreted, or ignored. While a revaluation of Marx's political thought is demanded by *Democracy Against the State*, Abensour's hypothesis is that we have arrived at a historical and theoretical juncture – as it were, a new figure of the "Machiavellian moment" – that allows us to read Marx as critically addressing our present political predicament.

Can we really think the Machiavellian and the utopian together? This may be judged an at best paradoxical endeavor. We need only recall *The Prince*, Chapter XV: "anyone who abandons what is for what should be pursues his downfall." But neither should we lose sight of the "constitutive principle" that upheld Abensour's new utopian spirit: "the critical resumption of and the recourse to heresy against the legacy and the structure of an orthodoxy."[5] Killing two birds with one stone, Abensour's reference to Machiavelli signals "recourse to heresy against the legacy "of both democracy and Marx. A normative critique of the State – for Marx, the State's disappearance is the fulfillment of democracy – is brought face-to-face with a permanent struggle that defines the specificity of the political realm in its finitude. The anti-politics of the "democratic State" (consensual liberalism) and the meta-politics of "fulfilled sociality" (the Communist and totalitarian mystification that fashions society beyond division) are in this way equally unsettled. The tensions implicit in this double-edged approach to political institution build the inner logic and fuel the movement of *Democracy Against the State*. The contentious wedlock of Abensour's "Marx-Machiavelli device" is meant to bring us to the heart of the question of politics proper, right to the sphinx-like enigma called "true democracy."[6]

At bottom, the "Machiavellian moment" in Marx represents a twofold movement: it has the positive function of designating a return to an Aristotelian conception of the human being as *zoon politikon*, and it has the negative function of criticizing the practical and theoretical alienation of this political nature. Starting from the humanist rehabilitation of civic life, from the revaluing of the human being as a self-determining political actor and historical subject, Abensour reveals a dialectical relationship between Marx's early radical liberalism and the more revolutionary position attained in 1843 through the critique of Hegel's philosophy of right. In Marx's 1842 writings for the *Rheinische Zeitung* , the center of gravity of the State is found *within itself*, in that the concept of the political State is secularized in its independence from both the theological realm and the ideological encroachments of private property. Yet the logic of secularization and the autonomy of political affairs compel Marx to relocate the center of the State's gravitation *outside itself*, insofar as the political self-consciousness of the *demos* signals the self-consciousness of an instituting power that is already overcoming the sham mediations of the State. Marx's political thinking thus winds up radicalizing the republican model of the *zoon politikon*: emancipating political reason from the vestigial metaphysics of bourgeois reason also means freeing the citizen of politics from the mystification of the State. The problem, then, is to think the conditions of this new political temporality, that is, to think the very indetermination of the democratic institution of society as a self-conscious focal-point for politics.

It is common coin that Marx himself made very little explicit use of Machiavelli. At the risk of stating the obvious, Abensour's reference to a "Machiavellian moment" has more to do with Marx's attempt to rediscover, or to reconstruct, a politics derived from classical and republican sources than with a historical account of the role of Machiavelli in Marx's thought. The Machiavellian moment in fact functions as a test for Marx's thought in a very straightforward sense: at issue is defining the respects in which Marx's political writings constitute a legitimate figure of civic humanism, in roughly J. G. A. Pocock's determination of the term.[7] That is, at issue is the extent to which Marx thinks political affairs against theology, without then making the logic of a secular, public realm subordinate to some other meta-historical norm. In this way, Abensour reveals in Marx a thinking of politics distinct from any metaphysics of history, whether it take the cover of the antagonism of productive forces and the mode of production which leads ineluctably to the emancipation of the proletariat, or whether it be a neo-Hegelian "end of history" in the "sufficiently" rational actuality of laws and institutions in "democratic capitalism." By contrast, the wager of Marx's civic humanism would have the advantage of bringing politics back to the temporality proper of the public realm, to the demands that the institution of political equality in a *res publica* make here and now on human freedom.

Yet Abensour pushes the civic paradigm of political temporality by applying it to Marx, and notably to the worry that political "representation" itself betrays a tendency of political power to withdraw from its finitude – from the contingency of public accountability – and to claim for itself a legitimacy it in reality lacks. Or more exactly, Marx himself tests the classical republican paradigm as he gains a more thoroughgoing comprehension of its inner logic and requirements. In Abensour's lights, this inflection of the Machiavellian moment represents the great accomplishment of the *Critique of Hegel's Philosophy of Right*. The passage from the criticism of religion to the criticism of politics culminates in a theory of political institution that makes the self-criticism of emancipation an indelible principle of politics. The Machiavellian problem of a "real humanism" that takes its bearings from actual relations of force here resounds by anticipation with the question raised by Maurice Merleau-Ponty: "Does all power tend to 'autonomize itself,' and is this tendency an inevitable destiny in all human society?"[8]

This dual character of the Machiavellian moment – as that which tests Marx, and as that which is tested by Marx – is important to keep in view, for it guides Abensour's study from beginning to end; it directs the care with which Abensour brings out the nuances of Marx's thought, as well as the constancy with which he thinks Marx's early writings independently of extraneous interpretations (not least of which are Marx's own). It is no surprise, then, that Abensour's close reading of the 1843 Critique has only a polemical relationship to the evolutionist dimension of Marx's later writings, where the political realm is subordinated to the economic infrastructure of society and its laws of development. But above all, the dual character of the Machiavellian moment emphasizes the tensions proper to Marx's texts from 1842 to 1844. It is as though the Machiavellian moment in Marx were continually threatened by a facile resolution of the forces on which it depends, which in turn produced a renewed effort by Marx to clarify the stakes at hand. The criticism of religion must be wary of a religion of politics, just as the criticism of politics must be wary of a criticism that has ceased to be political. Indeed, it is precisely by means of this wariness that the dialectical movement of Marx's thought opens and reopens the most decisive inroads to a Machiavellian moment.

For Abensour, these centrifugal pathways never are blocked off by ideological closure. It is the Bolshevik and Stalinist retrogression, more than the predominance of the economic in Marx's writings, which hinder the most penetrating of Marx's readers from separating myth from reality and from gaining access to Marx's thinking of politics. Simmering in Marx's oeuvre, right up to his 1875 critique of the Gotha program, is a desire to move beyond what Hannah Arendt called "the theoretical foundations and practical ways for an escape from politics" – precisely, "the notion that men can lawfully and politically live together only when some are entitled to command and the others forced to obey."[9] It was the failure of the German socialists to render the spirit of command and obedience that provoked Marx to exclaim: "Free State – what is this? It is by no means the aim of the workers, who have got rid of the narrow mentality of humble subjects, to set the State free."[10] Marx, whose references to the people as the *demos* were historically deliberate and even polemical, was quite likely more concerned with the Athenian example of political freedom – "not to be subject [. . .] to the command of another *and* not to be in command oneself" – than Arendt ever imagined.[11]

Abensour, it could be said, writes in the wake of Maximilien Rubel, whose "unknown Marx" is wholly oriented toward "proving an absolute antinomy between the State and society."[12] Here too, however, the recognition of plasticity, according to which even the fixed distinctions of an absolute antinomy may be shown to break down in a complex and dynamic relation, distinguishes Abensour's thinking.[13] In Marx's critique of Hegel's concept of the State, Abensour warns, "the work of radical criticism is not to be confused with simple negation" (p. 48). It is the universal content of the Hegelian State that implies the State's abolition as "mere representation," or as the formal illusion of the popular determination of public affairs. And it is only as the practical and ongoing abolition of the illusions proper to the system of representation that the State "disappears" in true democracy. In terms that recall Hegel's account of conformity to law that moves beyond the merely "legal person" to self-determination – "it is now the law that exists for the sake of the self, not the self that exists for the sake of the law"[14] – Marx writes: "man does not exist because of the law but rather the law exists for the good of man. Democracy is *human existence*, while in the other political forms man has only a *legal* existence."[15] The critical inversion of the Hegelian State is its abolition as the "materialism of passive obedience," but also its realization/transcendence in the materialism of self-determining freedom, starting with "the drive for the most fully possible universal participation in legislative power."[16]

This *Aufhebung des Staates* should thus be distinguished from the so-called "withering away of the State" (Engels), and therefore also from the aim "to win the battle of democracy" as presented in *The Communist Manifesto*.[17] True democracy does not centralize political and economic power in the State to pave the way for a meta-politics in which "public power will lose its political character."[18] To the contrary, the so-called "battle of democracy," to the exact extent it is a battle of *true* democracy, is waged by a *demos* that recognizes in "political character" a dynamic for countering the resurgence of political bureaucracy and representation, for throwing a wrench in "the mechanism of an ossified and formalistic behavior, of fixed principles, conceptions, and traditions."[19] Or again, the battle of democracy is "won" precisely by a people forewarned that any dissolution of the political realm would be tantamount to annihilating the site for gaining and regaining a genuinely human existence. It is in this sense that the 1843 Critique may be considered a spearhead of civic humanism. Human beings are political animals whose specific nature is to find fulfillment in the *vita activa* and the *vivere civile*, in the creation of a space of radical political equality, and in the "drive" toward direct participation in political decisions and active engagement in the determination of common affairs. The Marxian dissolution of bourgeois civil society is not to be equated, in the 1843 Critique, with the dissolution of *politike koinonia* as such.

The key to Abensour's interpretation of this "human existence" – quite evidently, political being as the wellspring of *kommunistisches Wesen* – is suggested by one word: *reduction*. In true democracy, the abstract political State is dissolved because the State is politically reduced to what it is essentially: a constitutional objectification – nothing more, and it is important to emphasize, nothing less, than the political moment in the overall self-determination of the whole *demos*. If the people gain their identity by dissolving the heteronomy of bourgeois civil society, by reconstituting the political realm in the drive toward radically participatory legislative power, inversely the political form of democracy is permanently redirected to the material power of its institution. Far from being set in a position of "representing" the people, the State-form is at once placed on a par with all the other networks that make up the life of the people – and, in this specific sense, the institution of the State "disappears" within them. In a word, the redirection of the constitution to constituent power and the extension of this power to the other realms of the people's life are themselves made possible by the political moment.

This, precisely, is the paradoxical meaning of true democracy as the so-called unity of the formal and the material principle. Far from feigning the universality it in reality lacks and reproducing the State illusion, in true democracy the partial nature of the State institution, and the universal nature of the instituting activity on which it depends, have become equally self-conscious. By formally and practically restricting political power, the democratic constitution (the political realm as form) coheres with its originary subject (constituent power itself) and the democratic exigency materialized in the political realm becomes a springboard for universalizing constituent power in all the dimensions of a people's life.[20]

Randolph Bourne, an American civic humanist and a critic of the liberals' statist politics of reform in the late 1910s, once said that the direct challenge to the historic organs of political domination would come from a genuine experiment in democratic self-government, a revolution whose "liberating virus" would unfurl with the practical knowledge that it "worked *against the State*."[21] Bourne had in view the American experience, in which the progressive experiment in agrarian and proletarian democracy under the Articles of Confederation was cut short by a hostile force that "gripped the nation and imposed upon it a powerful form against which it was never to succeed in doing more than blindly struggle."[22] Babeuf made an analogous critique in the immediate wake of the French Revolution, and proclaimed against the newly powerful bourgeoisie: "those who govern only make revolution to continue governing. We want to make one that would ensure the people an everlasting happiness in a *true democracy*."[23] More trenchantly still, after the 1921 suppression of the refractory Kronstadt soviet by the Bolshevik army, Alexander Berkman wrote: "The political State, whatever its form, and constructive revolutionary effort are irreconcilable."[24]

Abensour, it seems, places "true democracy" under the banner of Machiavelli not only to emphasize a relationship with the civic humanist paradigm, but more specifically to measure Marx's own consciousness of this perseverance of social division at the heart of revolutionary praxis. In other words, democratic revolution would *internally* reproduce clashes like those between the senate and the plebs during the Roman republic. For Machiavelli, these clashes are indeed derivative of the two dispositions that set the stage of political liberty: that of the populace to be free and that of the governing classes to rule.[25] Does Marx succeed in thinking democracy as the elaboration of this conflict?

On this score, the elliptical Hegelian and Feuerbachian phraseology of Marx's 1843 Critique does not fail to take a position, to the point that thinking true democracy as "still a State form" would threaten to lead wide of the mark.[26] The locus of true democracy (to the extent that the continuous rupture here in play has a locus) is the becoming indeterminate of political form.[27] The "drive" toward radically democratic legislative power aims at dialectically liquidating State power in a kind of self-*aufhebend*, quite as if recognition of the "real subject" of sovereignty went hand-in-hand with thawing politics from the frozen relations engendered by State sovereignty. As civil society gains "political existence as its true universal and essential existence . . . the full achievement of this abstraction is at once also the transcendence (*Aufhebung*) of the abstraction."[28] In Abensour's ultimate analysis: "the point is not that democracy, unless we are to confuse it with a republic, succeeds where monarchy fails because of the change in form; rather, at stake is breaking with the very idea of [organizing] form" (p. 67). Against, then, Lenin's "temporary use of the instruments, resources and methods of State power," true democracy flows in the undercurrent of liberty that keeps the rising class, no less than the falling class, from ruling.[29] It is as if Marx already harboured the worry that, as Merleau-Ponty says, "revolutions are true as movements and false as regimes."[30] At the very least, it seems the open metaphor of true democracy would compel us to imagine with Hannah Arendt the "possibility of forming a new concept of the State" – not the finally discovered truth of political sovereignty, but the transfiguration of political truth according to which "the principle of sovereignty would be wholly alien."[31]

As such, the "reduction" of the State may also be viewed as a phenomenological operation, a "putting in brackets" of the "natural" or preexisting determinations of politics – as rule, dominion, instrumentality – and the opening of political thought to a historically unsuspected way for politics to be. Like the object without concept in Kant's "reflective judgment," the enigma of "true democracy" denotes a resistance to full conceptualization – but determinant judgment, precisely, may be deferred in order to welcome the event that tends toward *exemplary* signification.

We may go so far as to say that it is not the lack of a primacy of political thinking but the patience of its indwelling that makes true democracy persist "as a hidden and latent dimension of Marx's writings, ready to resurge, susceptible to awaken by the shock of the event" (p. 84). As Abensour points out, the epoch-making breakthrough in political organization of the 1871 Paris Commune not only illuminated an unprecedented political realm, it also brought Marx's political thinking into focus by giving it body. It is indeed the *fact* of the Communal Constitution that most impresses Marx: "whatever the merits of the particular measures of the Commune, its greatest measure was its own organization."[32] This exemplariness sparks political imagination and demands criticism – and for Marx even, self-criticism – of henceforth "antiquated" programs of class struggle. In his 1872 Preface to the second German edition of the *Communist Manifesto*, Marx cites his 1871 Address of the Workingmen's Association to emphasize: "One thing especially was proved by the Commune, viz., that 'the working class cannot simply lay hold of the ready-made State machinery, and wield it for its own purposes' (*The Civil War in France; Address of the General Council of the International Workingmen's Association*)."[33]

It is here, in Marx's analysis of the Paris Commune, that the Abensourian move to connect true democracy with a sort of anarchist *virtù* from within social division resounds most powerfully. Of course, the unity of a people's life in the 1843 Critique is equally dependent on the perpetual surmounting of social division, just as even the anti-state "indivision" of primitive egalitarian societies is made intelligible, as Claude Lefort argues, by "a division whose effects it was trying to cancel out."[34] In 1843, however, the negativity of division is in the last analysis too caught up in a kind of eschatological dialectic of self-reconciling identity ever to really break from the Hegelianism under critique. Marx's texts on the Paris Commune, by contrast, give political negativity a more empirically satisfying basis, since the drive toward a universally democratic power invents, in a situation of revolutionary rupture, a political arrangement at the center of which is the struggle against the State. In terms which speak to the question of political form raised by Merleau-Ponty ("Does all power tend to 'autonomize' itself?"), Abensour points to how the Communal Constitution, as it were, inaugurates "the specificity of a political form that as such promises to escape from the autonomization of form – not only because the members of the Commune are revocable, but above all because this form establishes itself, reaches its particularity and reestablishes itself by deploying itself *against* State power, in a permanent insurrection against the State apparatus" (p. 87). In Marx's formulation, the political arrangement of the Commune is not the harbinger of a "regeneration of mankind" that would "do away with the class struggles," but rather, in the fight to "do away with the State," the Communal constitution "affords the rational medium in which that class struggle can run through its different phases."[35]

For Abensour, the distinction is significant enough to reflect a change of paradigms. In 1843, true democracy is a dialectic in which "the disappearance of the State" stands at the pinnacle of an almost cumulative process of mediations. In 1871, a more temporal, agonistic and immediately political dynamic of democracy is outlined, with the emphasis falling on "action that consists in smashing modern State power" (pp. 87 and 96). In ways analogous to Pierre Clastres' anthropology of society against the State, Marx's writings on the Commune indeed detail a "collection of mechanisms whose function is to impede the sudden rise of a separate power, and whose aim is to block, at the site of the political, the advent of a division between power and society."[36] Rather than pointing to the millenarian disappearance of the State, Marx therefore reveals the working existence of the Commune as actively engaging, from within its own political bounds, an opposition between non-coercive and coercive modalities of power. True democracy, far from representing a quixotic escape from the universality of political power, would provide a new figure of emancipation by proving that the conflict between democracy and the State can be given body and meaning in the invention of an unprecedented political relation.

Marx's specification in 1871 that the "State-machine" is not to be appropriated but smashed is all the more suggestive as this action now forms the "rational medium" for class struggle. It is as though the fight against exploitation would henceforth gain its rational structure from the fight against domination, rather than vice versa. The emphasis on the struggle against the State as the "rational medium" for class struggle establishes again – as with the 1843 Critique, and as against the 1859 *Contribution to a Critique of Political Economy* – the formal and practical primacy of the political over the economic: or better, it highlights the nuance of the analysis of the State that now makes the primacy explicit. Rather than designating an essentially neutral mechanism, a form of governmental institution that owes its liberating or oppressive character to the class that gives it its stamp, the State signifies as ever an irreducible relation of domination. If the bourgeois State is mediated by the economic base, by the progress of industry and the national power of capital over labor, and is in this sense the clearinghouse of bourgeois interests, its internal logic is nonetheless consistent with the "State-machine" of every epoch. Social domination is the embryonic structure of the State. As such, far from representing the "main booty" of proletarian revolution, the "temporary" appropriation of this structure toward revolutionary ends is seen as only delivering that revolution's death sentence. Every revolution that sets out to annihilate class differences, while centralizing power in the hands of the State, only serves to bring out the autonomy of the "State machine" in broad relief at the same time as it fetters the emancipation of the working classes anew. The State, therefore, can only constitute for Marx "the great and single object of attack to the revolution."[37] The emblematic breakthrough of the 1871 Commune, Marx writes, is "revolution against the State itself," revolution against the very movement of power's separation from society, which is now identified with the "machinery of class domination itself."[38]

The primacy of smashing modern State power – as the primacy of creating a political liberty that would provide the "rational medium" for class struggles – is thereby made coextensive with the primacy of neutralizing the force of domination through the force of democratic action. And again, the question of domination does indeed become central as the failure to confront politically the self-separation of social power appears, in Marx's view, to condemn every revolution in advance of emancipation turning into its opposite. The historical breakthrough of the Commune is to have turned self-government into a living critique of social domination – domination as something radical, as socially diffuse and ubiquitous – and to have thus established the "rational medium" for multiplying the fields of class struggle in the ongoing test of a people to initiate themselves to "social revolution." Thus, smashing the State refers less to the particular locus of negation – as if the power of domination and the power of its centralization/formalization were not consubstantial – than to the double-edged movement of negation itself. The Commune brings into view a struggle of the people to "form their own force instead of the organized force of their suppression."[39] Or more explicitly, the smashing of the State now signals for Marx the eruption of a "rational medium" which awakens a people's vigilance and force against "their own force opposed to and organized against them."[40]

Without pushing matters too far, we can nonetheless see how, beyond Machiavelli, Marx glimpses in the Commune an attempt to grapple with the difficult truth stressed by Étienne de La Boétie: "no real or empirical foundation, that is, nothing positive is capable of accounting for servitude."[41] It is as though the enigma of democracy were entirely contained in the enigma of servitude, and the Machiavellian division between the powerful and the weak, the dominating few and the dominated many, were for Marx revealed in the ineradicable division of a people's power itself. To the non-localizable dynamic of the State would thus correspond the interminable movement of true democracy. Rather than "resolve" social division, democratic society in its "truth" would constitute itself reflexively. As Abensour has suggested by reference to Étienne de la Boétie, such a political society would establish itself in an "incessant self-return that would tend toward a continuous self-institution, recognizing in the political realm, which would have become the nodal-point of contention, the very space of an inextinguishable questioning of its social being."[42]

For this reason, we may agree with Alain Badiou when he makes the Commune of Paris the emblem of an "unknown capacity, a power without precedence . . . a subversion of the rules of political appearance."[43] In effect, the world of politics is confronted with that which does not, in this world, count as politics: a government (the "Communal Constitution") based not on the laws of State power, but on those formulated by the direct initiative of workers (precisely, the uncounted of politics). The members of the Communal government are directly elected and revocable; the separation of representative powers is terminated and replaced by delegations that are directly deliberative and executive; the professional army is banned in favor of the direct arming of the people – coincidentally, a move not far from the aims of civic humanism according to Pocock[44] – and so on.

Yet we may also go beyond Badiou by recognizing how the logic of dual power, as an embryonic power contesting the property of the old, is immediately radicalized, internalized, and as it were self-consciously redoubled. Starting with the proclamation distributed over the entire city on 19 March – "the proletarians of the capital, in the midst of the weakness and treason of the governing classes, have understood that the moment has come to save the situation by taking the direction of public affairs in their own hands" (*Comité central de la garde nationale*) – representational treason ceases to index the regrettable, but unavoidable, everyday state of political affairs. Instead, such treason is the turn of events the Communards struggle actively to prevent by instituting popular accountability *over their own political powers*. In Abensour's reading of Marx, the Communards constitute, from within the Commune's own political terrain, a methodic intensification of dual power. That is, the Communal form institutes itself and perseveres in time as "an agonistic relation that aims to forestall the State's return [. . .] thus mobilizing a critical knowledge and a *thumos* where desire for liberty and hate of servitude are mixed indistinctly" (p. 88). Or more precisely, the revolutionary situation of the Commune is played out in "a multifaceted arena of conflict at the heart of which the struggle for democracy is confronted by at least two adversaries: it rises against not only the State of the 'Old Regime,' but also against the one that is *in statu nascendi* during the course of the revolution itself" (p. 96).

The problem, then, becomes how to read Marx when he presents the Commune as the "political form at last discovered" of emancipation.[45] Is the enigma of emancipation resolved? Is it to be found in the regime of the Commune? Or is true democracy instead revealed in the political movement of the Commune, which succeeded for a time in destabilizing the very idea of the "good regime"? Is it really possible to locate this moment and body: "When the Paris Commune took the management of the revolution in its own hands"?[46] Or is the fluidity of the verbal adjunct the whole point, as though Marx were connecting the "hands" of revolution to the rise of an anomalous managing body – the Commune as the self-government of the popular masses – in order to emphasize how the count of the uncounted reinvents the political realm as a permanent object of dispute?

If we maintain the perspective of "reflective judgment," the

Commune in effect has an exemplary, as opposed to determinant, signification for true democracy. Indeed, could any political "model" incorporate the body of the people as a power, or configure the utopian body of true democracy?

In this light, Marx's line of enquiry appears to undercut the matrix of the model no less than the portraiture of the Commune as the harbinger of the "dictatorship of the proletariat" (Engels, Lenin, Mao, etc.). The node of disagreement would now be Marx's own estimation that the social measures of the Commune "could but betoken the tendency of a government of the people."[47] Either the "weakness" of the Commune in its inability to *localize*, to *stabilize*, in a word, to *centralize* power in a vanguard of revolutionary transformation is what forces the measures to an emblematic status, and the nonidentity of the Commune reveals the Communards as caught, despite themselves, in the immature stages of proletarian class-consciousness. Or to the contrary, as Abensour seems to suggest, Marx takes the nonidentity and unstable structures of the Commune as the strength and motor of its exemplary working existence. In this case, the finitude of the Commune begets exemplarity in the unfulfillment inherent to such self-government. In other words, it is quite precisely the "lack" of the Commune as a self-governing tendency that drives its "more" as a historical breakthrough in political organization. Or again, the Commune experiences an ongoing indetermination between subject and object (between the betokening measures realized and the self-government from which these measures are realized) only as democracy appears all the better in its truth.

In any case, we are compelled to note that for Marx the social measures of the Commune were not simply the *sign* of democracy but the sign of the *movement toward* democracy ("could but *betoken* the *tendency* of a government of the people"). The negativity of the Commune in relation to the promise of its form is therefore double. Or to the contrary, the Commune's measures are doubly negative – merely signifying a government of the people, and signifying a government that in turn is not the thing itself but its tendency – because the form of the Commune is the breach of this political movement, the sign of self-government as it appears in actuality. To borrow the terms of Etienne Tassin, we could say that Marx contrasts the *technical arrangement of egalitarian society* with a *society of equality in action*.[48] That is, Marx vindicates the Commune as a public space in which each political action awakens the general organizing principle at its heart. Marx would thus have in view a circuitous relation such that democracy is referred to each action that brings here and now the "government of the people" to existence. For the point is to make political self-determination presently actual, with all the risks this entails, instead of erecting a model of equality that, by subordinating political action to an extraneous organizing form, destroys the plurality and unpredictability on which political equality in truth depends.

The Commune cannot delineate a political model, then, because such delineation contradicts the subject of the model – the very working existence of the Commune – which itself had made a virtue of rejecting the ready-made systems of government then on offer. When Marx calls attention to the unique political existence of the Commune, he therefore has in mind what Abensour aptly names the "collective will in search of its very own political expression" (p. 86). By instituting this quest as its own working existence, a political form that acts as the State's living antithesis is created. To the uniqueness of the Commune's political experiment there would answer the uniqueness of the form of emancipation exemplified in it.[49] Everything hinges on what Abensour calls "the distinctive trait of the Communal Constitution *qua* political form" (p. 87). On the one hand, the point is clearly to break with the Jacobin tradition. With the primacy of the fight against domination, emancipation aims not to appropriate but to undermine the State, not to impose political form but to deliver it to democratic indetermination. On the other, the anarchist rejection of the political realm is itself rejected, since at stake is not rediscovering a spontaneous sociality deformed by politics but regenerating a political sociality against the State.

Against Jacobinism and with a thus qualified anarchism, the "distinctive trait" of the democratic constitution is again interposed – this is the continuity of the 1871 texts with the 1843 Critique – as the "weapon" of the reduction (p. 94). Once political sovereignty is short-circuited by the power of the people, or more precisely, once the State is unmasked as a dynamic form that transforms the power *between* human beings into a power *over* them, the political realm is restricted to its essential content and principle: "the position *against*" that must ever be renewed. Contrary to the lore of the "democratic State" – for Abensour, an oxymoron if ever there were one – liberty and equality do not flourish on the firm ground of juridical right. Instead, they proliferate in the political movement that "affirms *in actu* the possibility of annihilating the division between governors and governed, or of reducing it to almost nothing, inventing a public space and political space under the banner of isonomy" (p. 96). The "truth" of democracy would thus gather its forces from what Lefort has described as democracy's "savage" character. The democratic institution of the social realm, and the incessant reinvention of politics it demands, are themselves fueled by the polymorphous struggles of democracy against its domestication in the State-form (p. 99, and the appendix essay to this book, "Savage Democracy and the Principle of Anarchy").

If we look forward from 1871 to the "wildcat" strikes of students and workers – strikes that break out of bureaucratic control and endure politically through coordinated councils of action – that shook Budapest in 1956, Paris in 1968, Gdansk in 1980–2 and that returned to haunt France in November–December 1995, the "position *against*" Abensour distills from Marx may arguably be raised to a principle of democratic modernity. Indeed, Abensour's hypothesis of a *contemporary* Machiavellian moment gains salience against this backdrop, just as the hypothesis of a Machiavellian moment *in Marx* is informed by the "libertarian spirit" Abensour takes as Marx's ongoing contemporaneity (p. 100). We may then speak of democracy as "intractable," in the sense Jean-François Lyotard gives to this term.[50] The people in democracy appear, when they there appear, as politically refractory, as conscious of being both *above* the "nothing" the State would have them be and *below* the "everything" they in truth are, and in reality ought to be. And just as this excedent of the people, this utopian identity, underscores the irreducibility of democracy to the State, so too the situation of democracy corresponds almost exactly to that of the proletariat which, according to the Marx of 1843, was both inside and outside civil society.

PREFACE TO THE ITALIAN EDITION (2008): "INSURGENT DEMOCRACY AND INSTITUTION"

At a time when the term "democracy" is associated with bloody wars, the crusade of good against evil, and torture, it has become necessary, indeed urgent, to *delineate* democracy so as to dissociate it from these obviously anti-democratic undertakings, which P. Vidal-Naquet describes as the "cancer of democracy." Thus, already some time ago, in order to counteract the neutralization and trivialization of democracy, qualifiers were chosen to allow it to retrieve its difference, its separateness from the phenomena of domination trying to hide behind its name. Among the many qualifiers proposed, Claude Lefort's "savage democracy" stands out, along with radical democracy.

In any case, if left undelineated, democracy would risk losing any identifiable features, and would be swept away into the greyness of universal trivialization. Is it not constantly confused in the everyday language of contemporary society with the rule of law or representative government?

For my part, I propose the expression "insurgent democracy," which has the advantage of conveying two particularities. First, that democracy is not a political regime but primarily an action, a modality of political agency, characterized by the irruption of the *demos*, or the people, onto the political stage in their struggle against those whom Machiavelli calls the *grandees* and for the establishment in the city of a state of non-domination. Second, that this political action is not confined to a particular moment but continues through time, always ready to spring up due to the obstacles encountered. It involves the birth of a complex process, where the social is instituted and the institution directed at non-domination, one permanently inventing itself to better perpetuate its existence and to defeat the counter-movements that threaten to annihilate it and to effect a return to a state of domination. Insurgent democracy in contrast to insurrectionary democracy, which, though evoking a mode of action of the people, does not incorporate its ongoing insertion in time.

Hence, if we examine the revolutionary days that punctuated the course of the French Revolution – their succession and rhythm – the Revolution could be defined as an insurgent democracy that arose and continued from 1789 to 1799, once Babeuf's "Conspiracy of Equals" is taken into account. For during those ten years the people were compelled a number of times to irrupt onto the revolutionary stage to proclaim their mission to act against both the state of the Old Regime and its remnants, as well as the new State, the "revolutionary government," and thereby to reaffirm their commitment to a mode of being of the political bearing the stamp of non-domination. Historian Sophie Wahnich's latest work, *La Longue Patience Du Peuple*, tends in this direction.

Seen in this light, the last insurrections of Year III, of Germinal (April 1795) and especially of Prairial (May 1795) are remarkable. The people – that is, what was left of the Parisian *sections* – invaded the Convention with a double agenda, "*Bread*" and "*The Constitution of 1793,*" which was clearly articulated in a leaflet published prior to the event: *Insurrection du peuple pour obtenir du pain, reconquérir ses droits* ("Insurrection of the people to obtain bread and regain their rights"). By linking the constitution with the demand for bread, what else were the people doing but insisting on, among other things, their right to insurrection recognized in the Constitution of 1793? What else were they doing but fighting to regain the sovereignty, in other words, the constituent power, that belonged to them? Amid the general turmoil of the two first days of Prairial, one can recognize the hallmark of democracy in the process of being instituted: brutal opposition between the people and the *grandees* of the day.

According to K. D. Tonnesson, the historian of these insurrections, they amounted to a breach between the two components of the urban Third Estate, the bourgeoisie and the people. The Insurrections of Year III were carried out almost entirely by the people and gave rise to a dual power: the power of the Parisian *Sans-Culottes* whose aim was to replace the other power, that of the government. Indeed, the explicit political goals of the insurrections were the abolition of the revolutionary government, the immediate establishment of the Constitution of 1793, and the destitution and arrest of the current rulers. On a deeper level, the underlying principle of the insurrection can be discerned: the search for a political relationship, for a vital, intense, non-hierarchical political bond distinct from order, the struggle to preserve the people's ability to act and to prevent the bonds among citizens from degenerating once again into a restrictive, vertical, hierarchical, top-down order. The contrast between "bond" and "order" stands out in sharp relief in this excerpt from the pamphlet "*L'insurrection du people . . .*"

> The citizens of all sections without distinction will leave from all points in fraternal disorder, without waiting for the movement of neighbouring sections; they will march with them, so that the shrewd and treacherous government will no longer be able to gag the people as it usually does and cause them to be led, like a herd, by leaders who are sellouts and who deceive us.[1]

"*Fraternal disorder*" is in opposition to the power of the leaders. In sum, non-domination, a non-restrictive and egalitarian political bond, is in opposition to order.

One of the most frequent criticisms of my work is that insurgent democracy, above all a negativity anchored in the present of the insurrectional event, ignores the institution or, at least, makes little room for it. Insurgent democracy retreats upon the passage from negativity to institution, the "positive model of action," as though there were a necessary antagonism between insurgence and institution. Admittedly, this critique does point to an essential difficulty. But to represent the relationship between insurgent democracy and institution solely in terms of antagonism would be an egregious oversimplification, as if the former were always deployed in a momentary ferment and the latter, inevitably in the grip of a marble-like stasis.

An initial tentative reply is called for: The potential for compatibility between insurgent democracy and institution exists, so long as the constitutional act, the fundamental norm, recognizes the people's right to insurrection, as did the Constitution of 1793. Hence, to demand its reinstatement was to insist on the legitimacy of the insurrection. Yet the defeat of the insurrection of Prairial had precisely the effect that the new constitution of Year III, which entrenched the rule of private property, suppressed the right to insurrection, thus dealing an irreparable blow to the political imagination. Decades of strong government, totalitarian experiences, and authoritarian practices have rendered the enshrinement of a right to insurrection in a constitutional act almost inconceivable, as if constituent power were faced with an "impassable horizon," as the defenders of the established order like to say.

And yet, if democracy seeks to institute a political community that holds domination at bay, to institute the social under the banner of non-domination, which device is best suited to preserve this principle if not the right to insurrection, which is the appropriate recourse every time the grandees' desire to dominate threatens to prevail over the people's desire for liberty? This is a difficult truth to hear, but the difficulty stems more from the spirit of the times than from the thing itself.

To solve the problem, however, it is not enough for insurgent democracy to be tied to the institution of the right to insurrection. It must furthermore be acknowledged that the democracy of non-domination is not deployed in a politically empty and undifferentiated zone of space-time. There must be no illusion about its relation to ferment; ferment is not momentariness. Nor does it belong to the present alone. For to safeguard the people's capacity to act politically it can turn to institutions that, at their inception, were meant to foster the exercise of that capacity. Thus, during the events of Prairial, the insurrection depended on the Parisian *sections*, and the Montagnard deputies who supported it initiated a vote, on the first of Prairial in the invaded Convention, to make the *sections*, abolished by decree on 9 September 1793, permanent. Just as insurgent democracy can bring about an interaction between insurgence and institution, it can also set in motion a circular flow between the present of the event and the past, insofar as this involves encounters among emancipatory institutions holding out a promise of liberty. Here, the people rose up against the liberating institutions' lack of a present, demanding that these institutions be respected.

We therefore arrive at a more nuanced formulation: insurgent democracy, far from being hostile as a matter of principle to all institutions or connections to the past, is selective. Because it tends, like any political movement, toward enduring through time, it distinguishes between institutions that promote the people's political action and those that do not, with non-domination serving as the criterion. There is no systematic antagonism between insurgent democracy and institutions as long as the latter work to preserve this state of non-domination and act as dikes stemming the *grandee*'s desire to dominate and thereby allowing the people to experience liberty. Conversely, all institutions, governmental or otherwise, that are apt to encourage a new situation where new *grandees* hold sway, can only arouse the hostility of insurgent democracy.

A comparable level of complexity emerges if we approach the problem from an "institutional" perspective. To this end it may be appropriate to follow the trail that Saint-Just blazed in *Institutions républicaines*, that is, of opposing institutions and laws, with institutions being granted primacy while laws are mistrusted, as evidenced in the text: "A law that conflicts with institutions is tyrannical . . . To obey laws is problematic, because the law is often nothing but the will of he who imposes it. We have the right to resist oppressive laws."[2]

Without reviewing Saint-Just's reasoning in its entirety, we can see that the Republic must, first, be constituted out of an *institutional fabric*, a kind of primary foundation, distinct from both government, the "governing machine," and laws, always liable to conceal acts of arbitrary power. The institutions whose purpose is to connect citizens through *generous relationships* must incorporate, in their form as well as their content, something like an essence of the republic, of the republican principle, and of its prefiguration in the form of a dynamic totality. It is in this capacity that institutions are deemed to be the "soul of the republic."

Even though Saint-Just's thoughts on the subject were not fully developed, he was nevertheless able to bring to light a specificity of institutions, which cannot be reduced to laws or the governing machine. That specificity was moreover recognized by Marx in *The Class Struggles in France,* where he points out that the Republic of February 1848, a bourgeois republic, under pressure from the proletariat, was forced to create "*social institutions*" in which Marx discerns, if only to criticize its meekness, a movement that involved outdoing the bourgeois republic "*in ideas, in imagination.*"[3] The institution, more a matrix than a framework, encompasses an imaginative dimension, one of anticipation, which in itself has the potential to engender customs, or rather attitudes and behaviours, consistent with the emancipation it announces. It is in this sense that for Gilles Deleuze the institution is a "system of anticipation" opposed to the law, insofar as it bears within itself an appeal – the appeal of one freedom to other freedoms – that radically differentiates it from the obligation characteristic of the law, which entails a penalty when an infraction is committed. Hence Deleuze's definition of the difference between institution and law: "the latter is a limitation of action, the former, a positive model of action."[4]

One objection remains. Is there not an incompatibility, a contradiction, between, on the one hand, insurgence taking place in a present in ferment, affected by extreme mobility, and institution on the other? For one thing, the extent of the ferment would make it difficult for the institution to carve out a place for itself. In addition, the institution would tend perhaps not toward stasis but at the very least toward a stability resistant to change, to the temporality of democracy. On the first point, as already noted, it is possible that, due to a circulation between present and past, certain institutions informing a given political context serve to underpin insurgence. It is even possible that insurgent democracy, in order to endure and not be reduced to a flash in the pan, summons or in some way gives rise to the institution, for the purpose in this case of articulating the principle of non-domination and a certain anchorage in time, in the confrontation of two temporalities.

On the second point, we must guard against hasty conclusions. According to Merleau-Ponty, the institution endows experience with a sustainable dimension.[5] But this sustainable character, which goes on in time, is even less like a stasis inasmuch as the sustainability reveals a creative, innovative (in the Bergsonian sense) duration. This then raises the question as to whether the anticipatory character of the institution, its relation to the imagination, to the social project, does not operate from inside the "sustainability," such that the sustainable dimension, instead of being a resistance, an obstacle to change, is transformed into a launch pad, a base whose relative stability allows invention and innovation to be enacted.

Within this "anticipatory" conception of institution, the creative duration must be privileged over the slow and uniform duration at the source of deceleration and equilibrium. We owe the distinction between these two forms of duration, from the institution's viewpoint, to jurist Maurice Hauriou, who writes, "The institution is, in all respects, the category of movement."[6] In this case, the institution could easily acclimatize to democratic temporality.

But here an ambiguity arises: which element ought to be given precedence – dynamism or permanency and stability? Given the hypothesis of a democracy opposed to the State, of an insurgent democracy implying a distancing, in the name of the institution, from sovereignty and the law, the only avenue open to the institution is that of greater plasticity, more openness to events, and a stronger disposition to welcome the new.

Contrary to the criticism levelled against us, what can be glimpsed through the exploration of these two complexities, insurgence and institution, is how insurgent democracy, having its own temporality, and institution can both be conceptualized together. Because, to the extent that institution – it too understood in its specific temporality – far from being alien to democratic ferment or from thwarting it, can in fact respond to it better, if institution, like democracy, can be perceived and applied against the State, particularly if it takes the form of non-state or even anti-state law, of social law. In fact, the theorization of institution often includes the thesis whereby the State is not the primary source of the law. Saint-Just and his invaluable distinctions – not unfamiliar to philosophers of institution – between law, institution, and governing machine make clear that conflict and incompatibility exist between the law and the governing machine on the one hand and insurgent democracy on the other, but not between insurgent democracy and institution.

While taking care not to confuse State and government, let us turn to William Godwin, author of *Enquiry concerning political justice* (1793), who incisively described the irreparable conflict between government and the mobility of humanity:

> Government, under whatever point of view we examine this topic, is unfortunately pregnant with motives to censure and complain. Incessant change, everlasting innovation, seems to be dictated by the true interests of mankind. But government is the perpetual enemy of change (. . .) What was admirably observed of a particular system of government is in a great degree true of all: They lay their hand on the spring there is in society, and put a stop to its motion. Their tendency is to perpetuate abuse. (. . .) Man is in a state of perpetual mutation. (. . .) By its very nature positive institutions have a tendency to suspend the elasticity and progress of mind.[7]

FOREWORD TO THE SECOND FRENCH EDITION (2004) "OF INSURGENT DEMOCRACY"

Are we condemned to the alternative of either moderate democracy or classical anti-democratism? Let us say that we were faced with the following choice: democracy as long as it's practiced with moderation, reduced to an inescapable political framework for instance, or as an illusion and, as such, deserving neither to be preferred nor preserved if it were in peril, for its appearances of liberty would only make it an ever more pernicious form of domination.

Yet, isn't one of the many qualities of Marx's 1843 text precisely to open the way beyond this alternative and its constraints by formulating the question of "real democracy"? As though, before democracy could be submitted to the requirement of moderation or else rejected without further consideration, one would have to turn to a prerequisite. That is to question democracy in its truth, to discover the characteristics that disqualify the remedy of moderation as much as that of denial. Not through an essentialist approach but by a reflection on the destiny of democracy in modernity.

Exemplary research of Marx in 1843, which has the advantage of reminding us of an approach which has forgone our minds, busy as we are tallying the deficiencies of democracy or denouncing its illusions. Unless that, under the spell of the theme of the end of the political, we should consider with as much platitude as confidence that this form of political community is a "utopia" in the most vulgar sense of the word. Let us put aside the fatigue of reason and the acritical scepticism, which accompanies it. Let us return to the initial question: what is the truth of democracy? Relying on "the modern French," the author of the *Critique of Hegel's Philosophy of Right* comes to a surprising, enigmatic response, according to which the advent of democracy would go hand-in-hand with the disappearance of the political state. Moreover, instead of turning this thesis into a beautiful sunrise with no tomorrow, we might concede to recognize in it a latent, underlying, persistent dimension of Marx's political interrogation. Wouldn't we be led to perceive a shift, between the 1843 text and the 1871 address on the Commune, from a thought of process (*pensée du processus*) to a thought of conflict (*pensée du conflit*)? The coming into being of democracy wouldn't so much take place through the withering of the State than it would be constituted in a struggle *against* the State. The onset alternative comes out discredited. Thus understood, the truth of democracy opposes itself to the formula of moderate transaction, which represents the familiar expression of "democratic State." Be it in regard to the State or democracy, doesn't this expression betray a lack of critical analysis? Likewise, the rejection of democracy in the name of a critique of domination is unfounded, inasmuch as democracy works, in its deepest sense, against the dominant/dominated relation and towards the advent of a state of non-domination.

Thus oriented towards non-domination, wouldn't true democracy reveal itself in the "deconstruction of the political field"? That is, following R. Shürmann's analyses, in the caesurae between two political forms free action might emerge and deploy itself beyond all principial or referential influence. Relying on H. Arendt and her idea of the lost treasure of revolution, R. Shürmann writes, in regard to these breaches of modern history belonging to the council or communalist tradition: "Thus, the *princeps*, the government and the *principium*, the system it imposes and on which it rests, are suspended for a while. In such caesurae, the political field fulfils its disclosing role entirely: it reveals for everyone to see that the origin of action . . . is the simple coming into being of all that is present."[1] It deserves to be compared to Marx's thesis according to which "democracy is the resolved enigma of all constitutions." That is to say that to interpret a constitutional objectification correctly, it is always advisable to return to what produced it, to the *demos* and its free action. Isn't it precisely to maintain and safeguard the contact, the connection with the "real people" that, at the very moment at which it is instituted, real democracy leads to the disappearance of the political state, as an organizing form susceptible of substituting itself to the will of the people and, in the end, to rise against it?

In a way, "savage democracy," in Claude Lefort's terms, enlightened or rather resolved by the principle of anarchy could be a plausible figure, a name, for democracy against the State.[2] Indeed, if savage democracy defines itself by the dissolution of the ultimate markers of certainty, by the repeated test of indeterminacy – which implies a way out of metaphysical derivation, an emancipation from a foundational principle – it appears hardly compatible with the State whose existence requires foundation, certainty, and reliance on a primary principle. Moreover, how could the plural effervescence of savage democracy, strengthened and fed by the innate indeterminacy of the human element, accommodate itself to integration in the totalizing system of the State? How could the test of indeterminacy consent to the domination of One, abdicate before One? But possibility is not necessity. The logic of savage democracy is not necessarily anti-statist. Isn't the "savage" exposed to being confined and thus reduced to a mode of being, a mode of expression, to an epochal style characterized above all by a crisis of foundations, without drawing all the consequences from this crisis? Furthermore, isn't there some danger in binding the idea of savage democracy to that of the law, to the struggle for the upholding of vested rights and the conquest of new rights? Even if it is legitimate to dissociate the law from the idea of domination and to associate it to that of resistance; wouldn't this struggle for the law, which seeks ultimately the recognition and sanction of litigious rights by the State, come *volens nolens* to a strengthening of the State and, worse, to a permanent reconstruction of the State? It's only in turning to the idea of social right that savage democracy could remain true to its anti-statist vocation. This is one of the paradoxes, and not the least, of contemporary progressivism which in its renewed invocation of the "right to" inescapably ends up asking the approbation of the State and, at the same time, comforts it, as if nothing could be done without the approval of the State. Finally, is it on the side of human rights, even interpreted in a political manner, that we must discover the live source of savage democracy? Is the nature of this source able to ward off State control?

Considering these questions and difficulties, would it be advisable, instead of looking for the possible figures of democracy against the State, to return to this formula, to explore and make its dimensions and issues explicit? Without a doubt, this expression has the merit to revive Marx's fruitful intuition in the 1843 manuscript, to invite its assessment; however it may have been neglected or rendered common by the epigones under the Saint-Simonian theme of the withering away of the State. The point, for Marx, is not to announce that the administration of things will replace the government of men, but to observe with the modern French that the advent of democracy signifies the disappearance of the political state; and, if we consider the path taken between 1843 and 1871, to affirm that democracy can only exist inasmuch as it rises *against* the State. The Marxian thesis relies on democracy's exception, which expresses itself above all in the implementation of *reduction*. Modern democracy is democracy against the State because its specificity consists in practicing reduction. Without going into this complex mechanism, let us remember the essential, namely that reduction serves to block political objectification so that the latter doesn't turn, in spite of itself, into alienation. In other words, in democracy, thanks to this blocking, political action remains what it is inasmuch as it resists transfiguration into an organizing, unifying form, in short, into a State. By bringing to light reduction and its consequences, Marx was able to show as clearly as possible that the struggle against the State, as a form, is inscribed in the heart of democratic logic. Democracy is anti-statist or else it is not. Given this fact, it is not difficult to understand that its usual eulogists, more or less conscious of this phenomenon, recommend a moderate use of democracy; the mechanism of reduction thus hindered, the democratic exception fades making room for the contradiction in terms that is the "democratic State," understood as the rule of law or an inescapable framework. Let us add that the mechanism of reduction is paradoxical: the blocking that it produces and which forbids the transfiguration of political objectification into the State-form is at the same time, according to us, that which "makes possible the extension of what is at stake and shows in the political sphere – an experience of universality, its negation of domination, the constitution of an isonomic public space." As if, thus resourced, democratic action could express itself in the public space, modulate itself in the life of the people. There are three stages therefore: reduction, blocking, extension. It is this latter stage which allows for the irrigation of all the other spheres of the life of a people, according to a democratic mode of being, in such a way that we can say that all holds to democracy.

The stakes are high: the occultation of this impulsion against the State, the avoidance of reduction, the blocking of the blocking, can only thoroughly ruin the democratic institution of the social, void its logic, as much in its initial movement as in its effects. If such is the case, why not try another name, why not propose the name of *insurgent democracy* to those who continue to wonder about real democracy? Far beyond the souvenirs of the revolt of American settlers against England, during the war of Independence, the term clearly signifies that the advent of democracy is the opening of an agonistic scene which has the State as a "natural" and favoured target; or else that democracy is the play of a "permanent insurrection" against the State, against the unifying, integrating, organizing State-form. It is from reduction and in its prolongation that this agonistic deploys itself, ever more destined to last that, in this war, it might be that reduction fails and that the State wins in its struggle to neutralize democracy, to incorporate it to the point of producing the "democratic State," which will only keep from the initial reduction, a tendency to permanent contestation, a pale reflection of the original impulse.

In contemporary thought, which wrongly identifies democracy with representative government or the rule of law, only Jacques Rancière seems to preserve Marx's intuition as to the being, as to the anti-statist disposition, of democracy. Calling for a distinction between two logics of the community, the author of *La Mésentente* suggests to name *police* "all the processes by which the aggregation and consent of collectivities, the organization of powers, the distribution of ranks and functions and the legitimating systems of this distribution, operate."[3] This logic is opposed by another perturbing logic, namely that which relies on the presumption of the equality of anyone with anyone. On this side one finds democracy, a manner of being of the political: "more precisely, democracy is the name of a singular interruption of this order of distribution of groups in community that we have proposed to conceptualize under the extended word of police. This is the word for that which interrupts the good functioning of this order by a singular device of subjectivization."[4] The only difference with Marx would be that Rancière's police order refers more to the government or governmentality than to the State; as such it would resemble more an instrumental machinery, or even a "thing" susceptible to inspection, than to the State as a system, a unifying totality, thus endowed with an incontestable symbolic dimension. Aware of the "sublimity" of the State, at the very least of its elevation, Marx wanted to get in the way of its presumptuousness by denouncing the deception of universality on which it pretends to be built. Not to reduce the State to an empirical set of functions and ranks, but to incite the real people to proceed to a reappropriation of this universality which the State claims to be bearer of, in order to irrigate democracy until it reaches its truth. Nevertheless, an opposition does exist, even though the terms which constitute it somewhat differ. According to J. Rancière, democracy institutes a "polemical community" which puts at stake "the opposition of two logics, the police logic of the distribution of ranks and the political logic of the egalitarian trait."[5]

Regarding insurgent democracy, two comments must be made at

once. Firstly, a question arises: against which state does democracy struggle? Upon closer inspection, insurgent democracy struggles on two fronts. As in the French Revolution, with the popular societies and *les Enragés*, it rises against the state of the Old Regime and at the same time against the new state *in statu nascendi*, the one which brings to power new "nobles" hoping to dominate the people in their turn. But beyond Revolution, all political communities experience a similar situation in a way: they are engaged in a struggle against a state of the Old Regime, with its burdens, its relics, and in a struggle against the new state, in prey to innovation, making or reconstructing itself under the name of reform, of modernization or of rationalization. It is to acknowledge that insurgent democracy installs itself paradoxically in a place which defies any installation, the very place of the caesura between two forms of state, one past, the other to come. Just consider the repeated insurrections of the people after the 1830 Revolution which rises against the Old Regime as well as against the new, the "liberal" monarchy, in the hands of the "high capacities," as if it had been about opening the caesura of the July days each time. It is because it situates itself in this space in between that democracy is more apt to keep the way clear for the action of the people. More precisely, it is to safeguard this free action that insurgent democracy constitutes itself in a struggle on two fronts. A counterexample can help us better understand this strange situation. What was Trotsky doing in *The New Course* (1923), when he opposed the authoritarian logic of the State to that of the Party, but barring the way to another logic – that of democracy at war with the State as well as with the Party, the new figure of the State in formation? What is really significant rests at the micro-sociological level. An institution true to the logic of insurgent democracy constantly manoeuvres between two pitfalls: on the one hand, the relapse into inherited tradition, on the other, the hold of a form to come, that is in the making. Far from any state of grace, the caesura works to maintain itself in the opening to the action of the people. The temporality of such democracy wouldn't rest so much in presence, in the concordance of the self with the self, than in discordance – repeated, even harboured – inasmuch as this struggle against the emergence of the State-form meant to, and would, preserve the non-identity of the people with itself. Admittedly, this is an exhausting temporality, even more so because it requires the systematic, the persistent practice of conflict – each conflict offering the possibility to maintain, better, to revive the caesura. All goes as if, thanks to this time of caesura, the question would be to interrupt the classic passage, described by G. Landauer in *Revolution*, from a utopia to a new *topia* and to make of our stay the nowhere of utopia, to open the greatest horizon of chances to the action of the people.

Secondly, insurgent democracy is not the equivalent of a variant of the radical-liberal project – the citizen against the powers – but rather a plural formula – the citizens against the State, or better yet the community of citizens against the State. In the words of La Boétie, insurgent democracy means the community of "all ones" (*tous uns*) – what it specifically terms friendship – against the "all One" (*tous Un*); and more precisely, if we take in charge the dynamic dimension of the political, the resistance of the *all ones* to the shift into *all One*, as if insurgency had amongst other functions the one of blocking, eradicating the ever menacing slippage of the community of *all ones* towards the unifying form of the *all One*, denying the plurality, the ontological condition of plurality.

Doesn't this attempt at a definition call for an immediate critical revision of the notion of civil society, as it is professed by the *doxa* of the day? Let us say that the fundamental character of the expression lies in putting the political into brackets. The term aims to designate a social ensemble – of groups, relations, practices – which work towards the reproduction of a given historical community, in various fields: technical, scientific, industrial, cultural, ideological; and as such would represent the real basis of today's states. This is where "it would happen," as if civil society had the monopoly over seriousness and efficiency. It would come to civil society to assume the durability of the historical community beyond the vicissitudes of the political. In the long run, it would not suffice for civil society and those who claim it to put the political in brackets; it would rather be a question of moving away from it, of opposing it so as better to substitute it if need be, if there were obvious shortcomings to the political. The project seems able to concretize itself, for a society which functions by excellence would spontaneously produce "elites" susceptible of taking over the politics; even more suspect that they now pretend to practice a profession requiring a certain technical know-how. The reduction of the political to governance, namely to the application of the methods of business management to the political community, only increases the alleged legitimacy of the "representatives of civil society." Ultimately, the notion of civil society, implicitly made up of a confused blend of anti-totalitarianism from the East, of anti-statism, of misunderstood liberalism, is an anti-political machine feeding more or less on the belief that politics has necessarily to do with evil. We can also wonder if the invocation of civil society doesn't play, in our society of domination and exploitation, the role of a simulacrum of liberty.

In the face of such a situation, wouldn't it be advisable to repoliticize civil society?[6] This is a complex operation that requires a range of critical interventions. In the first instance, to repoliticize civil society implies if not to return to the meaning of the term in the seventeenth and eighteenth centuries, at least to remember it. In seventeenth-century England, the expression *civil society* was synonymous with *political society*. John Locke entitled chapter VII of the *The Second Treatise of Government*, "Of political or civil society." Later, some of Rousseau's texts, particularly the *Discourse on the Origin of Inequality*, refer to the political society with the expression "civil society." Similarly, Diderot writes in the *Encyclopédie*: "Civil society signifies the body politic which the men from a same nation, state, city or else, form together and the political relations that unite them; it is the civil commerce of the world, the relations that men have, as subjects of a prince, as citizens of a same city and as subjects to the same law and participating to the rights and privileges shared by all who belong to this society." With Kant, the term civil society keeps, in the *Critique of the Faculty of Judgment*, its political meaning in the sense that it signifies a whole under the influence of a legal power. In other texts, Kant insistently invites us to distinguish the judicial civil society from the ethical civil society, failing which the organization of the State might be disrupted.

It is with Hegel, a careful reader of the English economists, that the concept of civil society shifts from the political to the economic, though preserving a political character. Civil society becomes the civil-bourgeois society, a system of needs resting on an antagonistic structure close, to some extent, to the war of all against all. Of course, mediating bodies mitigate these conflicts, but it is only at the level of the State, and because of the State, that the conflicts of the civil-bourgeois society could be overcome in such a way that the State manifests itself as an organic totality. The effect of the Hegelian shift is twofold: on the one hand, civil society having become economic, it is the political, in the Hegelian conception of the State, that has the responsibility for imposing its norm and foundation on the economic, rather than the opposite; on the other hand, Hegel historicizes the concept of civil society. With Hegelian philosophy, "the abstract notion of civil society takes on its true meaning: civil society is bourgeois."[7] Civil society cannot be its own end. Torn by its internal contradictions, it cannot accede to liberty, nor unity. The antagonism of wealth and poverty is the primary contradiction which divides it. In the *Philosophy of Right*, Hegel writes, 243: ". . . the accumulation of wealth grows on one side . . . while on the other, the specialization and limitation of particular work also grows and, with this, the dependency and destitution of the class which is bound to this work . . ." or yet, 245: "It thus appears that, despite its excess of wealth, civil society is not rich enough, that is that it does not possess as its own enough resources to prevent the excess of poverty and the production of the masses."[8]

Repoliticizing civil society therefore does not mean purely and simply to return to the political theorists of the seventeenth and eighteenth centuries, before Hegel. The operation is more complex, more subtle. Against the reduction of civil society to the economic, the necessary acknowledgment of the political signification imposes itself; but in stating two complementary demands at once. Firstly, the return to the synonymy of civil society and political society could not mean to profess, as the pre-Hegelian theorists did, an equivalent synonymy between the political society and the State. Indeed, hasn't the Hegelian fault line between civil society and the State revealed another possible fault line, which remained unacknowledged inasmuch as Hegelian statism had spontaneously concealed it, namely the one between the political community and the State? On this issue, critical work could demonstrate how the Hegelian concept of civil society holds within itself a political dimension that it tends to conceal, but that it can't entirely suppress. While the State is a possible form of political community, it is not its necessary form. It is to recognize that there existed, that there exists, that there could exist political communities other than the State, ones which don't find their accomplishment, their perfection, in the State. Non-statist, or even anti-statist, political communities. Forms of political communities which constitute themselves against the State, against the sudden appearance of a separate power, are indeed conceivable. Isn't it one of the lessons of new political anthropology, of the Copernican revolution of Pierre Clastres, in the study of savage societies, not of societies without State, but of societies against the State?[9] Isn't it what Rousseau sought when he calls for distinguishing between the "body of the people" and the "body of the state" and isn't it very precisely this body of the people which expresses itself in its opposition to the State, fighting against it to reappropriate political action as it deploys itself in the caesura between two forms of State? Isn't it this kind of affirmation of the political which is inscribed in all modern revolutions, concerned with the *in situ* expression of the "political capacity" of the people in action, the political capacity of the *all ones*? Isn't it what is at stake in the confrontation of the revolutionary positions, one, the Jacobin calling for a takeover of the State, the other, the communalist or councilist aspiring to break the State to give free rein to an anti-statist political community. For instance, is this not what Marx meant in regard to the Paris Commune with the mysterious wording "communal constitution"?

This affirmation of a non-statist political community leads to a two-fold struggle. If it is obvious that it struggles against the identification of politics with the State to which Hegelianism proceeds which reduces all political possibilities to the State; it nevertheless also rejects a "vulgar" anarchism, that of Martin Buber in *Utopie et Socialisme*, for instance, which, content with inverting Hegel by playing the social against the political, concludes that the renaissance of the social fabric, the advent of the social, must immediately lead to the end, to the disappearance of the political assimilated to State domination. Repoliticizing civil society is thus to discover the possibility of a political community outside the State and against it. In light of this possibility, the bracketing of the political is better understood – the depolitization practiced by the current neutralization of political society – as the antechamber of consensual governance. Isn't this neutralization about conjuring the "specter" of a non-statist, better yet, an anti-statist, political community?

On the other hand, in this work of repolitization of civil society, one could not return to pre-Hegelian thought, since we are indebted to him for bringing the antagonisms tearing civil society apart to the fore, the opposition between wealth and poverty being the main one. If repoliticizing civil society leads to disclosure of the existence of a political community susceptible of rising against the State, it couldn't evidently be conceived of according to the model of the State, an organic whole, a unified and reconciled political society. It is rather compelling to think of it as divided, either by reviving the Machiavellian tradition aware of the confrontation, in every human society, between the *grandees* and the people, or by considering this political community as an answer to the polemical question of equality.

Upon reflection, doesn't this choice to repoliticize civil society, that is to give back its political meaning, reproduce Marx's gesture in the *Critique of Hegel's Philosophy of Right*, as long as one accepts the hypothesis proposed? Marx's goal in 1843 would not have been, as he would assert it later in 1859, epistemological, the determination of the place and status of the political in the social totality, constitutive of a critical theory, but at once political and philosophical. It would be a question of substituting a democratic mode of thinking to a bureaucratic one, under the influence moreover of Hegelian logicism.

For Marx, it wasn't so much a case of defining civil society, following the English and Hegel, as the whole of the conditions of material life and to find its anatomy in political economy, than to search for the original subject from which family and civil society proceed, namely, the whole *demos*. "What is required is to start from the real subject and consider its objectification," declares Marx. It is in this quest for the real subject that true democracy appears as a form of political objectification, of political community which goes hand-in-hand with the disappearance of the political State, understood as an organizing form. Isn't it precisely to avoid the Hegelian shift that Marx envisions bourgeois-civil society, not in its materiality, nor in its facticity, but in its movement outside itself, in what he terms its "ecstasy," as if the political community, in the form of true democracy, could emerge from this movement, of which civil society is the bearer, on the condition, thanks to the political act, of coming out of itself.

Such are the broad outlines that allow for the tracing of the contours of what should be understood as insurgent democracy. In a Rousseauist vocabulary, insurgent democracy can be defined as an arising of the body of the people against the body of the State; in other words, the expression of the political rapport as it proceeds from the true subject, the "whole *demos*." Still, one should specify that, in moving away from Marx and of this expression, in preferring *all ones* (*οὶπλλοί*), the body of the people is not to be considered as a substantial organism, turning inward, but as a divided, split, body, embarked on the never ending quest for a problematic identity. It is indeed in the test of multiple conflicts that the political community constitutes itself with the goal of bringing to all spheres, thanks to reduction, democratic universality, namely an experience of liberty offering itself as a rejection of domination, as non-domination.

Three characteristics can be attributed to insurgent democracy:

– Insurgent democracy is not a variant of conflictual democracy, but its exact opposite. While conflictual democracy practices conflict within the State, a democratic State which in its very name presents itself as an avoidance of the original conflict, inclining as a result conflictuality towards permanent compromise, insurgent democracy situates conflict in another space, outside the State, against it, and far from practicing the avoidance of the major conflict, – democracy against the State – it does not shrink from rupture, if need be. Insurgent democracy is born out of the intuition that there is no true democracy without reactivating the anarchic impulse which first rises against the classic expression of *arche* – at once commencement and commandment – namely, the State. In this sense, insurgency is the live source of true democracy; as well as, according to Machiavelli, the permanent struggle between the plebs and the Senate, the tumults of the plebs were the source of Roman liberty.

- Insurgency corresponds to the time of the caesura between two State forms; it is to recognize that the democracy which is inspired by it works to preserve this time of caesura, in doing so maintaining action in the Arendtian sense of the term and to preserve it from its ongoing transformation. Insurgent democracy is continued struggle for action against fabrication.
- The distinctive characteristic of insurgent democracy is to change appreciably the stakes. Instead of conceiving of emancipation as the victory of the social (a civil society reconciled) over the political, leading at the same time to the disappearance of the political, this form of democracy gives rise, works steadily towards giving rise to, a political community against the State. To the opposition of the social and the political, it substitutes that of the political and the State. Dethroning the State, it erects the political against the State and opens the too often concealed abyss between the political and the State.

The State is not the last word of the political, its accomplishment. On the contrary, it is only its systematic and destructive form of the *all ones* in the name of the One.

PREFACE

Of late, the tendency to treat Marx as a "dead horse" seems to be abating. Returns to Marx or comebacks of Marx are being announced and prepared all around us, though with clearly varied intentions. Have the obituaries played themselves out? Are we entering a new period in which Marx is "explained" in his own terms?

There are, then, many different returns to Marx. But rather than distinguishing them according to their specific objectives, we might do better to begin by drawing a line between those who are in the Marxist camp, or who are aligned with a given form of Marxism, and those who take a distinctly neutral or even antagonistic stance toward Marxism; between those who continue to make Marx a catalyst for movements, parties and States, and those who, turning their backs on these ways of using Marx, are ready to examine Marx in his singularity and in his solitude.

Marx frequently declared: "All I know is that *I* am not a Marxist." It would be a great mistake to see in this declaration only a provocative witticism coming from someone who has falsely been erected into a founding father. Marx sufficiently denounced and attacked "utopian substitutionism" – whereby a utopian claims to substitute himself for the social movement – to make it plain that he would just as vehemently contest any "theoretical substitutionism" – the substitution of the patrimonial name of a "great theoretician" for anonymous emancipation, the self-emancipation of the dominated class. In this sense, Marxism represents the inversion of Marx's thought – a thought that was in reality closer to Flora Tristan's project of a *Union Ouvrière* than to the various partisan or statist revisions developed by his self-proclaimed disciples. From this perspective, the collapse of the Marxist regimes falsely claiming to be "socialist" may be seen as having, among other salutary effects, "returned" Marx to us – a Marx freed from the rigidified ideological layers that have constituted a barrier between him and us. But in truth the return to Marx, or more precisely the rediscovery of a Marx beyond Marxism, did not wait for this collapse. In their respective ways, Maximilien Rubel and Michel Henry have already helped us hear Marx's voice again.

For Michel Henry this voice is philosophical, and his sharp verdict could hardly be clearer: "Marxism is the collection of misinterpretations that have been made of Marx" – a long-standing misapprehension reinforced by the prolonged unavailability of Marx's philosophical writings.[1] As Henry insists repeatedly, the astonishing truth is that Marxism established and defined itself without drawing on Marx's philosophical thought, and even in complete ignorance of it. It was, in fact, only in the 1920s that David Riazanov discovered Marx's main philosophical writings. Starting from this simple observation, Henry offers a revolutionary reading of Marx. Marx's historical and political writings are shown to rest on concepts that are not foundational and the essential concepts of Marxism are revealed as in no way Marx's own, since for him they are neither realities, nor principles of explanation. In this way we are reintroduced to Marx's philosophical enterprise, the quest for a reality overlooked by both Hegel and Feuerbach, a reality that is nothing other than practice, that is, pure activity as such.

In the case of Maximilien Rubel, the voice is more explicitly political. Rubel's rejection of any attempt to link Marx and Marxism is so emphatic that he actually winds up presenting Marx himself as the original and most essential critic of Marxism. Once the author of *Capital* is freed from his mythical role as the founding father of Marxism and as the progenitor of the October "Revolution" – the transformation of Marx's critical thought into party and statist ideology – he reemerges as what he never ceased to be: the theorist of workers' self-emancipation, responding to the double ethical exigency of utopia and revolution.[2]

As we observe the traditionalist form the return to political philosophy has taken in France, there is some concern that the return to a non-Marxist Marx may ultimately lead to a neutralization of his thought. Might the next step be Marx's integration into the academic corpus, with his thought safely severed from its roots in revolt and messianism? This concern, expressed by Jacques Derrida, is understandable, but there is nothing inevitable about this neutralization, because the return to Marx at the same time raises once again the question and the necessity of emancipation.[3]

In what follows, I will side with this type of return, which in truth is more like a reactivation than a return. I will focus in particular on an outstanding essay of Marx's that was published well after the establishment of Marxism: the *Critique of Hegel's Philosophy of Right*, written very likely in the summer of 1843 and published by David Riazanov in 1927. In this text Marx criticizes Hegel's *Philosophy of Right* virtually line-by-line, specifically §§261–313 in the third section of part III devoted to the State. My goal is less to propose a new overall interpretation of Marx's 1843 *Critique* than to find an answer to two essential questions: What status does Marx give to the political realm when he attempts to free the political logic specific to it from the grips of Hegelian logicality? And what type of society does Marx have in mind when he envisions a "true democracy," a democracy that would develop in tandem with the disappearance of the State? It is as though Marx, by raising the question of true democracy, were at once taking over for himself and pushing to its extreme the enigma brought to the world with the French Revolution.

This brings us back to the rift between Marx and Marxism. For it was by proposing an analysis of our contemporaneous Machiavellian moment – which may be considered as establishing itself through a critique of Marxism in order to rediscover a political realm lost either in philosophies of history or in scientistic projects – that I first became aware that an earlier Machiavellian moment already existed in Marx. And this moment was not unconnected with the adventure of the Young Hegelian movement, which is one of the sources, or testing grounds, of political modernity. We need only recall that in the span of just a few years, this movement gave birth to radical political liberalism (Ruge, Marx), socialism and communism (Moses Hess, Engels, Marx), anarchism (Bakunin, and perhaps also Stirner) and Zionism (Moses Hess).

That said, my aim is not to provide yet another rereading of Marx in light of some external referent, but to reactivate his major concepts and insights by following his own line of thought. If we consider the relationship of Marx's thinking to Machiavelli and Spinoza, we find an ongoing questioning of the political realm, a practical will to emancipate the *res publica* from the theological-political and from the vestiges of feudalism.

How does Marx's text – in which the notions of the political and of democracy seem to be so strongly linked – hold up when confronted with the examinations of his most scrupulous critics? I have in mind Hannah Arendt, Claude Lefort, and Theodor Adorno – critics who were respectful of Marx in the same sense that Benjamin Constant respected Rousseau even as he criticized him. Is it true that Marx was inclined *brevitatis causa* to neglect the specificity of politics by focusing on social forces, or to derive politics from economics, or to cloister himself in a sort of quietism as soon as the matter of ending domination was actually posed? In *Negative Dialectics*, Adorno writes: "Economics is said to precede domination, which must not be deduced otherwise than economically . . . The revolution desired by him [Engels] and Marx was the overthrow of the economic conditions of society as a whole, rather than a change in society's political form, in the rules of the game of domination."[4] But is it not more true to say that true democracy can be examined and understood only in terms of radical political concerns and the unceasing questioning implied by them?

Democracy *against* the State: this title is deliberately paradoxical in the literal sense of the term.

Its first target is the *doxa* of those partisans of democracy for whom democracy and State go together like two peas in a pod. They identify the two so easily that they seem to have no problem speaking of "the democratic State." Yet the linking of these terms, which seems so natural, does not go without saying. Why would there be any inherent affinity between the State and democracy when the latter was born in the ancient Greek cities? The notion of the "democratic State" has enabled State sovereignty to appeal alternately to both democratic and authoritarian modalities of political power, depending on circumstances or the whims of leaders.

But is democracy, or can it be reduced to, the modalities of State power, that is, to a mere method of government? If this is not the case, if, on the contrary, democracy is essentially a political institution of human sociality, then tensions, conflicts and even contradictions emerge between democracy and the State.

What if we reverse the terms and tackle the question from the standpoint of democracy instead of that of the State? Can the expression "statist democracy" be imagined without difficulty? The opposition between political democracy and "social democracy" is easily conceivable. Even the pleonasm "popular democracy," which was turned into such a cruel joke, can be understood. But "statist democracy" immediately strikes us as incongruous. In this resistance of language itself, it is as though a hidden antagonism, a latent, subterranean antagonism between democracy and the State were revealed, making it apparent that the State is definitely not the best form for democracy. Our society has adopted a peculiar way of functioning that is close to repression: as soon as a situation presents itself as a problem, it becomes an unsurpassable horizon – or worse, an insurmountable obstacle. Hence the habit of forgetting, or of hiding, the breakthroughs that shake up the limits that have been set on the possible. When we pause to consider the State, who still will debate the good news documented by Pierre Clastres under the title of *Society Against the State*?

The title of this book also deliberately contradicts the *doxa* of the opponents of democracy – or "democratism," as they sometimes call it. Despite their diametrically opposed perspective, they too unquestioningly identify democracy with the State. They reject democracy in the same breath as the State, and they do so all the more readily because they remain oblivious to the mutual antagonism between democracy and the State, democracy's inherent tendency to rise spontaneously against the State. But the invitation to envision democracy as arising over the dead body of the State is one of the great merits of Marx's 1843 manuscript; Marx creates an opening that must be explored, so that we can access this extraordinary form of political experience and confront the enigma of true democracy.

If Marx, like many of his contemporaries struggling for emancipation, was tormented throughout his life by specters, he also never ceased to contend with enigmas. Moses Hess, Marx's collaborator on the *Rheinische Zeitung*, offered in his article from 19 April 1842 one of the best summaries of this enigmatic horizon of the nineteenth century:

> The French Revolution entrusted modern times with the task of finding the solution to this enigma. *Liberty and equality*, this is what I want, declared the world revolution (. . .) Yet it was not as easy as it had originally seemed. The first primitive, natural, crude form of liberty and equality – *sans-culottisme* – did not last long: the Empire was the sickness engendered by the Revolution, and the Restoration was its tomb. Only then did the real history of the enigma begin, which is the history of bringing about its resolution. What was the July Monarchy, if not the first reasonable and intellectual attempt to realize liberty and equality? (. . .) But when we consider the great changes that have taken place since 1830 in the French, English or German *nations*, we have good grounds for hoping that the enigma has taken a step toward its solution.[5]

The difference between the nineteenth and the twentieth century is that the former believed that it possessed, or could possess, the solution, whereas the latter makes the enigma its dwelling, forewarned that the historical and political domains are destined to remain endlessly in question.

INTRODUCTION

I

For those who made a point of thinking it through, modern democracy immediately appeared as an enigma, or as a chain of paradoxes. This holds true for Alexis de Tocqueville as much as it does for Marx.

In his *Democracy in America* (1835), Tocqueville interprets the democratic revolution as a "providential fact" that "each day escapes from human power."[1] His desire for clear-headedness notwithstanding, Tocqueville confesses that he feels "a sort of religious terror" at the sight of this "irresistible revolution."[2] As the quintessential example of democracy, the United States represents "the password of the great social enigma" that is affecting the modern world.[3] Tocqueville's call for a new political science is an attempt at mastering, at correcting democracy's "savage instincts" in order to make the revolution submit to civilization, rather than having democracy rise freely and anarchically against it.[4] From now on, according to Tocqueville, the alternative is not between an aristocratic or a democratic society but between a democracy submitted to order and morality, or a "disorderly" and "depraved" democracy "abandoned to its frenzied fury."[5]

The terms "democratic State," which surface as early as the Introduction, express succinctly Tocqueville's project, as if at issue were making the tumultuous tide of democracy return to the bed of the State. Indeed, doesn't associating democracy with the State amount to dissociating democracy from the revolution – is not the bed of the State a bed of Procustus for democracy? Attentively bringing to light its ambiguity, Tocqueville presents all of democracy's manifestations, carefully revealing its counterparts and paradoxes.

Thus democracy, which rests on the principle of the people's sovereignty, is nonetheless seen as bringing forth an original form of despotism, as yet impossible to name, a tutelary more than tyrannical power liable to introduce a "sort of regulated, mild, and peaceful servitude."[6] Thus the democratic revolution, far from carrying on in a permanent revolutionary movement, is actually destined to sap the revolutionary passions by replacing subversive passions with new passions oriented more toward preserving the *status quo*.

For Dr Marx, a young German philosopher then struggling to import the French political model to Germany, democracy appears, in the language of the 1843 manuscript on Hegel's philosophy of right, as the "enigma of all the constitutions solved." In truth, however, this enigma is not so much solved as redoubled, since once Marx turns his attention to his French contemporaries he notes the emergence of a new enigma in their writings. "In democracy the State as particular is only particular, and as universal it is the real universal (. . .) The modern French have conceived it thus: In true democracy the *political State disappears* [*der politische Staat untergehe*]."[7] I will later return at length to this mysterious formula in order to elucidate it. As democracy expands and experiences a real fullness of life, the State diminishes. For now we may keep a preliminary question in mind: how can a political community, in this case a democratic one, have as its ultimate truth the disappearance of the political State? How could a political society persevere with the State's disappearance? Is this to say that a difference is to be found between the political realm and the State? It will be seen that modern democracy is only intelligible once it is thought as being *against* the State – and once the term "democratic State," which appeared so naturally from Tocqueville's pen, is by the same stroke rejected. Democracy will be construed instead as going beyond the boundaries marked out by the State, as pointing beyond the State, as though its calling were to overtake the State's designated limits, to overflow like a fertile, generous river, and extend to the whole body of the social realms.

Recognizing the appropriateness of the French moderns' formula, Marx makes their analysis his own. His adherence, from across the Rhine, is no swallow wholly unrelated to the springtime of peoples preceding 1848; it is situated at the heart of that springtime, and to judge from Marx's political interventions of the period, in which the *res publica* features as a sort of battle cry, it seems he belongs to what may rightly be called a "Machiavellian moment." When applied to Marx, this term may take one aback or engender ambiguities. I will therefore offer a few preliminary indications for my reading of the young Marx's political writings during the years 1842–4.[8]

As will become clear, I do not intend to contribute to Marxist political science, or to a "regional science" of the political realm, as British and American criticism tried to do a few years ago. Legitimately concerned by the general neglect surrounding the political dimension of Marx's writings, sensitive to its real importance, these critics endeavored to bring this dimension out by means of a materialist theory of society and history. Nor do I intend to help elaborate a materialist theory of the State, as if the issue were to make up for a regrettable blind-spot, or to assemble dispersed features of Marx's writings in order to produce a coherent theory that existed only in fragments.[9]

This is to say that I will deliberately keep my distance from Marxism, and more specifically from those sophisticated forms of Marxism that try to do away with the economistic depreciation of the political realm, and which never really succeed in doing so. Although this updated Marxism shows respect for a plurality of instances, for their reality and effectiveness, it in the end amounts to flattening the political back down upon the economic all the same, or to encouraging a sociological approach to matters that are specifically political.

What will here be at stake, rather, is apprehending the political writings of the young Marx as a *work of thought* in Claude Lefort's understanding of the term, that is, as a work born by an intention to know and in relation to which language is essential. By virtue of the links between Marx's thought and the tradition of political philosophy, there is, moreover, a legitimate case to be made for interpreting his writings from the standpoint of that tradition, or better, in light of how these writings helped shape the ultimate orientations of political philosophy. As such, my approach is defined against two poles of thought that converge in one important respect despite their differences: (1) against those Marxists who welcome Marx for having abandoned the forms of political thought specific to philosophical speculation; (2) against those who view Marx as having put an end to the tradition of political thought. By way of the path opened between these two poles, I hope to reveal a hidden or occulted dimension of Marx's work: a philosophical questioning of the political realm and of its very essence. While this questioning was particularly pronounced in the years 1842–4, it runs through the whole body of his work, including the apparent exceptions represented by his specifically political writings. And my first hypothesis is that this dimension is best revealed once we connect it to the tradition of modern political philosophy as ushered in by Machiavelli.

The use of Machiavelli as a reference-point should not be interpreted loosely. It here signifies neither the foundation of a positive, objectivizing political science supposedly inherited by Marx, nor a "political realism" according to which political theory would be reflection on relations of force. According to the "political realism" approach, the reflection on relations of force would be common to both Machiavelli and Marx, the former in view of establishing the modern nation-State, the latter in view of the proletariat's emancipation. However, if Machiavelli cannot be reduced to realism, it would be equally misguided to reduce the Marx/Machiavelli relationship to a resurgence of so-called Machiavellian realism in another social-historical framework, with other players, following the thesis that Marx is the Machiavelli of the proletariat. Instead, I propose to show how the young Marx, by virtue of his philosophical questioning of the political realm, has an essential relationship with Machiavelli, inasmuch as the latter is the founder of a normative, modern political philosophy based on criteria and principles of evaluation distinct from those of classical political philosophy.

This, then, is how Marx's placement in a Machiavellian moment becomes a legitimate object of inquiry.

In his reflections on "Machiavelli today" (1951), Eric Weil encouraged us to distinguish between two possible forms of Machiavelli's presence in our civilization. There is the academic presence, the debates by scholars and specialists over the genesis of the work, its meaning, and so forth. And there is the public presence, when Machiavelli suddenly appears on the political stage, and his name is evoked as a possible answer to the problems of the day. In the latter case, Machiavelli's stature changes. Despite the difference in time, he becomes, to all intents and purposes, a contemporary to those who speak of him, and a new ordering of thought arises. The question is no longer to address the topic called Machiavelli, but to think Machiavelli through, or better, to think *with* Machiavelli the political issues of the present. "New moments emerge which reinvent the thinker who was until then only an author among others: we address our impassioned question of the being of politics to him, we begin a discussion with him as though we were talking to a living colleague . . ."[10] Thus a whole other approach is uncovered. By means of this conversation with Machiavelli, the questions *What shall we do?*, or *How shall we act?*, are put aside in favor of the fundamental question: *Shall we act or not?* What is the legitimacy of political action? Wary of the possible relations between politics and evil, we may decide to abstain from action. It is no longer this or that political option that is being questioned, but politics itself, the politics that a famous Machiavellian – Napoleon – introduced as the destiny of the modern human being.

It is in this fundamental sense that the question of Marx's participation in a Machiavellian moment of his time finds its most resolute answer, especially since the Young-Hegelian movement to which Marx belonged can up to a certain point be understood with the help of this category. Bridging philosophy and radical journalism, Marx raises "the impassioned question of the being of politics" to the author of *The Prince* and *The Discourses* while developing it in several directions:

- What are the conditions for a philosophical thinking of the political realm?
- How are we to think political affairs?
- What is the status of the political, its nature or essence?
- What is the place of the political in the constitution of the social realm?
- What is the specific character of political modernity?

On the basis of these questions a unique relation between Marx and Machiavelli is formed; with regard to Leo Strauss's analysis of Machiavelli in the first wave of modernity, we could say a veritable "Machiavellianizing" of political thought occurs in which Marx played an active role.[11]

Marx indeed acknowledges, in an article from July 1842, the extent to which contemporary political philosophy, or the thinking of emancipation, establishes itself in a relation to the tradition. The idea of the State – what Marx calls "the conversion of the concept of the State into an independent concept" – far from being the whimsical invention of the latest political doctrines, stems, once one examines it carefully, from a living relationship to a diverse, centuries-old tradition inaugurated by Machiavelli and Campanella. In a word, the independence of the concept of the State results from the Machiavellian institution of modern political philosophy.[12] Actually, this is also a more satisfying way to formulate Marx's relation to the tradition, since the term "Machiavellianizing" avoids only exceptionally, and with difficulty, the Straussian periodization of political philosophy in modernity, that is, a course of decline interpreted as loss, the narrowing or shrinking of the horizon.[13]

With this critical specification in mind, we may tackle our question concerning Marx's contribution yet again and try to improve on it. For doesn't Marx belong to a Machiavellian constellation in another, more powerful, more determined and specific sense? In this case, not only would the thematic of Marx's Machiavellianism be more open and generous than one that would refer to loosely connected periods of "Machiavellianizing," not only would Marx appear as more than the executor of a tradition, but it would be more complex than the one proposed by Eric Weil. Whereas Weil's analysis presents the periodic Machiavellianizing as a sort of unstructured, almost arbitrary movement, a more careful consideration of these resurgences, or more precisely, these Machiavellian constellations in modern history, brings in view a genuine current of political and philosophical thought. This is notably what results from J. G. A. Pocock's great work on the Machiavellian moment.[14] Pocock unsettles the classical presentation of modern political philosophy, hitherto completely under the sway of the juridico-liberal model, by revealing its "hidden side": the existence of another model, a civic paradigm at once republican and humanist. In the wake of Hans Baron's writings on civic humanism, Pocock brings to light an alternative modern political philosophy that extends, according to him, from Florentine humanism to the American Revolution by way of Machiavelli and Harrington; it establishes itself by affirming the political nature of the human being and by designating the goal of politics, over and beyond the "defense of rights," as the practice of this primary political nature through the active participation of citizens in public affairs.

This Machiavellian moment and the constellations that result from it present three distinct elements:

1. The movement by which political actors and thinkers have, over several centuries, worked to reactivate the *vita activa* of the Ancients, to liberate the *bios politikos* (life devoted to public affairs) from the primacy of the *vita contemplativa* and the discredit inflicted on the political realm by Christianity and the promise of the heavenly city. This rehabilitation of civic life, of life in and for the city, builds on the resurgence of the Aristotelian definition of the human being as a political animal that cannot attain excellence except in and through the condition of citizenship. In addition to the critical distance taken from the Platonic tradition and from the privilege given to the contemplative life, the rediscovery of the political realm implies a revolution of the medieval mentality. The medieval man had recourse to reason in order that he may, through contemplation, have the eternal hierarchies of an immutable order of the world revealed, and in the last analysis, in order to have his own place in creation set. Thus the world of

historical particularity and contingency was the irrational sphere, the flux from which every man was to withdraw. By contrast, the partisan of civic humanism breaks from contemplative life in favor of action and redefines reason simultaneously as the potential of action to give a human and political form to the chaos of contingency and particularity. Oriented toward making decisions in common, this new form of civic existence recognizes the linguistic nature of humankind and tends to consider access to truth as the fruit of free exchange; the role of rhetoric, which had been so present in the ancient city, here recovers its lost stature, and the saying *civitas facit legem* defines the new principle, in opposition to Dante's patriotism, his vision of a fulfillment of the eternal order, as much as to the demagogical syncretism of the Roman Cola di Rienzo.

It is almost in Arendtian terms that Pocock comprehends the specifically political dimension of this Machiavellian moment and the establishment of a new earthly city. "This book has told part of the story of the revival in the early modern West of the ancient ideal of *homo politicus* (the *zoon politikon* of Aristotle), who affirms his being and his virtue by the medium of political action, whose closest kinsman is *homo rhetor* and whose antithesis is the *homo credens* of Christian faith."[15]

2. The choice of the republic as the only form of *politeia* of a nature to satisfy the exigencies of the human being as a political animal destined to find fulfillment in the *vivere civile*, and those of a secular historicity. The opposition to Dante is thereby reinforced, since his ideal of universal monarchy aimed at blocking historicity for the sake of better preserving an eternal order and its contemplation. Beyond the revision of the myth of the foundation of Florence – Brutus the Republican, the hero of liberty, taking the place of Caesar – the point is to conceive a political community set apart from dominion, and through the choice of a republic to gain access to practical temporality. Against the rejection of time proper to Empire and universal monarchy, the republican idea is linked to a reaffirmation of temporality, or better, to an idea of action that, deploying itself in time, endeavors in its effective actuality to separate political order from the natural order of things.
3. This rehabilitation of the republican form therefore goes hand-in-hand with placing community in time. As a creative potential in history, the republic is by the same stroke withdrawn from eternity, open to crisis, transitory; moreover, as a form of non-universality, it appears as a specific historical community. The republican form

that results from the will to create a worldly, secular order subject to the contingence of the event is thereby vulnerable to temporal finitude, to the test of time. And thus a further line of questioning: Is the republic, which up to a certain point represents a reactivation of the Aristotelian *politeia*, a form of political community capable of experiencing stability in time? In other words, despite the blows of chance and the effects of corruption, can it persevere in its being thanks to the politicization of virtue?

It is therefore this Machiavellian centering of the political domain on itself that Marx welcomed in 1842, and he welcomed it all the more vigorously as he intended to repeat the Machiavellian move against the specters of the theological-political that continued to haunt his own day. Beyond this, Marx's goal was to bring back in view the great classical, Aristotelian discovery of the human being as a political animal.

It is this mingling of Aristotle and Machiavelli, then, that makes Marx's intentions approximate so closely the spiritual tenor of a Machiavellian constellation. A few questions may help us consider better Marx's placement in this more specific understanding of the Machiavellian moment:

- To what extent did Marx remain faithful to the Machiavellian aim to circumscribe an irreducible political domain, place of politics or political realm?
- To what extent did Marx really do justice to modern political philosophy's aim to make the political realm autonomous, or to borrow his own terms from 1842, to convert the concept of the State into an independent concept?
- Finally, to what extent did his rediscovery of the political realm in opposition to the feudal Christian State – his manner of conceiving political emancipation against that form of State which, in truth, is a non-State – participate in a civic, humanist and republican paradigm? Beyond this mingling of Aristotle and Machiavelli, beyond Marx's "Greek inspiration," is it legitimate to see a relationship between the "true democracy" of 1843 and the orientations of republican humanism?[16]

II

By contrast to the great majority of critics, who make Marx's social and political writings begin in 1843 with the *Critique of Hegel's*

Philosophy of Right, I will distinguish, at least for the purposes of the present inquiry, two constellations of writings, those from 1842, and the texts from 1843–4 which are separated by a veritable crisis, the crisis of 1843. The first constellation contains the texts corresponding to the utopia of the rational State; its end can be dated 25 January 1843, when Marx writes to Arnold Ruge: "I can do nothing more in Germany. Here one makes a counterfeit of oneself."[17] The second constellation designates the great writings of 1843 which focus on the critique of Hegel's political philosophy, as well as *The Jewish Question* and the "Critical Marginal Notes on the Article 'The King of Prussia and Social Reform. By a Prussian'" (August 1844) – which should be read in the context of the Marx–Ruge correspondence (from March to September 1843, published in February 1844 in the *Deutsch-Französische Jahrbücher*). By bringing out the theory of the modern State, that is, the thinking of the political realm as it appears in these first writings, we may grasp better the meaning of the ulterior criticism of politics. It is as though a comparison of the 1842 writings with those of 1843–4 were to reveal, with regard to the status given to the political realm, two constellations in which the second one functions as a critique of the original positions. Should we fail to make this distinction between the two series of writings, we would be unable to offer a proper account of the crisis of 1843, the stakes involved and the full significance of the innovation; we would miss, then, the change in perspective that Marx carries out at the beginning of 1843.

There are two constellations first in the sense that Marx's 1842 writings, far from just expressing a democratic tendency more or less accentuated at the level of the political positions taken, are theoretically oriented not so much toward political emancipation as toward *emancipation of the political from the theological*, that is, from the juggernaut of the Christian State. If this essential position concerning the independence of political affairs is expressed by an attempt to import the republican idea to the Germanic world, it moreover leads to a genuine rediscovery of the political realm. The place of the political is considered as irreducible, as having its own consistency and – from within the logic of this independence – as determinant. In this respect close to Rousseau for whom "everything stems radically from politics," Marx puts the political world back in its sphere, recenters it, so to speak, and in this way elaborates for himself a new figure of the Machiavellian moment.

Yet two constellations appear also in the sense that, by contrast to the theses of 1842, the writings of 1843 begin to question the determinant power of the political realm, at least to the extent that it is identified with the State. The critique of the modern State, worked out in view of the autonomy of civil society, opens the way to a new kind of decentering of the political realm. In view of this blow to the independence of the concept of the State, a new question will arise: What now remains of the Machiavellian moment?

According to Marx's Preface to the *Critique of Political Economy* (1859), it is the 1843 crisis that led him to the general conclusion that would guide his later writings. If we follow his own narrative, it is after the articles written for the *Rheinische Zeitung* and following the paper's failure that, in order to "dispel the doubts assailing" him, he undertook a first work, "a critical revision of the Hegelian philosophy of right." When Marx considers the upshot of this crisis, he formulates the famous propositions that make up the cornerstone of what Marxists generally call "historical materialism," one of the effects of which is to deny expressly the independence of the political and the juridical. In Marx's words, "neither legal relations nor political forms could be comprehended whether by themselves or on the basis of a so-called general development of the human mind; on the contrary they originate in the material conditions of life (. . .) in civil society; the anatomy of this civil society is to be sought in political economy (. . .) In the social production of their existence, men inevitably enter into definite relations of production appropriate to a given stage in the development of their material forces of production. The totality of these relations of production constitutes the economic structure of society, the real foundation, on which arises a legal and political superstructure and to which correspond definite forms of social consciousness. The mode of production of material life conditions the general process of social, political, and intellectual life. It is not the consciousness of men that determines their existence, but their social existence that determines their consciousness."[18] The crisis is therefore essential. It seems to allow for two different interpretations.

- When we read this practically "canonical" text, in which Marx offers his own interpretation of the 1843 Critique, we are compelled to note a decentering of the political, since it is construed as a derivable and in a sense secondary phenomenon. At the same time that he denies the independence of the political, Marx naturalizes it by inscribing it within the field of infra-structural necessity, or in a totality of relations of force. A rupture with the Machiavellian innovation thereby becomes apparent: the reference to the institution of modern political philosophy fades away to the point of leaving its place to an objective science of social totality.

– Yet, as Marx emphasizes in the same text from 1859, "one does not judge an individual according to the idea he has of himself." Instead of sticking to the ultimate result of the 1843 crisis, as Marx does in 1859, we may instead *rework our way toward the result,* independently of Marx's self-analysis. By following pathways that do not necessarily lead to the result presented and hailed by Marx in 1859, we may find ourselves in touch with another dimension of the 1843 essay, one forgotten or repressed by Marx when he began writing the *Critique of Political Economy.* By way of a close reading of the movement of thought, the critic may perceive a specifically philosophical dimension to Marx's critique of Hegel, an ongoing questioning of the political realm. This kind of reading quite evidently implies its own strategy, in that it withdraws from existing orthodoxies, from the project of mastering a text, and lets itself be led by Marx's own questions, without for all that sealing them up in an answer. The point is to play off the contradictions, the tensions and their lateral implications that run right through the text in order to give oneself fully to the labor of unsealing Marx's writing.

If we approach matters this way, if we keep the self-interpretation of 1859 at a distance, is it still possible to consider quite simply that Marx – after having returned to the political realm its proper consistency, after having established its independence by dissociating the modern State from the theological – would in 1843 take an opposite direction and deny the independence of the political by making it derive from the economic? Is it at all likely that the political realm put back on its feet in 1842 and freed from the theological-political, would be thrown off its center a year later, overturned by the project of subordinating this newly won independence to the socio-economic?

In short, does the crisis of 1843 amount to an epistemological crisis during which Marx would have sought and found a new base that would enable him to account "scientifically" for the political realm? Or is the crisis a properly political and philosophical one, during which Marx would have sought a new political subject, an alternative to the State that would bring to its zenith what he himself calls "the political principle"? A preferable site is available for judging the reality of the 1843 decentering and its effects: either the Machiavellian moment is canceled and effaced – which would reduce it to a mere stage in Marx's evolution and make it mostly of historical interest – or there is a shift and a reorientation of the Machiavellian moment, which would confer to this moment the status of a permanent dimension in Marx's oeuvre. This theoretical site is established in 1843 in the formulation of the question of democracy and in the enigma of the proposition I recalled from the outset, concerning the discovery of the French moderns. Do we here have an unprecedented placement in the Machiavellian moment, characterized by research on the milieu proper to politics that most aptly brings the enigmatic place of "true democracy" in view? The relationship that must be posed, and perhaps even maintained, between the criticism of politics and human emancipation depends, then, on our answer to this question. Without for the moment addressing it, we may note that if we observe a tendency in Marx to occult the political realm by naturalizing it – that is, a tendency to insert it within a dialectical theory of social totality – his work seems simultaneously to be haunted by a contrary orientation. It is as though the heterogeneity of the political, its radical instituting power, were to haunt Marx his whole life long – as the richness and the complexity of his political writings amply suggest – as if Marx never ceased to question the enigma of the foundation of political community, the life in common of human beings.

My reading will rest, especially in the second half of this book, on the 1843 *Critique of Hegel's Philosophy of Right*, which was published, as I have emphasized, for the first time in 1927. This text should not be confused with "A Contribution to the Critique of Hegel's Philosophy of Right," an incisive piece of writing, in which the discovery of the negativity of the proletariat is first announced, and which Marx published in Paris in the *Deutsch-Französische Jahrbücher* (1844), along with "The Jewish Question" and the correspondence with Ruge.

As for its audience, the 1843 Critique has received only a moderate reception. Whereas *The 1844 Manuscripts* inspired numerous interpretations – ranging from that of the young Marcuse, to Christian or spiritualist versions, inspiring anti-bureaucratic struggles against totalitarian domination – the 1843 Critique has for the most part been studied academically as an important phase in the genesis of Marx's thought, but only as a phase.[19] Of course, the 1843 Critique does not have the scope of the *Manuscripts*, since this work transforms the critique of political economy into a cohesive criticism of modern society. But the 1843 Critique is nonetheless an exceptional work in the sense that, by making Hegel's philosophy of right emblematic for political thought in the modern period, it simultaneously offers a veritable critique of political modernity under the banner of democracy, making it, in Michel Henry's view, an extraordinary text of unlimited philosophical significance.

Why then the relative disinterest? Shall we conclude that the "Contribution to the Critique of Hegel's Philosophy of Right," which Marx himself published, threw a shadow over the manuscript of 1843 by reducing it to the status of a preparatory work? Or did Marx's judgment in 1859 intimidate critics from exploring a route that would challenge his self-interpretation?

Perhaps the explanation is to be found at a more fundamental level. Would a careful and unprejudiced reading of the 1843 Critique throw Marx's standard image into question? Would it reveal an unexpected dimension to his thought, as though alongside the naturalization of the political, the "impassioned questioning of the being of politics" simultaneously persisted, as well as the no less impassioned investigation into figures of liberty that appear under names such as "true democracy" or "disappearance of the State"?

The questions addressed in this study on Marx are undoubtedly tied to questions of our own day. Are we at a Machiavellian moment that would constitute itself in the Marx–Machiavelli relationship, or in the opposition of these two ways of thinking? Before exploring the significance of this opposition in its own right, my purpose here is to show how the Marx–Machiavelli device works in Marx himself, to make it reemerge as an inner tension of his thought, and to reveal in Marx's writings, by way of this course, several possibilities of an unfinished modernity.

— 1 —

THE UTOPIA OF THE RATIONAL STATE

Marx's essays from 1842 and the beginning of 1843 (the 15 January article on the vine-growers of Mosel) may at first be interpreted as a complete and coherent expression of the theory of the rational democratic State – as it were, an epitome of the democratic movements' practical struggle during the French Revolution and the theoretical struggle of the German philosophers – written in the wake of those whom Walter Benjamin describes as "the Germans of 1789."[1] Marx's radical journalism put a theme into play that reappears as a leitmotif in the Left Hegelian movement: the present time is – or rather, must be – a time of politics. In 1841, Arnold Ruge welcomes the new movement, essentially Bruno Bauer and Ludwig Feuerbach, as the latest German equivalent of the *Montagnards*. And in the *Deutsche Jahrbücher*, in 1842, the same Ruge launches his critique of Hegel's philosophy of right by describing the character of the new era: "Our times are political, and our politics intend the freedom of this world. No longer do we lay the ground for the ecclesiastical State, but for the secular State, and the interest in the public issue of freedom in the State grows with every breath that humans take."[2]

This rediscovery of politics, or better still, this reawakening of the political element itself, is in Ruge's view the manifestation of a spiritual revolution whose fulfillment in a new form of life will depend on the rejuvenation of political virtue. It is in the name of this new life that Ruge criticizes the old-guard of diplomatic, compromising German philosophers, such as Kant and Hegel. "Their systems are systems of reason and freedom in the midst of irrationality and lack of freedom."[3] Ruge thus focuses on emphasizing Hegel's contradictions: he who understood the essence of the State as the realization of the ethical idea, who rightly flogged the Germans for their political nothingess and favored political *praxis*, nonetheless shut himself into a unilaterally theoretical viewpoint, was blind to the relationship between theory and existence, and conceived reconciliation only in the realm of spirit and in the form of speculative mediation. The new movement aims at overcoming these contradictions by working for the realization of reason in existence, by abandoning a purely theoretical point of view and giving priority to the free will of human beings. The new critical tendency – and in this respect it constitutes a profound reawakening of the political element – presents itself as the unity of free will and thought and proposes to replace the philosophy of spirit with a philosophy of free will and action.

In a polemical vein, it is this veritable faith of the young Hegelians that was targeted in 1845 by the critical arrows of Max Stirner's *The Ego and its Own*: "State! State! So ran the general cry, and thenceforth people sought for the 'right form of State,' the best constitution, and so the State in its best conception. The thought of the State passed into all hearts and awakened enthusiasm; to serve it, this mundane god, became the new divine service and worship. The properly *political* epoch had dawned."[4] Arthur Rosenburg is therefore quite right, in his *History of Bolshevism*, to bring out Marx's Jacobin inspiration, in the broad sense of the term. For Marx, editor of the *Rheinische Zeitung*, a daily founded in January 1842 by representatives of the Rhenish bourgeoisie opposing Prussian absolutism, the task of the present times is to bring the model of the French revolutionary State over to Germany, to create a rational State in which Germans, still submerged in the immaturity of spirit, would be raised to political modernity and transformed into a people of citizens. Announcing to Ruge in March 1842 his intention to elaborate a critique of Hegel's theory of natural right, and especially the internal political system, Marx writes: "The central point is the struggle against *constitutional monarchy* as a hybrid which from beginning to end contradicts and abolishes itself. *Res publica* is quite untranslatable into German."[5] And, tested by failure, shortly before his move to "Paris, capital of the nineteenth century," where he would collaborate with Ruge in editing the first and only issue of the *Deutsch-Französische Jahrbücher*, Marx confesses the absurdity of this project in the Germany of Frederick William IV: ". . . Germany is sunk deep in the mire and will sink still deeper . . . one has a feeling of national shame, even in Holland. The most insignificant Dutchman is still a citizen compared with the greatest German."[6] The reference to Holland should catch our attention, for it has a significant place in Marx's intellectual development; Holland is first of all the land of Spinoza and of the *Tractatus*

Theologico-Politicus, which Marx had cited extensively in a notebook from 1841. But at that time Holland is also a rare example of republicanism in the midst of absolutist Europe – proof, in other words, that the republic is not a mere ideal of the past but a possible destiny for the modern world.

Marx's contributions as a political journalist may therefore be analyzed, on a first level, as a harmonious conjunction of Jacobinism and Left Hegelianism. This means, then, a program that consists in emancipating the State from religion through the creation of secular political community, and destroying the political forms of the Ancien Régime – the hierarchical structures, the rule of privilege – in order to replace them with a democratic republic based on political equality.

Yet a reading of these writings in strictly political terms, no matter how exact, is evidently insufficient. For the political positions that are here asserted are in a sense *derived.* Indeed – and this is what legitimates seeing in this new movement the presence of a Machiavellian moment – we may perceive in this political thematic, beyond the opposition to the Christian State and the political forms of the Ancien Régime, the reactivation, or even the repetition, of a phenomenon of far greater breadth, since it puts the very being of society into question, reformulating the relationship of thought and action, philosophy and politics. In Claude Lefort's analysis, this movement of thought conditions the emergence of a universalist and rationalist conception of politics, in this case Florentine humanism. This is a groundbreaking phenomenon, since at stake is "a radical change not only in political thinking but also in the very categories according to which reality is determined."[7] With the rupture from the theological representation of the world, there is a disentangling "of the place of politics for thought, and consequently an attributing of reality to the place specific to politics. What could then be realized is a relationship to that place, not a new political discourse, but a discourse on politics as such."[8]

To justify this "maximal" reading and grasp the constitution of the Machiavellian moment, we will recall two essays, one by Feuerbach and one by Marx. Both of these essays indeed exemplify how the political discourse of the "modern French," held at the German scene in the years 1841–3, is the derived effect of a foundational discourse on politics, or more precisely, on the place of politics, and are completely inclined toward reclaiming the political dimension as a dimension constitutive of humanity.

In his essay on the "Necessity for a Reform of Philosophy" (1842),

Feuerbach calls for a transformation of philosophy; and to highlight the radical and innovative character of this project, he distinguishes between two types of reforms: a reform internal to philosophy, "the child of philosophical need," and an external reform that refers to the historical world outside the field of philosophy, and is therefore of a kind to satisfy a need of humanity. It is this second type of reform that he eagerly recommends, and its necessity is seen as stemming from two changes in the historical situation: on the one hand, a religious transformation in the form of a negation of Christianity, on the other, the upsurge of a new need of humanity, the need of political liberty, or simply, the political need. Feuerbach's reform therefore rests on a principled hostility between Christianity and the new fundamental need of humanity, and he describes this hostility in Machiavellian terms: "Men throw themselves into politics today because they recognize in Christianity a religion which destroys their political energy."[9] In a word, politics has replaced religion. From this conversion of the human gaze, redirected from heaven to earth, Feuerbach deduces simultaneously the exigency of a reform in philosophy and the tendency of that reform. Philosophy must now transform religion, or more precisely, it must elaborate the "supreme principle" that would allow politics to become a new religion, so that the political need is not simply registered in the mind but penetrates through to the heart.

It is political need, then, to which is given the status of the need for a new period in human history, that determines and demands the reform of philosophy. We may notice, moreover, the veritable reversal carried out by Feuerbach at the heart of this typically dialectical procedure. The negation of religion is posited as the condition of possibility for reclaiming the political realm. Yet the disentangling of the political from the theological, that is, the emancipation of politics from the hold of religion, itself expresses a preliminary moment of philosophy's transformation into religion by virtue of this very liberation. This new consecration of politics will determine through and through Feuerbach's construction of the concept of the State.

From the standpoint of its genesis, according to Feuerbach, the State is deduced from the negation of religion: it is when the religious tie is broken or is dissolved that the political community may arise. Or again, it is once the relation to God fades away that the inter-human relationship may establish itself. This is how the new supreme principle works in its negative form, as atheism.

From the standpoint of its very constitution – the supreme principle's realization in its positive form, as "realism" – the State is made up of a complex sequence of two overlapping processes. It is as if the termination of religious cohesion were followed by a splitting apart, by a separation or by an unlinking of the immaterial community, but in such a way that a whole new link would necessarily come about, a political connection, the link that establishes itself in and through politics. For Feuerbach, the theological-political is fundamentally inconceivable, since this combination attempts to keep two forms of consciousness together which work logically in opposing directions. "Ordinary religion is less the cohesion of the State than its dissolution." To posit God as father, provider, "regent and lord of world monarchy," is to make the interhuman link specific to the political realm an inanity, for in this case "man does not stand in need of man . . . he depends on God rather than on man. On this account, man is only accidentally related to man." It is only with the fading away of the religious form of social cohesion, with the moment of separation, that the establishment of the new form of union, the political link becomes possible. As the subjective genesis of the State is considered, a relationship between the dissolution of religion and the development of the State comes in view. "The reason that men came together is precisely that they do not believe in any God, that they negate their religious belief . . . Not the belief in God, but rather the doubt concerning him is the actual cause underlying the foundation of States. From the point of view of the subject, it is the belief in man as the God of man that explains the origin of the State."[10] The coming out from the theological-political thus occurs through a dynamic of rupture and reunion, of disaffiliation and renewed cohesion that returns human subjects to their finitude while opening a new ascendant sequence. The rise of the new infinite subject springs from the freshly appropriated incompleteness of finite subjects, and the characteristics of this new subject, of the human relationship brought back to itself, are remarkable. The State is posited as an infinite being, as a totality, as pure activity and self-determination, in short, as endowed with all the attributes of divinity. "The State comprehends all realities and is man's providence for him. Within the State, one man represents the other . . . I am surrounded by a universal being; I am part of a whole. The true State is the unlimited, infinite, true, perfect, and divine man. It is primarily the State in which man emerges as man; the State in which the man who relates himself to himself is the self-determining, the absolute man . . . human beings come together for the State because here they are without God, because the State is their God, which is why it can justifiably claim for itself the divine predicate of 'majesty.'"[11]

This text, then, is fundamental for our purposes:

Beyond the recognition of the political need as a specific need of modernity, there indeed appears here, on the ruins of the theological representation of the world, a *philosophical institution of the political realm.* As it were, the political realm, raised to the status of working out a new philosophical principle – "realism" – would be the place where the question that never ceases to haunt history is finally thought and resolved: the advent of a universal, wholly self-transparent subject, instituting in the identity of being the era of earthly reconciliation. Moreover, this very modern exaltation of the political realm undeniably brings out a dynamic that, according to Jacques Taminiaux, characterizes modernity, that is, its "set purpose for the obliteration and even the debarment of finitude," and that may arise even in the midst of a philosophy that admits finitude – in this case, Feuerbach's evocation of the "heart," source of affectivity, of need and sensuality.[12] Finally, this text seems to define best the spiritual climate in which the young Marx began to think and to write. It is as if the exaltation of the political formed the horizon, and perhaps the theoretical matrix, in relation to which Marx thought in succession – the modern State, "true democracy," and communism – as many names for the finally resolved enigma of history, the attainment of self-identity or what Feuerbach understands by realism: "Direct unity with ourselves, with the world, with reality."[13] It is in light of this rehabilitation of the political realm that "The Leading Article in No. 179 of the *Kölnische Zeitung*" (14 July 1842), which Marx wrote as a sort of succinct Machiavellian–Spinozist manifesto, should be interpreted. For the purpose of this essay, in fact, is to reply to an article influenced by the logic of the Christian State and that as such denies philosophy the right to treat political questions rationally.

I say Machiavellian–Spinozist manifesto, since Marx, an assiduous reader of Spinoza, and particularly of the *Tractatus Theologico-Politicus* during the year 1841, grounds his whole counter-attack concerning the right of philosophy to treat political questions on principles put forward by Spinoza, one of the first, as we know, to have recognized in Machiavelli the love of liberty (*Treatise on Politics*, ch. V).[14] In several instances, Marx engages in a virulent critique of the ignorance whose demonic power results historically in so much tragedy. But above all, he restates the Spinozist theme of the rightful separation between theology or faith and philosophy: while the former has as its object obedience and the ardor of conduct, philosophy aims at truth (Preface to the *Tractatus Theologico-Politicus*, and ch. XV). From this Marx deduces the vocation of philosophy to gain knowledge of truth, based on the model of the knowledge of nature. "Is there no universal human nature, as there is a universal nature of plants and stars? Philosophy asks what is true, not what is held to be true."[15] Thus the specific character of philosophical discourse; as the work of reason, it demands to be heard by reason: "You speak without having studied . . . philosophy speaks after studying . . . You appeal to the emotions, it appeals to reason."[16] Marx also deduces the right of human reason, or of philosophy, to address human affairs and the organization of the city not "in the obscure language of private opinion" but "in the clarifying language of the public reason." The "newspapers not only may, but must discuss political questions. It seems obvious that philosophy, the wisdom of the world, has a greater right to concern itself with the realm of this world, with the State, than has the wisdom of the other world, religion."[17] Not only is the central theme of the *Tractatus Theologico-Politicus* recalled – the freedom of philosophical inquiry – but also the idea that the foundation of the *Res publica* requires destroying the theological-political *nexus*. This impure mixture of faith, belief, and submissive discourse, this particular alliance of the political and the theological (such as the Christian State contemporaneous with Marx) invades the city in the name of divine authority and enslaves the political community; worse, the theological-political totally undermines the inner equilibrium of a political community by superposing over its logic a logic that stems from another order.

From Machiavelli to Marx through Spinoza, there is then a common thread that consists in the liberation of political community from the despotism of theology in order to reestablish the proper consistency of the political realm, and thus to allow for the advent of a rational State. This advent, according to Marx, "need only be derived from human relations, and this derivation is realized by philosophy." Consequently, one ought to "judge the rightfulness of State constitutions not on the basis of Christianity, but on the basis of the State's own nature and essence, not on the basis of the nature of Christian society, but on the basis of the nature of human society."[18]

It is all the more important to bring out this continuity given that it represents quite exactly the line of battle chosen by Marx in his offensive against the partisans of the Christian State. Which does not mean the issue is simply one of occupying a strategic position. Marx seeks, rather, to interpret the history of political philosophy from his own perspective, to define for himself the specific nature of modernity's contribution to political thought. Several remarkable formulas confer upon this article the look of a manifesto. Marx proposes to circumscribe the *initium* starting from which it becomes possible to think political affairs. In his view, at stake is a veritable Copernican revolution: "Immediately before and after the time of Copernicus' great discovery of the true solar system, *the law of gravitation of the State was discovered, its own gravity was found in the State itself* (. . .) Machiavelli and Campagnella, and later Hobbes, Spinoza, Hugo Grotius, right down to Rousseau, Fichte and Hegel, began *to regard the State through human eyes and to deduce its natural laws from reason and experience, and not from theology.*"[19] This is to say that the legitimacy of questioning philosophically the political realm is based on its independence. Inversely, the independence of the concept of the State is to be brought into a relationship with the critical labor of philosophy, with the movement of emancipation that allowed for the constitution of secular knowledge of the political realm in its independence. Marx in fact links the establishment of secular knowledge to the modern theory of balancing powers. Thus the discovery of the modern political system is inscribed in the general movement by which the sciences are emancipated from revelation and religious belief, a movement instigated by Bacon of Verulam who, according to Marx, had the foresight to emancipate physics from theology. It should nonetheless be noted that, while Marx recognizes the modern innovation as such, he insists on its relation to classical political thought, as though modernity had leaped over Christianity to resume a form of questioning proper to antiquity. "Recent philosophy has only continued the work begun by Heraclitus and Aristotle."[20] Socrates, Plato, Cicero represent for Marx as many summits of historical culture, symbols for those moments when the blossoming of popular life was coextensive with the rise of philosophy and the decline of religion. This relation to the Ancients is important, for it indicates well enough the complexity, if not the ambiguity, of a text in which the relation to modern science, and the independence of the concept of the State inspired by Machiavelli, coexist without implying a commitment to empiricism. Actually, the opposite is the case. Marx enriches the so-called independence of the concept of the State with other determinations, or rather, he elaborates it in a speculative direction. To consider the State through human eyes, to discover the law of the State's gravitation, to discover this law as something internal to the State itself: these key propositions have a twofold meaning: that in order to apprehend the logic of the State it must be emancipated from the theological, and that this emancipation is not only a liberation in the form of separation and negation but must also lift itself to the level of a *position,* to an affirmative liberty. In other words, once the independence has been gained, it is imperative not to bring the logic of politics over to realms that are non-political and of a kind to offer an empirical genesis of the State; otherwise, the political dimension retrieved by thought would be occulted all over again.

This is why Marx purposefully takes his distance from those modern theories of natural right (Hobbes, Grotius, Kant) that, despite their divergences, all represent the State according to an empirical genesis of a socio-psychological kind. "The earlier philosophers of constitutional law proceeded in their account of the formation of the State from the instincts, either of ambition or gregariousness, or even from reason, though not social reason, but the reason of the individual."[21] Marx, to the contrary, chooses to follow the new philosophy that expresses "the more ideal and profound view" – undoubtedly the Hegelian view – of elaborating a speculative concept of the political realm.

The State is construed by Marx as an organic totality, as a being whose specific modality is the system. Thus the unity of the multiple realized by the system of the State, or by the State *qua* system, is not to be considered as a unity-result stemming from the association or the linking of multiplicity, whether it be harmonious, or, from the empiricist's standpoint, whether it be conflicting. Instead, it would be the unity that would have an organic character. The most ideal idea of the State, by which Marx means the speculative idea of the State, is constructed starting from the idea of totality, or from "social reason." Another result of the speculative conception of the State is that all thought of a separation, of an externality between the individual-citizen and the universality of the State is rejected in favor of an integration of singularity in organic unity, or, more exactly, the recognition of a perfect adequacy between individual reason and the reason of the State-institution, which is itself the work of human reason.[22] The speculative framework of Marx's thought is worth emphasizing, for we may then measure quite closely the dimension in which the idea of the State's independence should be placed. The idea of the independence of the concept of the State should in fact be understood in two senses. In its negative meaning, establishing the independence of the State implies a rejection of an empirical genesis as much as a refusal of a contractual model, or of a genesis based on individual reason. In its positive meaning, thinking the State according to its concept, as a primary form at once integrative and organizational, demands thinking this independence at its highest level, so that it may cover all its implications, to the point of recognizing in political community the instituting power of the social realm.

To view the State as the "great organism," to position it beyond all derivation, is by the same stroke to admit its primacy and to place it in the very place of instituting sociality.

Marx's essay remains more sober than Feuerbach's. Nonetheless, we may notice that in the thought of both the struggle against the theological representation of the world opens the way for a rediscovery of the political realm, for "attributing reality to the place specific to politics," even though the requirement explicitly stated by Feuerbach – that "politics must become our religion" – reveals that the question of the links between the political and the religious has never been settled within modernity.

— 2 —

POLITICAL INTELLIGENCE

The full import of the independence of the concept of the State is revealed once we no longer examine the constitution of the Machiavellian moment in Marx and focus instead on how Marx contributes to it, in his reflection on the press, and in his theoretical elaboration of the State's reconstruction. Let us begin with this last point. If the State is the self-becoming of reason, the standpoint of reason alone constitutes the legitimate perspective from which to articulate a theory of the State. This is to say that in the young Marx's writings, political criticism is dependent on philosophical criticism, and the criticism of private interest is dependent on the criticism of empiricism. "The State, this natural realm of the spirit, must not and cannot seek and find its true essence in a fact apparent to the senses."[1] In order to submit "the rights of young trees" to human rights, Marx will develop a theory of "political intelligence." Political intelligence indicates the operation of spirit by which the facts apparent to the senses are interpreted, adjusted, and organized. Said otherwise, a fact apparent to the senses can only have a meaning in and by the operation of political intelligence. This means that, to the extent that a legislator is on a par with the properly modern worldview, far from judging facts empirically in their immediacy he will apprehend them through the eyes of the State and determine their meaning by carrying them over to its spiritual terrain. Political intelligence is a *principle*, in the sense both of a beginning and a foundation; that is, it is "the organizing soul." Political intelligence designates the new faculty that corresponds to the Copernican revolution in politics: it defines the center about which all objects encountered by the legislator must turn; the horizon of meaning according to which they must be understood and shaped. "Political intelligence will, for example, regulate landed property according to State principles, but it will not regulate State principles according to landed property. Political intelligence will assert landed property not in accordance with its private egoism, but in accordance with the State nature of landed property."[2] Reductive of all exteriority and an organ of totalization, political intelligence is that which allows for the homecoming of spirit in and by the State-form. "For intelligence nothing is external, because it is the inner determining soul of everything."[3]

The political effects of such a standpoint are easily anticipated. The rule posited for property – political intelligence must criticize and dominate property – applies to every element that would allege an exception to its exteriority in order to escape from the process of totalization and universalization. Contrary to the logic of private interest, Marx will define the logic of the State as a realm of conscious organization, or more precisely, he sets up a break between the standpoint of private interest and that of the State. The State is an independent, luminous, even grandiose realm that can be reduced to narrow limits, to the paltry dimension of interest or of private property, only at the cost of losing its dignity, its identity, its specific mode of being. "If the State, even in a single respect, stoops so low as to act in the manner of private property instead of in its own way, the immediate consequence is that it has to adopt itself in the form of its means to the narrow limits of private property."[4] The least transaction, an even partial renunciation of the means and soul of the State would produce necessarily a debasement, a degradation of its institutions, and could only engender a confusion between two mutually heterogeneous orders. In keeping with this independence of the State from any of the impinging interests that constitute civil society, in keeping with this heterogeneity of the State, Marx defines political modernity as the era of public right.

To the principle of private interest, "May right and freedom perish," Marx opposes the directly contrary principle, "Rather private interest should perish." The vocation of the State is not to remedy the fragility of this-worldly affairs; the guarantees the State provides for private interest have their limits and are subordinated to the State's vocation of universality. Marx reminds the forest owners that "compared to the State the greatest tree is hardly more than a chip of wood," and should any damage fail to be compensated, the immortal interest of right must prevail over the mortal right of interest.[5] "The world will not be unhinged on that account, nor will the State forsake the sunlit path of justice."[6] In the writings from 1842, Marx the theoretician of political idealism or of political elevation always sides with the political solutions, with solutions that are able, in the presence of material conflicts, to rise above simple appearance and make the rational standpoint of totality prevail. Yet it would be erroneous to consider this relation of the State to private interest according to the modality of an external domination of an authoritarian kind. On his guard for conflicts between private interest and right, Marx elaborates the fundamental phenomenon of "political transubstantiation" coextensive with the very nature of the modern State. In Catholic theology, the transubstantiation that occurs during the sacrament of the Eucharist represents the change in substance of bread and wine to the body and blood of Christ. At bottom, a similar operation is realized by the modern State. The State makes possible a change in substance such that it permanently realizes a function of mediation between human beings and their liberty – such that a process of transformation permeates all the problems, all the questions that stir and divide civil society. The placement of private interest in the realm of the State therefore makes it undergo a transformation, a spiritualization that by the same stroke reduces its externality, making the issue of its domination or subordination superfluous. The point, then, is less to repress or smother private interest, as State intervention would do, than to bring interest out from the obscure depths of civil society to the light of the State. Taken in the spiritual milieu of the State, private interest sheds its prosaic skin – ineluctably, its crude appearance is abandoned in favor of the garments of the State. At the heart of modernity, according to Marx, there is a conflict between the logic of private interest as he defines it in the article on the law on the theft of wood (from October to November 1842), and the logic of political regeneration as presented in the essay on the Prussian estates (December 1842). To borrow Marx's organic images, in one case – the logic of private interest – the political body is dissolved in favor of the repressive body of the proprietor. Parallel to the dissolution of the political body an abasement occurs, a downward fall.[7]

In the other case – the logic of the State – we find the phenomenon of transubstantiation that produces a veritable statist reconstruction, or political regeneration, of a kind to wipe out materiality, passivity and dependence. The elements of the State would be made to take an ascending course to a realm where they would henceforth revolve about the sun of liberty and justice and experience an irresistible metamorphosis.

> In a true State there is no landed property, no industry, no material thing, which as a crude element of this kind could make a bargain with

> the State; in it there are only *spiritual forces*, and only in their State form of resurrection, in their political rebirth, are these natural forces entitled to a voice in the State. The State pervades the whole of nature with spiritual nerves, and at every point it must be apparent that what is dominant is not matter, but form, not nature without the State, but the nature of the State, not the *unfree object*, but the *free human being*.[8]

The system of metaphors to which Marx resorts, itself indicative of the philosophical premises of his political thought, shows well enough that the phenomenon of political regeneration is posited as a culmination-point for the independence of the concept of the State. To think through this apogee is to measure the full breadth of this independence, the extent to which this idea of independence, not on the level of the State's genesis but on the level of its nature and operation, is entirely marked by a speculative conception of politics. Are not the terms of "political rebirth" and "resurrection" themselves indicative of a theory of the State based on the model of organic totality?

By virtue of the relationship Marx establishes in these texts between nature, the unity of nature and the State, there is reason to conclude that, for Marx, the system of liberty reaches the status of a genuine political cosmos. In a sense, the specificity of modernity is to pursue at the political level the path taken by self-consciousness at the level of nature, to go from the first sense perception to the rational perception of the organic life of nature.[9] Adult thought, by which is to be understood speculative thought, is able to rise above the chaos of interests to the spirit of living unity; it comes to understand the process specific to the State according to which the particular turns about the general. It is in this respect that Machiavelli would have achieved for politics what Copernicus achieved for nature.

As for the nature of the State, all the characteristics of organic totality are found within it:

1. The State is not to be thought in a juxtaposition, faced with heterogeneous, fixed, or ossified elements that exist in separation, and that the political structure would encompass only mechanically and superficially, thus failing to transform and integrate them in a cohesive tissue.
2. To the contrary, Marx posits the inner structure of the State, the "public organism," "public life," as primary – not in the chronological sense but in the sense of a condition of possibility – in relation to really existing differences. "They are members but not parts, they are movements but not states, they are differences of unity but not units of difference."[10]

3. The life of the State, as a spiritual life, consists in the complex process of differentiation-unification. The moment of differentiation is subordinated to unification, since difference would come to being only as difference of unity, as a furthering of the unity of the whole. Thus difference is understood only as an object of transformation that results in a superior type of unity: namely, political unity.
4. The movement of the State, the process of the State (these dynamic metaphors are important because they highlight how the unfolding life of the State consists precisely in destroying, in shattering reified divisions) may thus be analyzed as a kind of continuous self-creation, as a great organic process or spiritual metabolism that blends everything stemming from materiality, the past and necessity in order to allow for the transformed resurgence of these metamorphosed elements in the everyday recreation of a unifying nervous tissue.

This, then, is the speculative basis for understanding the process of transubstantiation that, from within the modern State, transforms material parts into organs of the spiritual whole.

Undoubtedly, this conception of the State expresses a metaphysics of subjectivity. True to the modern conception of the system, Marx thinks the State according to the framework of organic unity. And it is by reference to the properties held as characteristic of human existence (representation and free will), by reference to the model of the systematizing human, that Marx structures this theory of the State. From this perspective, a strict correlation emerges between the State *qua* organic totality, and political intelligence *qua* totalizing faculty and architectonic structure, "the soul that animates and determines everything" according to Marx. This placement of Marx's first conception of the State in the metaphysics of subjectivity is worth emphasizing, since by bringing out its speculative basis, we may determine the legitimacy of attributing, in the structure of this thought, the institution of society to the institution of the political realm. By reconstituting the philosophical pathways that lead to Marx's theory of political regeneration – according to him, the only theory capable of producing social resurrection through spiritualization – we discover the extent to which this new aim of the political is rooted and philosophically founded in Marx, the degree to which he made it consubstantial to his thought. In short, the position taken does not reveal simply the political tendencies of the young Marx. At issue is a political theorizing on the logic of the State that takes its bearings from both the modern conception of the system and the philosophy of subjectivity. The State is subject; it is as such that the State is considered pure activity, spirit, integrative totality, reduction of externality, the aim of self-identity, the site where the homecoming of spirit is actualized and fulfilled.[11]

This is the matrix of Hegelian speculation, it may rightly be said. We may add, however, that whereas Hegel makes the political relative by subordinating it to absolute knowledge, Marx conceives the political as the real absolute. In this sense we may speak of a "*political absolute*" that, in the wake of the young-Hegelian project, and in the name of the philosophy of *praxis* or action, aims to transform philosophy into politics, and thereby also to replace the phenomenology of spirit with a phenomenology of free will. Political life must affirm its universal supremacy, wrote August von Cieszkowski at the same time.[12]

Marx's contribution to the Machiavellian moment is equal, then, to what the constitution of this moment means to him; it is the unfaltering application of this new way of thinking the political realm, which asserted itself through the double critique of the Old Regime and the Christian State.

If we follow the movement of Marx's political thought, it seems that starting from a critique of political theology and a concomitant recovery of the independence of the political realm, Marx discovers the law of the State's gravitation, the centripetal movement of the State as a self-sufficient totality. Unsatisfied with separating two spiritual realms from each other, unwilling merely to free the political from the hold of religion, Marx goes on to play out this newly won independence in all the dimensions of the social field. Generalized and extended to other areas, the independence of the political realm is a universal law, valid for all the realms and therefore also for the material realms. If the independence of the concept of the State is able to gain such a considerable extension, to the point of leading Marx to a veritable rediscovery of the political realm, Marx owes this rediscovery to the speculative field in the midst of which he carried out his struggle. Because, after the modern idea of system, he thought through the State as a great organism and because, after the philosophy of subjectivity, he thought through the State as subject, Marx was able to posit the State's independence in relation to the social field as a whole and to think the State as an independent realm, or even as a heterogeneous realm, an ideal, spiritual one, and in that sense fully active, capable of surmounting antagonisms and of creating a community beyond social divisions. And because Marx decided to save philosophy by transplanting it into the field of politics – just as Themistocles saved Athens by transferring its power into the marine element – Marx was able to think *the political element* both in an upward direction, in the sense of elevation, and under the sign of transfiguring light (Marx obviously being dependent here on the problematic of vision, wherein references to the eye and to the mirror alternate).

Finally, this way of thinking the political realm – as mediating matter and form, nature and the State, the material and the spiritual – is undoubtedly a direct outgrowth of what Robert Legros, in his book on the young Hegel, terms a philosophy of reconciliation. Marx inherited the project of a "terrestrial realization of the intelligible, of form, of the universal, of the infinite," and places it on the side of the revolutionary movement.[13] A question immediately arises: If the political realm is in this way saved from the materialist denial and reclaims its irreducibility, does it not lose its identity by being transformed into an absolute? For we may reveal in Marx the same paradoxical reversal found in Feuerbach: starting from a critique of political theology, the independence of the political realm is stressed to the point of making politics our new religion. "An enthusiast of politics" (these are his own terms), intoxicated, carried by the religious tonality of his enthusiasm, does Marx thereby leave the real ground of politics? Perhaps, indeed, the identity of politics is maintained only by being careful not to occupy the "sublime point" later suspected by Merleau-Ponty as the illusory place in which all oppositions are resolved and abolished.

— 3 —

FROM THE 1843 CRISIS TO THE CRITICISM OF POLITICS

Does the Machiavellian moment change radically in the passage from the crisis to criticism? If we now turn to the 1843 crisis, we may interpret it directly as an attempt to deconsecrate the State in two senses. For one, Marx appears to break with a conception of the State determined according to the model of the infinite, self-determining subject, integrating all exteriority and coinciding with itself. In this light, his comprehension of the press as a pluralistic organ of mediation already opens the door to an element of passivity and finitude. Yet Marx strives simultaneously to block the resurgence of a sacred structure in the realm of politics, to throw into question a vertical and dualistic conception of political space, the view that political space is to rise from its base, profane life, to its summit, the heaven of the State. To understand the 1843 crisis, then, it is necessary to examine the reorganization of the political space that takes place in favor of a horizontal dimension, the substitution of the vertical model with a horizontal one. At stake is the emergence in Marx's thought of a political stage at the center of which is a subject radiating from a plurality of points and in multiple directions, or what Marx names "true democracy."

The 1843 crisis is first of all a political crisis. Beyond the rupture with the young-Hegelian utopia of the rational State – a utopia still promulgated by Marx in 1842 – the thinking in the Kreuznach period produces a remarkable constellation of essays. Differences notwithstanding, these texts are held together by a central argument: the denunciation of political revolution in favor of a radical form of revolution. In the "Contribution to the Critique of Hegel's Philosophy of Right," published in Paris in the *Deutsch-Französische Jahrbücher*, Marx declares: "It is not a radical revolution, universal emancipation, that is a utopian dream for Germany, but rather a partial, merely political revolution, a revolution that leaves the pillars of the edifice standing."[1]

Marx draws a conclusion from his experience in Germany that applies to modern society as a whole: today it is necessary to criticize political emancipation, the form of emancipation which the bourgeois class, as a revolutionary class, had brought to the world. And this form of liberation is limited since, as a determined class, the bourgeoisie thinks general emancipation starting from the conditions, from the narrow content, which characterize its particular historical situation.

More fundamentally, political criticism becomes *criticism of politics*. It is in effect in this same article that Marx states the transition from the criticism of religion to the criticism of politics. From now on, the task of philosophy in the service of history is "to unmask self-estrangement in its *unholy forms* . . . Thus the criticism of heaven turns into the criticism of the earth."[2] At this point in Marx's itinerary it is as if there were a retreat from the standpoint of 1842, as if following the over-interest in the political realm which led to its rediscovery, there were not so much a loss of interest, but another way of being interested. One must be careful not to think this movement as a reversal, or of considering it quantitatively in terms of a lessened emphasis. That is why the term *loss of interest* does not fit, and even less that of its effacement. We would do better to grasp the complexity of the passage and to consider how Marx, far from burning what he once adored, attempts to save the political realm from its excrescence in order, as it were, to prescribe its limits. This, then, is quite exactly what the project of a criticism of politics aims for and designates on several levels. First, on a socio-historical level, the modern State is permanently haunted by a secret defect, the reminiscences of the Ancien Régime that make the State function beyond its real capacities. It is confronted, moreover, with a new and major problem, "the relation of industry, of the world of wealth generally, to the political world," which itself points to an incurable social division at the heart of existing structures. Upstream or downstream, the modern State, then, is weakened by a double focal-point of imperfection. Second, at a philosophical level, Marx denounces the repetition of religious alienation in a profane form, such that the product – the State – withdraws from its producers – human beings – and turns against them by establishing itself as a foreign power. Lodging itself in the place the criticism of religion left unoccupied – the place of *theos* – the State engenders a veritable self-idolatry. Reclaiming the human powers wasted in the heaven of politics; deconsecrating the State; reorienting emancipation with the help of the Copernican turn again, so that humankind no longer revolves about the illusory sun of the State and at last revolves about itself: these are the directions opened by this new phase of Marx's criticism. It is through the critique of Hegel's philosophy of right that Marx believes himself able to realize this project since, according to him, it is in the theoretical field and exclusively there that the Germans are equal to the task of the modern present. By criticizing the Hegelian theory, Marx deals a blow to the abstraction of the German conception of the State – which is no more than a particular expression of the abstraction of the modern State itself – and the socio-historical phenomenon of political alienation. If we define Marx's task in this way, the criticism of the modern State, mediated by the criticism of Hegel, appears to hold as a critique of Marx's own positions in 1842, as if the historical impossibility of political emancipation in Germany simultaneously revealed to Marx the imperfection inherent to that project. That said, if with the help of the1843 letter-program to Ruge we heed the very method by which Marx undertakes his criticism, it becomes clear that the enthusiasm for emancipation, far from canceling the enthusiasm for politics, actually includes it as a necessary and, so to speak, indelible moment. The political relationship to the Greeks is intensely present (letter to Ruge, May 1843): "Man's self-esteem, his sense of freedom, must be reawakened in the breast of these people. This sense vanished from the world with the Greeks, and with Christianity it took up residence in the blue mists of heaven, but only with its aid can society ever again become a community of men that can fulfil their highest needs, a democractic State."[3] The reference to Aristotle is particularly poignant and relevant, since it functions as a critique of the philistine world of Germany, a world whose lack of "political sense" would have reached the point of rewriting a political treatise. "A German Aristotle who wished to construct his *Politics* on the basis of our society would begin by noting, 'Man is a social but wholly unpolitical animal'."[4] The revelation of this typically German confusion shows the extent to which Marx, faithful in this respect to the beginning of *The Republic*, is careful to distinguish between a "city of swine" and one of human beings – that is, between sociability and political sense, the political link properly speaking. Harking back to this distinction, Marx strikes against German apathy and refuses to confuse the human being with any animal in its gregarious state, or what amounts to the same, to conceive the sociability of human beings in terms of the reproduction of the species. In the world of the German philistines, "the political animal world" as Marx puts it, no more is necessary than living and reproducing. To be Greek and republican *à la française* is to be in excess of this idea of living, to be beyond this neutrality of living. As such, the living-together of the city is construed in the form of a break, of an irreducible difference between mere living and the good life, understood in its modern acceptation as living in accordance with liberty.

In the terms of the letter of September 1843, the task of criticism consists in making each particular form of existing reality, whether it be a form of theoretical or practical consciousness, acknowledge the effective reality toward which it tends. At stake is harmonizing in its inclination each form of reality with the movement that produced it, inciting reality to give full vent to what underlies it, to the superior form *in statu nascendi* of existing imperfection and incompleteness. This means, for example, pushing constitutional monarchy to recognize democracy as the truth of the principle, the political principle, which upholds it. "Hence . . . from this ideal and final goal implicit in the actual forms of existing reality the critic can deduce a true reality."[5] The goal of this criticism, very clearly elaborated from the perspective of historicism, is thus not so much to abandon political revolution in favor of social revolution but rather to see how political revolution, providing one knows how to interpret it, itself points to social revolution.

The publicly announced program in this fundamental letter of 1843 thus elaborates the criticism of politics on the model of an emancipatory hermeneutics. Without now going into the details of the intersection that brings the perspective of criticism – the task of present times is the "ruthless criticism of the existing order" – together with the hermeneutical viewpoint, we may note that the work Marx here undertakes is oriented more toward the self-interpretation of humanity's own struggles and productions than toward the criticism of ideology. Marx refuses the dogmatic retreat that would place the critic outside the world to be judged. "Our program must be: the reform of consciousness not through dogmas but by analyzing mystical consciousness obscure to itself, whether it appear in religious or political form . . . It will then become plain that our task is not to draw a sharp mental line between past and future but to *complete* the thought of the past. Lastly, it will become plain that mankind will not begin any *new* work, but will consciously bring about the completion of its old work."[6] With respect to politics, this position implies that criticism – by contrast to the writings of the "crude socialists," who only disdain this realm – should not turn away from political questions, but should on the contrary penetrate them in view of revealing, through the work of interpretation, the stakes and the true signification. "It is therefore anything but beneath its dignity to make even the most specialized political problem, such as the distinction between the representative system and the Estates system, into an object of critique. For this problem only expresses at the *political* level the distinction between the rule of man and the rule of private property. Hence the critic not only can but must concern himself with these political questions."[7] The path toward a superior form of criticism passes necessarily through the criticism of politics precisely because of the particular nature of the modern State. For the modern State is the site of a permanent contradiction between its aim of universality, its rational demands, and its real presuppositions. This is to say that the criticism of politics must play out this contradiction, at once take the State seriously, believe in its vocation, and catch it in its own snare so as to produce from within political illusion, from within the tension of political idealism, the results that bypass the limits of the political State. For the critic who has emancipation in view, the State, then, is a strategic object of interpretation insofar as it opens a political arena where social struggles abound and find expression. "This internecine conflict within the political State enables us to infer the social truth."[8]

But more essentially, it would seem that for Marx the political State, by virtue of its aim and as a result of the very intentionality that constitutes it, is threatened by an *over-signification*, as though it were haunted by an unsuspected horizon situated beyond the State. Just as thought tied to innumerable things, to the implicit, "thinks of infinitely more 'things' than the object which it focuses on" (Levinas on Husserl's notion of intentionality), we may say that political intelligence "thinks more than it thinks," that the political State obeys an implicit principle of a kind to make it break its limits, to go beyond its defined boundaries.[9] As such, the political State is a special object for criticism in two respects: as the stage on which conflicts are expressed; and as a place wrought by an intentional movement that overwhelms it, pregnant with a "more" that in its movement tends toward the fulfillment of a principle, the political principle. This principle includes the political State while superceding and extending beyond it. In relation to real life, it is precisely the *political State* – even when it is not yet filled with socialist demands in a conscious way – that encloses in all its modern forms the demands of reason.[10] This is to acknowledge that, by virtue of its relationship to the implicit, the State carries within it the horizons of its meta-State implications. The complex aim of Marx's criticism of politics is thereby made more accessible. Marx does not to turn away from what in 1843 Victor Considérant named *the old politics* – in the vocabulary of the publicists, "the nature, the form, the constitution and the composition of power" – in order to devote himself to social questions, to "the totality of matters that make up the State, the nature and structure of society." Rather, he seeks to throw a bridge between the most specialized politics and the political realm, understood broadly, in Victor Considérant's terms, as "the organization of all the elements of life in society." Reinserted in this hermeneutics of emancipation, the criticism of politics, or Marx's effort to put into practice the alliance of the French heart with the German mind, has as its task to play off the tension internal to the State and to elaborate this of the State over itself. Or again, the task of the criticism of politics is to clarify as accurately as possible the trajectory of this movement of over-signification and illumination and to make explicit the *telos* that the State pursues *volens nolens*: the full blossoming of the political principle. "So inside its republican form the political State expresses all social struggles, needs, and truths."[11] Said otherwise, the task of the critic is to interpret every political question so as to translate the particular language of politics in the more "general" language of emancipation. On the basis of this over-signification – by means of the very movement of the modern State's self-transcendence – the question of political representation would be made plain: "In that he raises the representative system from its political form to a universal one and thus gives force to its true and fundamental meaning, he compels this party to go beyond itself, for its victory implies its dissolution."[12] Although the enigma is far from being explicitly resolved, we are nonetheless offered a better glimpse of how the political State, admitting to its own limits, can by the same stroke admit the horizon to which it is brought by the movement which exceeds it, and can designate "true democracy" as the end of this dramatic passage from the political to the universal form.[13]

Understanding the shift in the criticism of politics in this way does not suggest, then, a loss of the Machiavellian moment but its inflection, its more thorough comprehension even. The political domain is neither deserted, nor decentered; it surfaces rather as the key site for interpretation, since for Marx it is within it, and within it only, that the implicit horizons of modern reason may be revealed. Besides a still impassioned questioning of the being of politics, this criticism oriented at once toward the Greeks and the French moderns works for the resurgence of the human being in his uprightness *qua* political animal, that is, for coming out from political immaturity and for striking down the enclosure in species reproduction sociability. The point is not to choose a republic as a stable form that would resolve the fragility of human affairs but to seek the political community capable of the greatest opening, in the sense that it would express best the "more" that pushes the State beyond itself. In other words, at issue are the forms of emancipation that, instead of representing the liquidation of politics, place us before a new question: What are the emerging stages of universally human emancipation? And just as Marx deems it necessary to read, to recognize "the socialist demands" that haunt the modern State, he is simultaneously wary of their reification in a new dogmatism and rejects pre-packaged systems such as Cabet's *Voyage in Icaria*. "Our program must be: the reform of consciousness not through dogmas but by analyzing mystical consciousness obscure to itself, whether it appear in religious or political form."[14]

The failure of radical journalism, the dead end of the young-Hegelian movement and the retreat to Kreuznach: all this undoubtedly helped reveal the crisis of modern society and the scission proper to it. Marx's response to this crisis is to set course for human emancipation. But the criticism of politics depends on a hermeneutic model. Far from leading to a rejection of political emancipation the exercise of this criticism submits political emancipation to interpretation, and makes Marx acknowledge the oversignification with which it is pregnant. Marx must sketch the contours of this barely discernable realm, situated beyond the modern State, where democracy would come about in its truth.

— 4 —

A READING HYPOTHESIS

Against those who have claimed that they could derive Hobbes's political philosophy from a science of Nature and could offer a scientific reading, it has been shown that the Hobbesian philosophy has a moral foundation and that this philosophy really rested on an experience of human life at whose heart lies a fear of violent death.[1] Might the same conclusion hold for Marx's 1843 Critique? Rather than opt for a scientific reading that sees in this critical text on Hegel's philosophy of right the first elements of a materialist criticism of society and the State, might we see an impassioned and difficult quest for an anti-Hegelian political philosophy built on the experience of modern liberty as it appeared in the revolutionary movement?

If we adhere to the self-interpretation Marx offered in 1859 regarding his thought in 1843, we can conclude that the perspective from 1842 had been overturned and a new critical science had been born. As such, the law of the State's gravitation would no longer be situated within itself but in the material conditions of life and civil society, on the side of the economic structure of society. This "self-withdrawal" of the political realm to another order is certainly present in the critical review of 1843. It could even be considered the result of applying Feuerbach's transformative method to the criticism of politics. Yet the reference to Feuerbach should alert us, for it situates Marx's critical work in a context that has little to do with scientific aims, even if it is critical sociology. In 1842, Feuerbach's *Preliminary Theses on the Reform of Philosophy* defined the transformative method as consisting in the inversion of speculative philosophy, as making "the predicate into the subject and thus as subject into object and principle."[2] The criticism of politics, by applying this method to the speculative philosophy of right in order to reach "pure truth," obtains the following inversion: the true subject is the real human being – the human being inserted in the relations of bourgeois civil society and the family – and the predicate becomes the State which Hegel had wrongly made the subject as Idea.[3] Already in the *Preliminary Theses on the Reform of Philosophy* Feuerbach had written: "Man is the fundamental being of the State. The State is the realized, developed, and explicit totality of the human being."[4]

Marx begins his critical review with the unresolved antinomy between Hegel's two determinations of the State: on the one hand, the State is in a relation of external necessity to bourgeois civil society and the family, on the other, it is their immanent end. This unresolved antinomy makes the presentation of the State a duality. With respect to external necessity, there is dependence and subordination; the autonomy of civil society and the family are made externally subordinate to the State, that is, the identity of the State with civil society and the family is external to the extent that it is obtained by violence. With respect to the immanent end, there is neither dependence nor subordination but a harmonious identity, an inner identity, since the family and civil society represent but moments in the rise toward the Idea: the objective universality of the State.

Unsatisfied with highlighting this contradiction, Marx contests the idyllic vision of the immanent end according to which rights and duties would be coincident at the heart of the modern State. Contrary to Hegel, for whom the State produces its own differentiation in the particular determinations of civil society and the family, Marx calls attention to the arbitrary circumstances of mediation and reverses the perspective: the State is not the subject that posits itself and makes itself apparent in civil society and the family. Following the characteristic movement of the critical inversion that is mindful of addressing the issue of origins, Marx substitutes Hegel's backward and mystifying schema with real relations and writes the well-known formulas that makes the State dependent on the realms from which it emerges. "Family and civil society are the presuppositions of the State; they are the really active things; but in speculative philosophy it is reversed."[5]

"Family and civil society are actual components of the State, actual spiritual existences of will . . . They are the active force. According to Hegel they are, on the contrary, made by the actual Idea . . . This is to say that the political State cannot exist without the natural basis of the family and the artificial basis of civil society; they are its *conditio sine qua non*; but the conditions are established as the conditioned, the determining as the determined, the producer as the product of its product . . . the fact is that the State issues from the mass of men as members of families and of civil society."[6]

For the Marx of the 1843 Critique, the State's center of gravitation is situated outside of itself in the "active force," in the family and bourgeois civil society. On one level, we may therefore read in this position an inversion of Marx's own perspective in 1842. We seem to hold a first answer to the fundamental problem of modern times, defined as the relationship between industry and the world of wealth to the world of politics. A road is conspicuously opened for including the political realm in a dialectical analysis of social totality. Yet – and this point is essential – the road is not pursued; an open road is not the same thing as one that is actually taken. Is it really legitimate to view this text as a first draft for a "scientific" conception of the State and its relationship to civil society? Is this the point of the manuscript? Is this really the goal pursued by Marx, as if we need only note its unfulfilled state in 1843?

In truth, the road is not taken because at that moment in his development Marx had not yet decided in an unequivocal way on the apparently sovereign direction he attributed retrospectively to the unpublished manuscript of 1843. That is, he had not publicly given it one and only one meaning, to the detriment of the tensions and the multiple possibilities of this unfinished essay. It is as if in this self-interpretation of 1859, as reductive as it is "official," there were a slip, or rather, a confusion doubled by a loss between a "sociological" effect that made the text only possible – that is, the inclusion of the political realm in a dialectical analysis of social totality – and the text's otherwise more complex design. An alternative reading is legitimate and in a sense more productive. For, the proposition according to which the State's true center of gravitation is located in the "active force" represented by the family and bourgeois civil society may be interpreted in two ways. Either the State's gravitation is brought back to a *sociological* force or to a *political* force, to a determinative force or to an active power. We may certainly read the *Critique of Hegel's Philosophy of Right* as fundamentally epistemological, shaped by the "scientific" aim of denouncing the Hegelian inversion and by the further goal of locating within this inversion the veritable determinative force of social relations in history. The sociological perspective would, in the broadest sense of the term, then aim at designating within the family and civil society the levels that shape the State. But if we try to apprehend the text in its movement and contemporaneousness, the criticism he works out appears to be placed very exactly in the union of a philosophical and a political critique. By political critique I mean Marx's adherence to a political aim that involves opposing a bureaucratic mode of thinking politics and the political world to a democratic way of thinking them, and in this way to elaborate at once a theory of democracy and a theory of politics that would harmonize with the logic of democracy. Marx struggles against Hegel's bureaucratic knowledge as knowledge sullied by esotericism and formalism. Thus, with respect to the presentation of governmental power and bureaucracy, Marx detects philosophical deficiency: in this section, everything upheld by Hegel is devoid of originality; worse, his analysis only mirrors the organization of the State. Hegel offers a strictly formal description without considering the specific logic of political organization and its development in governmental power, since most of the paragraphs of this section are borrowed from Prussian law. But, beyond the denunciation of the platitude of Hegel's empiricism, Marx's criticism aims at the specific structure of bureaucratic thinking. In Marx's view, the conceptual apparatus of Hegel's *Philosophy of Right* reveals a bureaucratic representation of the world and of social totality that considers the State as a separate, independent entity, endowed with the exorbitant privilege of being the only agent, the unique place of activity in society. For Marx, the distinctive character of the bureaucratic representation of the world is this way of assigning every social element external to bureaucracy to the level of passivity. Or more precisely, the hypertrophy of bureaucracy results necessarily in occulting from the viewpoint of bureaucrats themselves the least source of activity that would rise spontaneously from the heart of society. "He [the bureaucrat] considers real life to be purely material, for the spirit of this life has its separate existence in the bureaucracy. Thus the bureaucrat must make life as materialistic as possible . . . Real knowledge appears to be devoid of content just as real life appears dead, for this imaginary knowledge and life pass for what is real and essential. While the bureaucracy is on one hand this crass materialism, it manifests its crass spiritualism in its will to do everything, that is, in its making the will the *causa prima* . . . The bureaucrat has the world as a mere object of his action."[7] Hegel's *Philosophy of Right* is read as an incredible product of bureaucratic solipsism. It is, then, the political will that motivates Marx's criticism and that compels him to offer a different conception of politics. An anti-bureaucratic impulse leads him to bring in focus the independence of the material and spiritual realms, and to support the aim of real emancipation with a new theory of history, so that in the name of democracy the Hegelian poles of activity and passivity are displaced. Thus the remarkable exchange that occurs in Marx's thought between the transformative method and the revolutionary will. If revolution can be defined as the intervention of the transformative method in the field of practice, inversely the transformative method itself represents a revolutionary intervention in the field of theory. A note very certainly contemporaneous to the 1843 manuscript expresses quite nicely the link that makes the revolutionary movement and the critical inversion cohere; by the same token, it reveals the extent to which Marx's 1843 quest for a determining principle clears a path away from all sociological intentionality, a properly political path delimited by the poles of revolution and reaction. "Under Louis XVIII, the constitution by grace of the king (charter imposed by the king); under Louis Philippe, the king by grace of the constitution (imposed kingship). In general we can note that the conversion of the subject into the predicate, and of the predicate into the subject, the exchange of that which determines for that which is determined, is always the most immediate revolution. Not only on the revolutionary side . . . the reactionaries as well."[8] It is therefore at the heart of an essentially political perspective, in relation to the conceptual antithesis revolution/reaction, that Marx thinks and determines the possible permutations of the subject and the predicate. But insisting on the primarily political grounding of this text, and thereby withdrawing it from a reading of a sociological bent, does not imply enclosing it in a purely political conceptualization either. On the contrary, the emphasis placed on the political referent immediately introduces the connection between political criticism and the criticism of religion. The struggle to win recognition for the independence of society's material and spiritual elements – a struggle that is waged against the thesis of the omnipotence of the State – indeed repeats the philosophical gesture aimed at affirming the independence of humanity in opposition to divine omnipotence. Whence also the pertinence of the encounter between political and philosophical critique. For, at the same time that the permutation of the subject and the predicate aims at designating the determining principle of politics, this permutation is also intended, beyond that goal and at a more fundamental level, as a response to the question of origins. Marx's goal is to lead the political (in this case, the constitutional), cultural, or material realms of objectified life back to a source of originary spontaneity that would, as it were, be the nodal-point of the inversion, the base on which it would henceforth be legitimate to carry out this inversion, since here, finally, we would be grasping the foundation whereby modern history would be illuminated in its truth. This is why focussing on the family, bourgeois civil society, and erecting these into determinant stages, would amount to bringing Marx's analysis arbitrarily to a stop and would end up interrupting the movement of radical regression, which goes off in search of an authentically originary subject, or what Marx himself calls the root. Following Marx on this journey toward the originary, we may note that, while he turns his attention at first away from the State in order to focus on civil society and the family, far from leaving off at this level he pursues his analysis until he is able to relate civil society and family – which, in this perspective, themselves appear derivative – to a subject, a center of originary activity, the *demos*, or more exactly, the whole *demos*. "Human beings as a mass . . . the mass out of which the State is formed." This formation of the State is here presented as an action of the Idea, "the fact is that the State issues from the mass of men existing as members of families and of civil society."[9] If we keep in mind the philosophical principle Marx so clearly stated in the 1843 Critique – "one has to start from the real subject and examine its objectification" – we may rightly maintain that, for Marx, there is a perfect appropriateness between democracy *qua* self-determination of the people and the philosophical principle proper to it.[10] For, with the *demos*, the real subject comes to existence in its truth – that is, as the "root" of history in modernity. "Here [in democracy] the constitution not only in itself, according to essence, but according to existence and actuality is returned to its real ground, actual man, the actual people, and established as its own work. The constitution appears as what it is, the free product of men."[11] Democracy thereby figures as the form established in the political realm by the transformative method, just as the transformative method itself figures as the work established in the realm of theory by the democratic principle. The interpretation of the criticism of politics as a hermeneutics of emancipation bolsters this reading hypothesis. The question is not to connect the political universe and its forms to the force of social totality in order to explain the political realm in a sociological fashion. To say that the center of the State's gravitation resides outside of itself indicates instead that the State should be returned to the movement that overwhelms it and pushes it beyond itself, that is, to the over-signification of the State and its real subject, the active life of the *demos*. For Marx, the real people preserve the secret of the over-signification that haunts the modern State. The center of the State's meaning, that which in the form of an implicit horizon gives the political State its meaning (and by the same stroke makes it relative), is revealed to be the plural, massive, polymorphous life of the *demos*.

Now that the movement of Marx's thought has been delineated

and the founding subject named, the object of Marx's criticism of Hegel comes in view. Marx wants to think the essence of the political realm – and this specification is key – from the viewpoint of the real subject as *demos,* and no longer, as Hegel does, in terms of a subject defined by the deployment of the Idea. Therefore, far from giving in to some sociological "*techne*," Marx's project is to break with Hegel's logic, and simultaneously to unveil the specificity of the political realm in terms of the activity of the political subject. If Marx maintains, then, the idea of the State as an organism, he criticizes Hegel no less for having done only one part of the journey by replacing the question of the political realm's essence with the deployment of logic. For the crux of the matter is to question the political realm. If we confront the critical essay of 1843 with other writings of the period – the correspondence with Ruge, *The Jewish Question*, and so on – we may notice that Marx's fundamental preoccupation during this period, as much theoretical as practical, is to disentangle successfully the essence of modern politics, or more precisely, the historically specific figure of the modern State as a political State. In this respect, the criticism that Marx levels against Hegel's presentation of the Idea of the constitution is particularly significant. Hegel does not think the constitution as the development of the State that determines the different powers that make it up in their particular essence (legislative power, governmental power), and he avoids the task of showing how, tested by the real differences of each power, the political organism as such can be constituted. Once again, the Idea is made subject, the different powers are grasped only as its result. For Marx, by contrast, the presupposition, the subject, are the real differences or the various aspects of the political constitution; and it is only starting from the relations between these singular essences that one may question the relationship between the idea of the constitution and that of the organism. Marx consequently accuses Hegel of not thinking the political realm, of missing it altogether: the movement of Hegelian thought corresponds only to a logical schema, that of the relations of the Idea and its moments, without any grounding in the *political element*, without confronting any of its determinations. "The point of departure is the abstract Idea whose development in the State is the political constitution. Thus it is a question not of the political idea, but rather of the abstract Idea in the political element . . . he [Hegel] tells us absolutely nothing about the *specific idea* of the political constitution."[12] Hegel's determinations are not thought out because they are not thought in their specific essence; his propositions are just as appropriate to the animal organism as to the political organism. The logical idea functioning everywhere the same, be it in nature or the State, Hegel misses the essence of the political realm and the political essence of each power in particular, since the different powers are determined by the nature of the concept and not by their own nature as political powers. Hegel's philosophy of right therefore offers only the false appearance of a real knowledge of the political realm. "He does not develop his thought out of what is objective [*aus dem Gegenstand*], but what is objective in accordance with a ready-made thought which has its origin in the abstract sphere of logic. It is not a question of developing the determinate idea of the political constitution, but of giving the political constitution a relation to the abstract Idea, of classifying it as a member of its (the Idea's) life history."[13] Marx concludes that an explanation that fails to provide the *differentia specifica* is not an explanation. By having failed to do justice to a dialectics of political experience, Hegel could only construe the State according to logical-metaphysical determinations. "Thought is not conformed to the nature of the State, but the State to a ready made system of thought."[14] To construct this organic unity, that is, to put this historically constituted – and problematic – unity to the test, the deployment of a logical definition is hardly adequate. In a first instance, a quasi-phenomenological description of the different powers must be offered: "The various powers each have a different principle, although at the same time they are all equally real."[15] It is necessary, moreover, to locate the collisions and the antagonisms between these different powers and to develop their unity neither in an imaginary realm situated beyond real conflicts, nor in the denial of conflict, but precisely through the conflict of the different powers, for it is by their confrontation that their real unity may come about.

In Marx's terms, the philosophical labor here consists in allowing for the embodiment of thought in political determinations. Bringing to light what Marx himself designates as "the logic of the political body" demands unveiling the *eidos* of political affairs in a sort of permanent confrontation between "the political element" itself and the *eidos* of the forces that, in their complex and differentiated game – political energy being the specific nature of legislative power, the practical energy of governmental power – constitute the modern State as distinct from the city of antiquity and the Middle Ages.

In this sense the ceaseless intertwining in Marx's investigations of the polemical with the affirmative is fundamentally geared toward finding an answer to the question: What is the *differentia specifica* of the political organism, once the philosopher no longer thinks the political world according to the logical idea of the organism but instead according to the specificity of the "political element"? Here the questions come fast and furious, or rather, in order to get at the question of the specific difference itself, that question must be posed in a particular mode. How does the political element in its specificity lead to developing the idea of totality? What becomes of the idea of the organism once it is referred to this particular subject, to the theoretical and practical energy of the *demos*? Can we perceive here an alternative form of totality that breaks with the logic of identity? In short, is the idea of system maintained despite the change of subject, or does this change result in undermining the very idea of the system?

It is at the site of "true democracy," which here figures as a sort of extreme point that plays out the logic of political affairs, where we may take our bearings to find an answer to this question.

If we accept my reading hypothesis, it seems that the 1843 Critique, despite the distance taken from the independence of the concept of the State, is not situated outside the Machiavellian moment and in a sense confirms Ernest Grassi's thesis which, starting from an analysis of the 1843 Critique and its Feurbachian roots, points to a neglected relationship between Marx and the civic humanism of Italy. Grassi discerns at least two areas of affinity: a same denunciation of every form of *a priori* philosophy that privileges the dialectic of the Idea to the detriment of the world of real human beings; a same primacy of the terrestrial, and that in both cases results in thinking history in a new way, even if historicity is thought according to different activities.[16] In reading Marx's 1843 text and noticing the "return" of political affairs that drives it, we might then judge that his critique of Hegel's philosophy of right confronts us with another figure of the Machiavellian moment, one in which, in the name of Machiavelli, we are being introduced, as Merleau-Ponty says, to the "milieu proper to politics."[17]

— 5 —

THE FOUR CHARACTERISTICS OF TRUE DEMOCRACY

We may now return to the enigma of "true democracy" and attempt an interpretation of the formula: "The modern French have conceived it thus: In true democracy the *political State would disappear*. This is correct inasmuch as *qua* political State, *qua* constitution it is no longer equivalent to the whole."[1] These phrases are, as previously noted, indeed enigmatic: Marx invites us to think a paradoxical situation such that the disappearance of the political State would only occur in and by the full self-attainment of a political community that has reached its truth. In other words, the question is raised as to how the disappearance of the State could coincide with the advent of a political form that, in 1843, Marx views as the consummate political form. The stakes are not slight, since we here witness for the first time the theme of the disappearance of the State together with – and it is well worth emphasizing this point – the contrast between the political State and democracy. Echoes of this theme may be heard throughout Marx's work: in *The Poverty of Philosophy* (1847), Marx evokes the post-revolutionary classless society and declares that in such a society "there will be no more political power properly so-called";[2] in the *Civil War in France* (1871), and in 1875, in the critique of the program of the German workers' party, the disappearance of the State is thought more in terms of an inversion-transformation than as a simple negation: "Freedom consists in converting the State from an organ superimposed upon society into one completely subordinated to it . . . The question then arises: what transformation will the State undergo in communist society? In other words, what social functions will remain in existence there that are analogous to present State functions?"[3] I have suggested that Marx's project in the 1843 Critique is to think the essence of the political from the viewpoint of the real subject as *demos*. This is to say that research bearing on the essence of the political realm and research bearing on true democracy coincide necessarily, or even amount to the same. To question the essence of the political realm is to raise the question democracy; to grasp the specificity of democracy in relation to all other forms of regime amounts to confronting the very logic of political affairs. It indeed seems that in this text Marx adopts for himself the equivalence stated by Leibniz, "democracy or politics."[4] True democracy – by which is to be understood democracy that has reached its truth as a form of *politeia* – is politics *par excellence*, the blossoming of the political principle, its apotheosis. Consequently, to understand the logic of true democracy is to grasp the logic of political affairs. The quest for the essence of the political realm, as much as the choice of democracy as the form capable of presenting the secret of that essence, are hardly minor decisions for Marx. At the very least they testify to a complex thinking of the political realm – the work of radical criticism is not to be confused with simple negation – as well as to an investigation into the status of the political realm that is all the more solid as it seems to be developed in a triangular relationship between Hegel, Moses Hess, and Spinoza.

I shall focus on four characteristics of true democracy. The triangular relationship I spoke of will be examined as I make headway in my analysis.

I

First characteristic: "Sovereignty of the monarch or of the people, that is the question . . . But then it is not a question of one and the same sovereignty taking form on two sides but rather of two completely opposed concepts of sovereignty."[5] By contrast with Hegel, Marx opts for thinking the political realm from the perspective of the sovereignty of the people. The people are the real State. Marx systematically inverts Hegel's propositions: first, with respect to the determination of the progress of political forms, Marx contradicts the thesis expressed by Hegel in §273 of the *Philosophy of Right*, according to which "the development of the State to constitutional monarchy is the work of the modern world, in which the substantial Idea has attained infinite form."[6] Far from seeing democracy as the symptom of a people lingering in an arbitrary and non-organic state, Marx on the contrary considers the democratic form as the crowning phase of modern history understood as the history of liberty. He even makes democracy the *telos* toward which all modern political forms are tending, whether it is a constitutional monarchy or the Republic. Consequently, Marx would recognize along with Hegel that the key issue in constitutional monarchy is the political principle – in Jean-Luc Nancy's terms, the *relation* – the union as such that "designates the 'surplus' of the specific nature of the *zoon politikon*."[7] However, and this is where the divergence is located, the political principle exists in monarchy only in a mutilated form, and even a mystifying one, since it generates illusions.

From a theoretical standpoint, it follows that monarchy cannot be understood starting from itself but only from the horizon, the implicit principle at work within it: the democratic principle. Therefore, if understanding monarchy demands a decentering since only the logic of democracy holds the key to monarchy, democracy by contrast can understand and know itself since, centered on itself on its own level, it is not dependent on any superior form; the real subject, the *demos*, institutes itself in a full self-relation. Still better, it is at the site of democracy that the political principle itself is revealed in its perfection. If we adhere to the parallelism of religion and politics – and inasmuch as we accept the Hegelian hierarchy of religions – the hierarchy of political forms may be presented as follows: in the field of politics, democracy occupies the same place at the summit as does Christianity in the field of religion. Just as Christianity is the religion *par excellence* and a hermeneutics of Christianity would deliver the essence of religion, so democracy is the constitution *par excellence* and its interpretation would provide the essence of the constitutional form itself. We thus arrive at the following propositions: the essence of religion, as it emerges through the interpretation of Christianity, is man deified; the essence of politics, as it emerges through the interpretation of democracy, is man socialized – a somewhat obscure formula to which I shall return.

These positions of the young Marx are relatively well known, but perhaps their implications have not really been gauged. People generally retain mostly the *political opposition* of Marx to Hegel without questioning what is engaged by, or is the engagement behind, Marx's thesis that democracy is the consummate form of politics, in terms of the thinking of the political realm and in terms of *its very status*. A first implication to be drawn is that only a complex thinking of the political realm could serve as the condition of possibility for Marx's proposition concerning democracy. By a complex thinking, I mean the way Marx apprehends the political realm according to a double postulate: if the political can be thought in terms of the domination/

servitude relationship – political evil being the domination of man by man – it is nonetheless thought as irreducible to domination only. For what is at stake, what becomes a question in and through the political realm, is how people might live together in a way that would meet the requirements of liberty and free will. It is precisely here that the triangular relationship I spoke of can be enlightening.

In the same year of 1843, Moses Hess's *The Philosophy of Action* openly broke with the utopia of the rational State and, in a single critical gesture, defined religion and politics simply as forms of the master/slave relationship. "Domination and its opposite, submission, are the essence of religion and politics, and the more perfectly this essence is made manifest, the more religion and politics acquire a fulfilled form."[8]

This refusal of politics is equally present in *Socialism and Communism* (1843) where Hess equally sweeps aside the attainments of the enlightenment, the State of right, and the religion of reason.

"Any politics, be it absolute, aristocratic, or democratic necessarily maintains the opposition of domination and submission for its self-preservation; it has an interest in oppositions because it owes its existence to them."[9] Past history is but the repetition of a lie – namely, dualism, the split between an abstract universal and an individual without truth and lacking all spirit. Practicing *la politique du pire* in the field of thought, Hess agrees with Hegel that monarchy is the apotheosis of all political forms, and that Christianity is likewise the most complete religion. Yet Hess falls in line with Hegel only to break with him: monarchy is the pinnacle of politics to the very extent that the essence of politics is the master/slave relationship. As domination by a single master (*monos*), monarchy becomes the paradigmatic form of politics understood as domination. Thus in the name of the Spinozist axiom – "that is good which favors activity and increases the appetite for life" – Hess's conclusion proceeds logically as a veritable *initium* of modern liberty toward anarchy as the negation of all domination in both spiritual and social life. The anarchy that Hess has in mind is situated at the intersection of atheism (Fichte) and communism (Babeuf); turned into a precise term by Proudhon, it is defined by Hess "as the negation of all political domination, the negation of the concept of the State or of politics."[10] A political atheist rather than a political rationalist, Hess dismisses the State of right, even in its republican form, since he views it as the resurgence of the domination/submission relation in the form of the division between those who govern and those who are governed. Hess likewise rejects democracy explicitly. "This democracy, is it anything other than the rule of individual despotism in the name of 'subjective' or 'personal' liberty? How does it distinguish itself from the domination of the One?"[11] To shatter the "closed circle of submission," Hess evokes Spinoza and takes as the horizon for a truly human history the end of religious and political alienation, conceiving action as a goal in itself, opening up a "philosophical ethics that would illuminate all of life." "This malediction, which appeared with religion and politics, will also disappear with the end of the reign of religion and politics."[12]

In this way the principle of modern times, the absolute unity of all life, would be fulfilled.

Marx's difference from Hess seems to consist in an alternative working relationship with Spinoza. If Hess pulls Spinoza over to the side of anarchy metamorphosed into ethics, Marx by contrast leads us back to Spinoza's thinking of democracy. In fact, by opposing the crowning position of monarchy in the Hegelian hierarchy of political forms, and by handing this position to democracy instead, Marx is repeating quite exactly Spinoza's own position. As we know, for Spinoza, democracy – "a united body of men which corporately possess sovereign right over everything within its power" – is the form of regime, the form of institution of the social realm that seems "the most natural . . . approaching most closely to that freedom nature grants every man."[13] Thus the priority and the preeminence given to this form of political community in Spinoza's treatise. Democracy as the most rational and free regime is the political community *par excellence*; for upon close analysis all sovereignty is in its essence democratic (and in this light aristocratic and monarchical regimes are derived and insufficiently elaborated forms of political institution).[14]

This resumption of Spinoza against Hegel on the level of the political position taken becomes meaningfully an argument against Hess in the context of the thinking of the political realm. If for Marx, as for Spinoza, democracy is the most natural regime and figures as the paradigm of the *politeia* – or even as a "hyper-model of true political life"[15] – it is precisely to the extent that the essence of politics cannot be limited to the master/slave relationship. Rather, democracy consists in working out the union of human beings, in the institution *sub specie rei publicae* of a being-together oriented toward liberty – what Marx names "human exchange" or the mediating activity of human beings. In this sense, Marx apprehends the political element as a specific link irreducible to a dialectics of needs or to a derivative of the division of labor. The political element is indispensable to a free human society and, according to Marx, its loss would come at the cost of sinking back to the political animal world (mere living and reproduction). In and through this element a space is cleared where "real man" – in the form of the people, the universality of citizens – is permanently set before the test of universalization.

The point of contention between Hess and Marx is readily perceived.

Everything hinges on the interpretation of the *monos* of monarchy: either the essence of politics is domination and by *monos* is meant the domination of a single master – in which case monarchy is the apotheosis of politics as a paradigm of domination and democracy is a spurious form of politics, a shameful transaction. Or the aim of politics is the institution of a community among human beings, the institution of a monadology, and by *monos* is meant unity. In this case – and Marx's whole movement in the 1843 Critique is in truth right here – the point is to play out the transformative method on the model of permutation of the subject and the predicate: "God is love," whence "Love is god." And applied to the political field: "The King is unity," whence "Unity is king" – to which should be added that the real subject *demos* replaces *monos*, since constitutional monarchy as Hegel conceives it is an inconsistency that bears fruit on the condition that it is overcome. In this case, democracy, as the perfect self-attainment of the essence of politics, is raised to the summit of the hierarchy of political regimes, with monarchy falling back to the rank of an imperfect form.

If one granted these implications, if this inter-expressive reciprocity between true democracy and the essence of politics is granted, it will also be granted that – at least at this moment in the evolution of his thought, and regardless of whether this is to be blamed or praised – Marx cannot be said to deny politics.

One may then also grant that it is certainly legitimate to read the 1843 Critique – with the help of the Feuerbachian categories and the parallel between democracy and Christianity – as a work guided by Marx's strong will to effect through Hegel (but this passage is not just any kind of passage) and against him a transition from *the dogmatic essence of politics to its ethical or anthropological essence.*

In this sense Marx, like Hess, can take the side of political atheism – but with this single but weighty difference: whereas Hess has a uniquely negative relation to politics, Marx is able to elaborate a *critical* relation such that he distinguishes the true from the false and thinks through the disappearance of the State *qua* advent of true democracy.

II

Second characteristic: The relationship between the activity of the subject, the whole *demos*, and the objectification of the constitution is different in democracy than in other forms of State. This remains true even if, without knowing it, the sovereignty of these forms is also democratic in its essence.

In democracy this relationship expresses itself in an alternative articulation of the whole and the parts, and its result is also the basic distinctive criterion of democracy. In other words, the objectification of the constitution – the objectification of the *demos* in the form of a constitution – is in democracy the object of a *reduction*. This is one of the meanings of the proposition: "Man does not exist because of the law but rather the law exists for the good of man. Democracy is *human existence*, while in the other political forms man has only a *legal* existence. That is the fundamental difference of democracy."[16] In other words, it is in view of maintaining an adequate relation with its specific essence – law is the existence of man – that the constitution is subjected to a process of the reduction. We would be mistaken to confuse this reduction with an effacement or diminishing of the constitution. It seems, rather, that the reduction has two interrelated meanings: first, it is a reduction/resolution, in the Feuerbachian sense of the term. By responding to the question, "What is the essence of the subject that recognizes itself in the activity that, in this case, gives rise to the political object?", and by its anti-dogmatic interpretative aim, the reduction has a liberating effect. But by reduction is also meant that once the objectification is brought back to the instituting subject and this recognition has occurred, it is necessary to *reduce* this objectification to what it is – a mere moment of a more global process – and to determine quite exactly the limits of the objectification in order better to control the theoretical and practical energy dispensed in the political realm. It is therefore because Marx has a high standard for what is at stake and for what takes place in the democratic constitution that he comes to see the reduction as necessary, since it alone assures the unfettered development of the actual operation. But what is this actual operation? Let us return to the formula stated above: democracy as a particular form of State (and not only as the truth of all forms of State) reveals the essence of every political constitution: "socialized man." This proposition is all the more worth interpreting as it can easily be misunderstood as expressing a typically modern error. In Hannah Arendt's terms, the Aristotelian definition of man as *zoon politikon* is nowadays understood in the sense of *animal socialis*, so that the political realm is mistakenly thought (and thus glossed over) in terms of the *oikos* instead of the *polis*.[17]

Yet the significance of the 1843 Critique, to the very extent that this text is indeed Machiavellian, is that it stays away from this modern tendency. We are not before a problematic of social right of the "society against the State" type, such that, with the advent of "socialized man," the political constitution would disappear because it had become null and void. The problematic proposed by Marx is on the contrary specifically political, in that he offers a political theory of sovereignty as well as a philosophical thinking through of subjectivity. Against Hegel who, careful to fulfill the modern principle of subjectivity, makes man (in the figure of the prince) the State subjectivized, Marx argues that in democracy man as species-being, as the people, or as *demos* (the use of the Greek term is not superfluous) attains, in and through the State, his objectification. The proposition according to which democracy "makes the State man objectified" signifies that in this political form the State is the stage on which the figures of human social existence become objective. Man knows himself and recognizes himself as universal being – man is man only among men, to recall Fichte's formula – only to the extent that he attains the political realm, only insofar as he participates fully in the political element. It is *sub specie rei publicae* and only as such that man reaches his destination as social being. The constitution acts simultaneously as a purifying and a disclosing element. Therefore the advent of *societas*, far from rendering the *civitas* useless or obsolete, is itself the result of the *civitas* – it is by having attained the *civitas* that the emergence of the *societas* occurs. In other words, it is not because man is an "*animal socialis*" that he gives himself a constitution; rather, it is by giving himself a constitution – because he is a *zoon politikon* – that he reveals himself actually to be "socialized man." We should take matters further still. Upon close analysis, the political essence, socialized man, turns out in reality to be the essence of man. It can manifest itself to the extent that it frees itself, to the extent that it liberates itself quite specifically from the limits of family, civil society, and the determinations engendered by them. It is thus not through relations developed in civil society that man succeeds in fulfilling his social destination; rather, it is by struggling against these relations – by rejecting them politically in the name of citizenship in a political State – that he can regain his essence as species-being. The political mode of being leads, consequently, to the experience of the true universal existence, the essential experience of community, the unity of man with man. Subordinated to the principle of possession, bourgeois civil-society certainly produces links, but they remain marked by an irremediable contingency. Only the "unlinking" at the level of bourgeois civil-society, and the concomitant entrance into the political realm, allow for the experience of a species link. In his political role, Marx writes, "the member of civil society rids himself of his class, of his actual private position."[18] It is only in the political realm that the member of society "acquires significance as man. In other words, his character as a member of the State, as a social being, appears to be his human character."[19] The gap between the political realm and the social determinations grows even wider once the question of representation is examined. Distinguishing representation by estates from political representation – the modern principle – Marx emphasizes that it is not starting with the facticity and the social texture of civil society that there can be representation in the modern sense but, to the contrary, through their negation and through the negation of their determinations. Marx even goes so far as to conceive this accession to political existence, this political act, in the form of a decomposition of civil society, as a sort of de-socialization, one would be tempted to say, doubled by a veritable self-transcendence of bourgeois civil society – an ecstasy. "Its political act . . . is an ecstasy, an act of political society which causes a stir."[20] Thus, it is quite evidently in a context of discontinuity that Marx thinks the relations between the political and what presents itself as the social. The constitution, the political State, does not come to crown or to bring to a conclusion an imperfect sociability that would be in gestation in the family and civil society; rather, it places itself in a position of rupture with this inessential sociability. "Class in civil society has neither need – and therefore a natural impulse – nor politics for its principle. It is a division of the masses whose development is unstable and whose very structure is arbitrary and in no sense an organization."[21] Two moments are isolated in this political act which he defines as a total transubstantiation. In a first instance, civil society is put in brackets: "in this political act civil society must completely renounce itself as such, as unofficial class."[22] Second, there is the advent of "socialized man" in and through the political element: from within it society must "assert a part of its essence which not only has nothing in common with the actual civil existence of its essence, but directly opposes it."[23]

The political site is thus constituted as a site of human mediation between man and man, and as the site of *catharsis* in relation to all the inessential links that keep man at a distance from man. We thereby arrive at the paradox that man experiences his species-being inasmuch as he turns from the contingency of his social existence to take on the being of citizenship, or rather, the necessary becoming of citizenship. In this sense, we may paraphrase a later declaration of Marx's and say: the *demos* is political or is nothing. We should not forget that Marx suspected a German Aristotle incapable of distinguishing between man as social animal and man as a political animal. Only once the paradoxical character of the political act is properly emphasized is it possible to grasp the no less paradoxical operation of the reduction.

Because democracy is the "the enigma of every constitution solved," the manifestation of "socialized man" that knows itself to be this solution – the moment of self-consciousness as well as the moment of self-consciousness specific to a philosophy of subjectivity – it succeeds in keeping constitutional objectification from degenerating into political alienation. Indeed, in democracy political alienation is conjured away. For, on the one hand, the constitution is recognized there for what it is; on the other, the constitution is reduced to the full self-attainment of human commerce in the political mode, thereby making it impossible to confuse constitutional objectification with self-objectifying activity. By being brought back to what is fundamental and connected up with the energy of the subject, the democratic constitution does not reify, crystallize, erect itself as a force, an alien form situated above the subject and directed against it. The resolution of the constitution (socialized man) eliminates the danger of petrifaction since it brings about a reduction of the constitution, a determination of its limits as a moment – since it assigns the constitution *the status of being a moment*. The question remains, however, whether the reduction of the constitution to a moment means this moment may be considered as homogenous with those other moments that make up the process of the total objectification of the *demos*. For the same reason, the replacement of the constitution, its immersion within the process that produces it – and this is, for Marx, what defines the democratic institution of the social – will bypass the level of the properly political realm and spread out to the totality of the realms, including the non-political realms. When examining Marx's analyses, we seem to find ourselves in the presence of a very complex movement that may be decomposed into several moments: the moment of the reduction, "the going back" to the originary activity that, in a second instance, will allow for what is realized in the constitution to extend over to the other realms of the life of the *demos*. Yet the reduction understood as a determination of limits seems, simultaneously, to be the condition of possibility for the extension. It is as if the movement of the return to an originary subject triggers a release, a retroaction of the subject's activity into every field that requires its energy. Marx writes: "In democracy none of the moments obtains a significance other than what befits it."[24] If this definition applies to all the moments, it appears nonetheless to have primarily in view the political moment. The political moment, in fact, is revealed as the moment most liable to gain an excessive meaning, to go beyond the meaning proper to it. It is in this respect that democracy differs from those other forms of State in which the political moment, precisely because it is not subjected to a reduction, is given a particular and exorbitant status. In democracy each moment is really only a moment of the whole *demos*. Democracy is indeed thought as a system centered on a unifying subject whose energy, as much theoretical as practical, constitutes the principle of unification.

By contrast, for having failed to carry out the anti-dogmatic reduction – which would show that, there too, sovereignty is essentially democratic – monarchy presents a flawed relation between the whole and the parts. "In monarchy one part determines the character of the whole; the entire constitution must be modified according to the immutable head."[25] This part is evidently the monarch, "the absolutely decisive moment of the whole" according to Hegel (§279). To this is added a flawed subsumption: "In monarchy the whole, the people, is subsumed under one of its modes of existence."[26] Inversely, "in democracy the constitution itself appears only as one determination, and indeed as the self-determination of the people."[27] Thus in monarchy the determinative relation is mystifying and consequently paralyzing, since the determinant (the people) becomes the determined, and the determined (the political constitution) becomes the determinant. In monarchy we have the people of the constitution, that is, not the people as they are in their being, but the people as posited, recognized, identified, in short determined by the constitution. Furthering the parallel between the criticism of politics and the criticism of religion, Marx writes: "it is not the constitution which creates the people, but the people which creates the constitution."[28] We can thus see the extent to which the 1843 Critique is carried forward by a generalized struggle against any vision – be it of monarchical or bureaucratic inspiration – whose effect would be to place the human species *qua* people on the side of passivity and immaturity by obscuring and thereby inhibiting the subject's own activity. Democracy, on the contrary, introduces a relation of the determinant to the determined that is satisfying, in that it is in continuity with the actual movement of objectification: the political principle is defined here as the emergence of species unity from within the constitution, in the name of the *demos*. Democracy presents a juridical and meta-juridical constitution of the people, since the people are endowed there with the threefold status of principle, subject and end. In this self-relation that is worked out in the self-constitution, in the self-determination of the people, the constitution (the political State) represents but a moment – an essential moment, certainly, yet only a moment. The people offer the particularity of being a subject that is also its own end. This self-constitution of the people – which does not become frozen into any compact, which must not become frozen into any contract – also displays an element of ideality. The political realm is all the more characterized by ideality as "the people" do not correspond to a sociological reality and are nothing social, but consist entirely in their political will-to-be. "The people" exist, acquire the identity of people, inasmuch as they will themselves as people. The greatness of the people is their political existence.

This is why democracy rightly appears as the solved enigma of all constitutions. What is fundamentally at issue in all the constitutions is indeed the self-determination of the people. But as a matter of fact, it is an issue (when it is an issue) only unconsciously, as a mystification, as a form of denial. Thus the job of democracy is to bring the partial work of other forms of regime to its full conclusion, to make of it its own work, and it does so because it recognizes that the subject of every political society is the activity, the energetic power of the people. An enigma resolved not only knows the solution, but it knows and recognizes itself as this solution. It is therefore in the logic of this self-return, in the fullness of this self-consciousness that the complex movement of reduction originates. And again, this is a complex movement because, once the truth of the political constitution becomes conscious, limits to the constitutional objectification of the *demos* must be assigned so that, in the very same sequence, this democratic action can, thanks to these very limits, launch into all spheres of existence. Thus the objectification of the *demos* wins out in all domains where it is meant to manifest itself, in the multiplicity of its being.

III

Third characteristic: This aim of a self-constitution of the people, of an objectification of human dealings in a political mode that would never deteriorate into political alienation culminates in a conception of the democratic self-institution of society following the model of a self-institution of an ongoing self-determination.

According to Marx, in its essence but above all in its very existence (a democracy that does not realize itself is not a democracy) the constitution is constantly "returned to its real ground: actual man, the actual people, and established as its own work."[29] Marx here introduces the question of democratic temporality which he conceives in the form of ongoing creation, as a full self-adherence, between the focal-point of power, the foundation (the real people), and its work. At stake is a subject that would coincide continuously with its work, better, a subject that would be coincident with its "workings," as if time were not to inscribe any lag in the realization of this power. In democracy, every objectification is permanently brought back to its foundation, to its focal-point of activity, in a sort of total presence and in a way such that the relationship between the subject and its work is not weakened in duration, and instead voids any passivity with respect to time. In the course of political realization, no temporal gap, fault-line, or breach that would be liable to let heterogeneity set in is admitted. Thus, through the constant movement of "going back" to the source, the process of petrifaction is brought to a halt. A barrage is raised against any slip from objectification to alienation, so that the energy of the *demos* may maintain intact its nature, its life force, its mobility, its plasticity and fluidity. Marx's position is reminiscent of that of William Godwin, the author of the *Enquiry Concerning Political Justice* (1793) whom Marx often associated with the idea of a criticism of politics. Godwin contrasts the true interests of mankind that demand constant change, unending innovation – man lives in a state of perpetual mutation – with the principle of stability inherent to government. "Government is the perpetual enemy of change."[30] Whence the criticism of the idea of constitution that, in the name of the distinction between fundamental and ordinary laws, feigns a relative permanence in an illegitimate manner. This same opposition is to be found in Marx's 1843 Critique: the people have the permanent and unconditional right to give themselves a new constitution. "The constitution becomes a practical illusion the moment it ceases to be a true expression of the people's will."[31] Beyond this connection to Godwin, there emerges a conception of democracy wherein the *demos* – at once principle, subject and end – can permanently meet the test of self-recognition, that is, the *demos* should be able, in relation to each of the objectifications of its being, to recognize itself in a perfectly reflected image that no residuum or remainder would disturb or confound. Marx is really touching here upon one of the requirements of democracy when it is thought on the basis of the subject-people or the people as subject. He seems to be transferring to the totality of the people's actions the social narcissism that, according to Rousseau's *Letter to M. d'Alembert*, is given free expression in the ecstatic moment of the popular festival, for at this moment the people abandon themselves to the joy of contemplating on the surface of the mirror – the lake of Geneva – their own image. The republican spectacle has no object: "Nothing, if you please," writes Rousseau, besides the people's self-constitution, the emergence of their sensuous presence: "Let the spectators become an entertainment to themselves; make them actors themselves; do it so that each sees and loves himself in the others so that all will be better united."[32]

By thus emphasizing this imperative of plasticity, this flexibility specific to a shared democratic life, we grasp by another route the fundamental importance of the reduction. By virtue of this specific operation, democracy avoids any obscuring of the relation between the part and the whole that would bring about an illegitimate excrescence of that part, and that would engender an exorbitant claim to rule over the other realms in a dominant fashion. It is by virtue of the reduction, moreover, that the political subject puts a check on the constitutional objectification from a temporal standpoint, which is to say that the moment of alienation can be avoided during the very time of effectuation. The reduction satisfies the requirements contained in the idea of ongoing creation since by this route the constitutional moment, instead of withdrawing into itself, opens itself up to a more essential level, to the activity and energy of institution, the original focal-point that produces the constitutional moment itself. What constitutional monarchy and democracy have in common is that in both of them the constitution is the free production of man. In monarchy, however, the free product closes upon itself; the constitution becomes that which forms the State and the people are reduced to a moment. In democracy, by contrast, the free product is open to the very activity at the origin of this process, and it is as such oriented toward the subject-people that objectifies itself. Consequently, once the constitution is grasped, encompassed, and rooted in a movement that is much more radical – the self-attainment of the *demos* – it is reduced to a moment, to a particular form of the subject's existence, rather than being erected into an organizing form that passes for the whole. As it were, there emerges a self-interpretation connecting up to a self-radicalization, since true democracy is upheld permanently by the demand to regain productive activity, to be on a par with the acting subject. This conception of democracy is quite certainly influenced by the "philosophy of action" developed at the same time by Moses Hess. What holds for spirit must equally hold for action: Hess shows how the principle of activity requires that spirit never be held in, that far from giving in to petrifaction it must perpetually regain itself over its own determinations, in order to go beyond them and assert its infinitude. "Spirit constantly transcends its own products because it is something greater than the finite and determined world, because as active spirit it always conceives itself anew, even if each time it does so in a determined manner."[33] By being thus oriented to the infinite, this philosophy of action is a philosophy of liberty. Moses Hess could hardly state more plainly the principle that evidently drives the labor of reduction in Marx's 1843 Critique. "The precise distinction between the free act and servile labor is that in servitude creation binds the creator, whereas in liberty, each limit in which spirit alienates itself is surmounted in *self-determination* rather than becoming a form of *natural constraint*."[34]

I have framed this question in terms of democratic temporality. But is the question really one of temporality? Can the temporality be thought in the present alone? Can we consider with Feuerbach that overturning "the principle of stability" and substituting it with the principle of ongoing foundation is enough for introducing time to politics? In the words of the "Preliminary Theses on the Reform of Philosophy"(1842): "Space and time are the first criteria of praxis. A people that banishes time from its metaphysics and deifies the eternal – that is *abstract*, time-detached existence – *excludes in consequence time from its politics* and worships the anti-historical principle of stability which is against right and reason."[35] Yet this choice of ongoing self-institution reveals Marx's ambiguity. For one, it is easy to recognize in this thinking of democratic temporality, so careful to conjure away, to chase off the non-coincidence introduced necessarily by effectuation in time, a radicalization of the modern idea of liberty, of the idea of autonomy, to the point of confusing it with the aim of an ongoing self-foundation. Whence the primacy of the present that leads to conceiving the subject-people as absolute being, as pure act, that is, as a liberty that in its deployment is sheltered from all passivity. But while it is true that the present may be thought as the fundamental mode of a shared democratic life that gives itself the task of liberty, and while it is true, too, that the affirmation of the present is a condition of liberty, it is nonetheless necessary to add that the rehabilitation of the present holds only to the extent that the present specific to the democratic institution is posited as a regulative ideal, as a practical ideal to be realized in history, and not as an existence or an objective reality. This is to say that the identity presupposed in the primacy given to the present should be understood more as an imperative becoming than as an actual existence. For if it fails to "dereify" itself and take on the meaning of a regulative practice, this valorization of the present would then be exposed to the blows of a double criticism: besides being caught in the grip of the principle of identity, incapable as it is of admitting differentiation, it would partake totally of the modern tendency to occult finitude. Evidently, the valorization of the present relies on the idea of unconditioned being, and the result is a valorization of transparency, identity and self-adequacy. Thinking true democracy under the banner of ongoing self-foundation implies thinking the people on the model of the infinite subject. It is as if Marx, by severing the ties of the present to the other dimensions of time, had sought – by a route other than that of stability, but one that is no less metaphysical – to chase off the time of politics. In this respect he had forgotten about Feuerbach's theses, which demanded a passive principle in philosophy.

Yet perhaps a judgment without appeal on the Marx of 1843 in the name of finitude would be hasty. As Jacques Taminiaux warns, finitude "may make itself manifest where its most heedless disavowal seems to prevail."[36] A twofold postulate seems to govern Marx's thought: as dependent as it is on a conception of the subject as self-causality, his thought undeniably obliterates finitude; and yet, to the extent that there is a perpetual emphasis on the will for ongoing self-institution, it inevitably admits that this self-identity depends on winning out incessantly against the dispossession that is itself constantly reintroducing time. Thus true democracy, which is governed by the principle of ongoing self-foundation, is thought not as some kind of definitive fulfillment but as a unity that must perpetually make and remake itself against the constant threat of heteronomy's resurgence. In a word, the unity of true democracy is carried off in the movement of its infinite striving.

IV

Fourth characteristic: It seems we hold the guiding thread that should allow us to elucidate the formula of the French moderns. All the preceding analyses tend to bring out the specific difference of modern democracy in relation to any other form of State, be it a constitutional monarchy or a republic. I shall now attempt to review and systematize these analyses in several propositions that account for the *exception* of democracy.

Democracy is characterized by an unprecedented relationship

between the political State or the constitution and the totality of the other material or spiritual realms, which Marx designates sometimes as the "non-political State." In democracy proper the whole, by which is meant the whole existence of a people, is never organized in terms of a part, in this case the constitution (the monarch in constitutional monarchy or the public realm in the republic that remains a form of alienation or that *qua* form testifies to continued political alienation). And it is precisely because democracy never allows for the advent of a mystifying confusion between the part and the whole – between the political State and the *demos* – that it will leave the field open for the instituting activity of the subject that is its own end.

Only the implementation of the reduction allows one correctly to subsume, that is, to think a particular element, the political State, as encompassed, included within the whole – the whole *demos*. But reduction does not quite simply mean disappearance; or rather, we have to agree on what exactly disappears, for the meaning of the political State's disappearance is not exactly obvious. Before trying to answer this question, we may return to the components of the reduction so as better to avoid an error of interpretation: (1) The political State undergoes a reduction to the extent that it is brought back to what it is, to its proper dimension as one and only one element of the whole. "The specific difference of democracy is that here the constitution is in general only one moment of the people's existence, that is to say the political constitution does not form the State for itself."[37] Or in other words, "in a democracy the political State . . . is itself merely a particular content, like a particular form of existence of the people."[38] (2) It follows that the constitution is only one part of a whole and that the logic of democracy prevents a subsumption that would result in an inversion of the whole and the part. "Insofar as we speak of the constitution as a particular thing, however, it must be considered a part of the whole."[39] (3) Finally, the consequence of this is that, by contrast to what occurs in other forms of State, the political State having been *reduced* in this way no longer functions as a whole dominating and determining its parts: ". . . *qua* political State, *qua* constitution it is no longer equivalent to the whole," and "in democracy the abstract State has ceased to be the governing moment."[40]

Inversely, in other forms of State, by want of the reduction, we encounter systematically opposite characteristics. In monarchy: (1) This particular moment experiences an excrescence such that universality is attributed to it; (2) its true character is misrepresented, the part passes for the whole, "in monarchy we have the people of the constitution"; (3) transfigured in this way, the particular moment acquires an efficiency that enables it to dominate and determine the parts, "In all States distinct from democracy the State, the law, the constitution is dominant."[41]

Excrescence, misrepresentation, dominance: these are the three characteristics of political illusion that result in setting up an unbalance in the form of an improper hierarchical relation between this particular moment and the other elements – that is, between the political State that thereby acquires the status of an organizational form, and the other realms that remain mere particular moments. Moreover, this political moment, raised wrongly to the status of the universal, does not refer to the other realms as a unifying form on the model of reason, an architectonic faculty, but refers to them through the analytic and separative modalities of the understanding. The political State in monarchy (the prince) or in the republic (the public realm that, specifically as the dominant realm, here ceases to be a uniquely political constitution) appropriates for itself the role of the dominant without really dominating, without "materially permeating the content of the remaining non-political realms."[42] This organizing form functions as a separative faculty that establishes itself in the dualism of the political and non-political State – and it does more, for it accuses this dualism only to better assert its imaginary universality in the view of unassimilated particulars.

But this picture of the forms of State, in which the political State is not subjected to a reduction, may be misleading if connected to certain propositions of Marx concerning the specificity of democracy. Marx indeed writes, "In democracy the formal principle is simultaneously the material principle. For that reason it is the first true unity of the universal and the particular."[43] Is this to say that democracy, the real universal that would surmount the dualism specific to modernity, is an organizing form that would function as a unity, as a cohesive whole on the model of unifying reason?

To conclude this way would be to ignore the reduction, to make slight of this operation situated at the heart of democracy, and therefore to overlook the meaning and the intentionality of Marx's investigation in the 1843 Critique.

Marx's argument, rather, is that because in democracy the political moment remains a particular moment – because it does not experience an elevation to the status of an organizing form – the political principle is able to win over the other realms. It is quite precisely the reduction of the political State to a moment that opens the possibility for the democratic institution of every realm. But this process is at the least surprising. How can a reduction result in making possible the democratic institution of the totality of society? The answer is twofold to the extent that it takes into account the two aspects of the reduction. In a first instance, there is a negative effect: as a determination of limits, the reduction consists in blocking the transformation or even the transfiguration of the political moment into an organizing form that would take on the role of an abstract universal. Or again, it consists in blocking the type of imaginary community that engenders the dualism specific to political emancipation, according to Marx's critical account of it in *The Jewish Question*. This is followed by a productive effect: for by bringing the political moment back to what creates it, by compelling it to "go back" to the self-determination of *the whole demos*, the reduction turns this activity away from any focalization on the political realm and thus any crystallization over it that would, as Marx knew well, be realized only to the detriment of the other realms. The question is to save *the "fluidity" of instituting activity*, to avoid a situation in which the political moment – the moment of bourgeois civil society's self-transcendence, of ecstasy, the exemplary accession of "socialized man" – would become an object of hypostasis. The question is to enable instituting activity as such to reach all the other realms, to rush on to them, or better, if we keep to the metaphor of fluidity, to irrigate them. It is as though the reduction only, at once retraction and reappropriation, allows for a retroaction of this energy that would thus remain active in all the other realms. Moreover, is it not the life, the existence of the people that is at stake? Is it not a model of life that makes the 1843 Critique meaningful – like the one presented by Feuerbach in *The Essence of Christianity*? "As life in general consists in a perpetual systole and diastole; so is it in religion. In the religious systole man propels his own nature from himself, he throws himself outward; in the religious diastole he receives the rejected nature into his heart again."[44]

Let us return to the question: when the French of the modern era posit that in true democracy the political State would disappear, what disappears? Is it the political State *qua* particular moment, or is it the political State *qua* organizing form, that is to say, *qua* political realm raised to the level of the universal, to the level of a whole dominating and determining the parts? The question may appear scholastic, but if we discern the stakes it is far from being so. How should this disappearance of the State be interpreted? Should it be understood in the play between democracy and "true democracy," such that the advent of democracy in its truth would at the same time mean that democracy has bypassed itself, abolished itself to the point of leaving the political realm behind and making the State extinct? By virtue of the self-transcendence of true democracy – as the simultaneity of the formal and the material principle, and as the true unity of the universal and the particular – would the social realm finally be given back to itself, returned to its spontaneity, so that this comeback or this emergence of human community would make the political henceforth useless, forevermore knocked down to decrepitude? In this case, the extinction of democracy in the advent of its truth would inaugurate, depending on the critics, either the sunrise of anarchy or that of communism.[45]

Yet the course of Marx's impassioned investigation, entirely drawn to the truth of democracy in its essence and in its existence, is more complex, more nuanced and also more restrictive. In order to avoid any abusive simplification and to alert the critic, let it be said that Marx welcomes the formula of the French moderns in definite terms. The advent of "true democracy" signifies only the disappearance of the political State *qua* organizing form and separate realm, and not at all the extinction or the disappearance of the political. The political State persists as a particular moment in the life of the people, but it is above all with the advent of "true democracy" that the political principle reaches its fulfillment. It is as if the reduction on which democracy depends were to result, by way of the restrictive force of the reduction, in paradoxically liberating the over-signification that haunts the State. Thus a path beyond the political State would be opened by the democratic institution of society, such that the *demos* manifests and recognizes itself as *demos* in all realms of human life while respecting the specificity of each one. In the 1843 Critique, however, this distinction between the two meanings of the political State is essential. If we keep to Marx's argument right down to the details, we find that the requirement of differentiation remains intact. The advent of true democracy is not to be confused with either the infamous night where all cows are black, nor with the sunrise that is dazzling to the point of blurring all outlines. We may consider several propositions that support this reading.

(1) We should be wary of interpreting the simultaneity of the formal and material principle – the real unity of democracy in its opposition to monarchy – as the passage from an organizing form based on the understanding as a separative faculty to one based on unifying reason. The unity engendered by democracy has nothing to do with the unification that would result from the imposition of a unifying form to a content threatened by division. Marx's criticism of monarchy turns out to have two facets. Not only does monarchy fail to really dominate, to materially permeate the content of the other

non-political realms, but it moreover has the drawback of conceiving the relation between the political and the non-political State in terms of the imprint of a form on a content. The point is not that democracy (unless we are to confuse it with a republic) succeeds where monarchy fails because of the change in form; rather, at stake is breaking with the very idea of form, be it organizational in the mode of separation or in the mode of unification.[46]

(2) In democracy, the operation of the reduction does not mean that the constitution or the political State disappears in the sense that there would be a leap beyond the political realm; rather, the political State disappears as an organizing form and is restricted to the limits of a moment of the people's existence. In other words, in true democracy the reduced and limited political State does not persist and persevere any less; it exists. Once the confusion between the political State and the whole of the people's existence is eliminated, once the political State is made relative, not only does this political State exist, we may even add, without forcing the meaning of the text, that by regaining its veritable function and its right place, it exists all the better: it sets itself next to the non-political content, and by setting itself as a particular content in coexistence with the other particular contents of the people, it distinguishes itself from them in its irreducible identity. In this way we grasp better the reduction's meaning: while it changes the *status of the political realm* and ceases to claim for itself the authority of a form that would be equivalent to the whole, it does not for all that efface the specificity of this moment that, as a moment, deserves and requires to be distinguished from the other moments of the people's life. The political moment "dethroned," fallen from the exceptional status of being the organizing form of the people's existence, is no less a particular element in the existence of the people that, in its very particularity, remains ineffaceable. As it were, once an end is put to what Marx would in 1844 call "the presumptuous exaggeration of the political factor,"[47] we may say that this moment experiences a sort of opening out that reveals its complexity. Subjected to the work of the reduction, the political realm remains what it is and no longer tends to transform itself from part to whole. This means that it does not accede to the rank of a dominant element, nor to the rank of a determinant element, "In democracy the State as particular is only particular." But the State exists also as universal, "as universal it is the real universal." We may first understand this proposition according to its negative meaning: in democracy the political State as universal does not exist as a formal universal. We here find again the previous declarations regarding the simultaneity

of the formal and material principle, and democracy as the true unity of the universal and the particular. And in a decisive way Marx specifies that as a real and not formal universal, the political State in a true democracy does not act as an instance of determination of the non-political content. "As universal it is the real universal; that is it is nothing definite in distinction from the other content."[48] But the positive meaning is more enigmatic: how can a moment become a real universal without setting itself up in a position of dominance, nor of efficaciousness or determinacy? We are compelled once again to return to the operation of the reduction. By blocking, so to speak, the transformation of this particular moment into a form imposed on a non-political content, the reduction by the same token opens an unprecedented alternative path toward universality. In other words, the inhibition of the excrescence the reduction brings with it, which is reinforced here by the effort to lead this particular moment back to its originary focal-point – the life of the people – genuinely makes it possible to convert this particular moment in such a way that it can produce an effectively actual universality. The conversion in question constitutes, indeed, an opening, for it could be said of this moment that, drawn back into its originary source, it rises up again beyond the reified and reifying opposition of content and form and crashes back down as pure acting, pure creation. From this perspective, and by virtue of its connection with Moses Hess's "Philosophy of Action," and through it, with Fichte, the 1843 Critique seems like it can be read as the implementation, in the political field, of an ontology in which being is thought of as action or, to express this better by privileging the verbal form, as *acting*. Criticism of the idea of form and a valorization of action are the two conditions of true democracy. The political State is deformalized at the same time that it is generalized or, more exactly, it is generalized because it is deformalized, because by virtue of the reduction it can take a route other than one of formal universality. As the working out of the practical and theoretical energy of the people, the power of the political State is defined by an essentially dynamic dimension: brought back to its originary focal-point the State reemerges as instituting activity itself. The enigma we are up against is none other than the democratic institution of the social realm. We could understand this process of institution as the self-determination and self-constitution of the people that intends in the other realms (the non-political realms) that which is at stake in the political realm: namely, the advent of "socialized man." Yet we are not before a schema of a generalized politicization of all the realms either. With respect to the question raised by and in the political realm, the aim is to allow for a resonance, an answer, a solution or specific translation in each one of the other realms. It is as though, through the impetus of the political realm, the different moments that constitute the pluralistic existence of the people were to mutually reflect, like as many mirrors, the image of the socialized human being or of man as species-being. The "tendency" of true democracy consists in demanding that the *demos* be the political figure, the name that would signal the advent of a human existence, beyond the division of political existence and social existence.

If we accept this interpretation we may take full measure of the restrictive preciseness Marx brings to his restatement of the French Moderns' formula. In true democracy, the political State would disappear as a form that attempts wrongfully to take the function of a determining authority or an organizing form. It is in this respect only that Marx adopts the theme of the State's disappearance. But the political State does not disappear, and it persists, then, to the extent that it keeps to its task and remains what it is: a particular moment in the life of the people. By considering Marx and the problem of politics in this way, we are therefore as far from anarchism as from communism, as far from a self-regulating social spontaneity as from a species-community that would exist beyond politics, beyond the political realm. The thesis of a "crude" disappearance of the State (in the sense of Marx's 1844 criticism of the "crude communism" of the French) is even less compelling when we consider that Marx recognizes simultaneously a heterogeneity of the political moment and a specificity that, if maintained, makes the political realm essential to the emancipation of all other realms. Marx, in a spirit akin to Machiavelli's admirable letter to Vettori (15 December 1513) – in which the political realm is raised above the facticity of everyday life mainly devoted to the reproduction of life – wants to acquaint us with "the milieu proper to politics," to help us think the essence of the political realm and bring out its particularity. He is wary of conceiving this particularity as homogenous to the other moments and is careful to make it access heterogeneity. There is indeed a kind of *sublimity* of the political moment for Marx. Elevation is proper to the political realm: in relation to the other realms, it represents a beyond. It is therefore legitimate to recognize in the political realm the characteristics of transcendence: the political realm is a situation distinct from the other realms, on a different level, and it is the solution for bringing the other realms into a continuity, one highlighted by Marx once he focuses on the explosive, ecstatic character of the political moment. "Political life is the life in the air, the ethereal region of civil society."[49] In and by the political realm, the rudiments of universal reason are instilled, making possible, under the name of the people, the experience of human unity. The political State as a constitutional realm is displayed, then, as the element where the people's epiphany can take place, where the people make their species-being objective, universal, free and unlimited to the point that they appear to themselves as an absolute, divine being.

"The political constitution was until now the religious sphere, the religion of popular life, the heaven of its universality in opposition to the earthly existence of its actuality."[50] It is quite precisely by perceiving the particularity of the political moment in this way that Marx introduces the possibility of going adrift, of turning off course. By insisting on the sublimity of the political, Marx designates by the same stroke the point where a turn from objectification to alienation could intervene. It is, exactly, because of its sublimity that the political realm is exposed to the dangers of excrescence. That is, by virtue of its relation to the sublimity of species-life, the political realm is affected by a tropism of presumptuous exaggeration. But then again, this is why Marx considers that, compared to the various moments of the life of the people, the political State was the most difficult to elaborate. We may then understand what is at stake in the restrictive interpretation proposed. The question is to maintain the impulsion toward the sublime while avoiding the drift off course, the "folly" of the political realm that, intoxicated by the high realms – what Marx terms "the high taste of the life of the people" – would declare: "the community is me," and immediately bring about an impoverishment of the non-political realms.

It seems all the more unlikely that Marx would aim for the dissolution of the political realm as a particular moment in the life of the people when we consider that he welcomes the people's "demand" for political life as a necessary historical task. Marx praises the French for the production of the political principle itself, for their "rediscovery of political feeling."[51] This abstraction of the State as specifically political is a necessary moment, historically and theoretically – and the French are not to be criticized for it, for without this abstraction the passage from nature to culture could not have been realized, nor could the political principle have been made manifest. This is not to say that the abstraction of the political State is the last word on a people's life, nor is it to say that we here hold the ultimate figure of emancipation.[52] Said otherwise, as soon as it is acknowledged that it is in the political realm that the people may experience their universality, their liberty and infinitude, it is immediately necessary to transform this ecstatic experience of human unity into an effective experience, to generalize it and make it continuous with all the non-political realms. In short, the "ceremony" of the political should be *converted* to the species-life of the real and total being of the *demos* – the *demos* that, in its people-being belongs at once to the political principle and the sensualist principle, and that as real living being, as both head and heart, aims for reality in its totality. The design of Marx's analysis, then, is clearly drawn out: in Feuerbachian terms, the people who in the constitutional systole expel their own essence – "socialized man" – are to regain this essence in what could be called an instituting diastole, letting it spread out to the totality of life, in a multifarious and pluralistic life, "exposed to the vivifying and refreshing waves of the ocean of the world."[53]

"In true democracy the political State disappears." It is a narrow path that is chosen by Marx in this proposition:

- Neither a dissolution of the political into the social, for it is out of the question to deny an element that, in its heterogeneity, is unsurpassable by virtue of its capacity for instigation and exemplariness, qualities that are indispensable to any modern society. The political realm alone can designate and place on center stage what is at stake and what never ceases to make itself at stake: the life in common of human beings, the demands of liberty. It is here that the autonomy or heteronomy of the *demos* – its existence or dissolution – is played out. Would it be pushing matters too far to discern, in the specificity of the political element as a particular moment, the emergence of a symbolic dimension, a totality of expressions and reference points that sketch the contours of the place, as Claude Lefort writes, "for apprehending what is presented as real," the place where the question of the making of the *demos* is posed?[54]
- Nor an objectification that would turn into fetishization and alienation, that would deepen a chasm between the excrescence of the political realm and the impoverishment of the other realms; the whole point is to avoid this hypostasis of the political moment, the turn to a form that would set itself up as the keeper of universality.

Marx's labor consists, then, in restraining to modesty a moment that, by virtue of its privileged relationship with human "communal being," with the "linking" of political sociality, presents a constitutive tendency toward immodesty. Yet Marx maintains, without concessions, the necessity of this moment for the self-realization of the *demos*. Without nourishing the illusion of an offshoot, we may find an illustration of the Critique's problematic in the 1956

Hungarian revolution. One of the distinctive traits of this revolution, in fact, was to demand a persistence of the political principle – that is, of political power – while practicing the "reduction" of the political realm. This realm was forced, on the one hand, to the status of a particular moment that is a moment only, and, on the other, to coexist with other forms of institution corresponding to other moments of the people's life.[55]

In relation to Marx's position in 1842, the 1843 Critique gives rise, at the very heart of the criticism of Hegel, to a sort of replay of the Hegelian dynamic, but one that would gain its distinctive characteristic by being brought over from a philosophy of spirit to a philosophy of action. While with Hegel the path to make an absolute of the political realm is barred because the political is made relative to absolute knowledge, in Marx's 1843 Critique the political realm drops a level and is consequently made relative, but this time in relation to the absolute activity of the subject as *demos*. Evidently, the relativization of the political realm that takes place in the logic of the philosophy of action should not be confused with a derivation from a sociological instance that would be posited as dominant and determinant. If, between the 1842 texts and the 1843 Critique, a shift becomes evident from a political to a democratic absolute, this meaningful move itself seems to require the rise of a new subject, the real and total subject, the *demos* that as both head and heart takes the place of a subject that was only head, and only reason: political intelligence.

— 6 —

TRUE DEMOCRACY AND MODERNITY

Marx refuses the theory of the State of right as developed in his time by Lorenz von Stein, in which he could only too easily discern an excrescence of the political State, its transformation into an organizing form. As we have seen, however, he does not opt for Moses Hess's ethical anarchy either, which dismisses indistinctly the concept of the State and that of politics. Marx's position is situated between these two antagonistic poles: the disappearance of the State as an organizing form, but the persistence of the political realm – the moment of the life of the people – such that liberty and universality can extend to all realms to penetrate into them. This, in brief, is the choice Marx makes in the name of true democracy.

I will here raise a last and legitimate question: does Marx have in view a modern democracy or a theory of modern democracy? If we turn our attention to the requirement of differentiation specific to democratic modernity, the answer can only be affirmative. Marx is not only careful to distinguish the different moments of a people's life, he moreover characterizes democracy precisely as the political form where it is seen that each moment does not exceed its powers and does not encroach on the other realms.

In democracy no moment takes on a meaning that is not proper to it – from this perspective, the reduction of the political moment is exemplary, and what is true of this moment is equally true of the others. By virtue of this reduction, the particular realms that have heard the call to a free community arise from the site of politics may respond to it in the specificity of their being. Exalted by the *illumination* of the political, they may in turn blaze fully. The self-constitution of true democracy in and by the political realm is neither a socialization, nor a politicization but the advent of species-existence, the advent of human existence, and far from blurring the differentiation, this advent aims to elaborate it. In other words, a respect for the specificity of each realm is made to cohere with the imperative of allowing for the appearance, according to the modalities of the respective realms, of the unity of man with man. The perspective of differentiation never ceases to uphold Marx's text. Marx develops quite well the opposition between the States of antiquity – in which the political State is completely separate from the other realms of life – and modernity, in which the State is separate as a necessary abstraction, but in which simultaneously there is an accommodation that occurs by way of the constitutional mediation such that, through this mediation, the characteristic movement of the democratic institution of the social realm is realized. True democracy, then, is a form that surmounts the abstraction of the modern State – without for all that denying the existence, nor the necessity, of a political realm – attaining, like the Middle Ages, an identity of a people's life and the life of the State, while rejecting the authoritarian model of organic unity and making unity instead wholly dependent on the inexhaustible demands of modern liberty. The free human being, the free, non-alienated and unlimited *demos*, is the real principle of this political community. Marx, morevoer, is careful to describe as faithfully as possible each of the different powers that contribute to the practice of democracy.

However, a careful look at the question of unity immediately makes the answer to this question more problematic. On the one hand, the theory of true democracy shows that no modern society devoted to liberty can endure without, so to speak, an ongoing difference between the political realm and all the others. Yet, on the other hand, there is no getting around the fact that Marx nonetheless thinks true democracy according to a model of unity, and that the self-identity of the people structures the 1843 Critique from beginning to end. In this respect, Marx's conception of democracy is at odds with a theory of democracy as a form of society that welcomes social division, and that distinguishes itself precisely by recognizing the legitimacy of conflict in society.[1]

It seems a chasm is here deepened, if not between Marx and the Italian humanists, at least between Marx and Machiavelli. In chapter IX of *The Prince* and chapter IV, Book I, of *The Discourses*, Machiavelli in effect posits that every human city regulated and constructs itself starting from an originary division expressed best by the opposition of desires: the desire of the great to command and oppress the people, and that of the people to be neither commanded nor oppressed – the desire for liberty. This division of desire at the heart of the city is all the more in gestation given the originary division of the social it implies, as if every manifestation of society were indissolubly an exposure to division.[2] And from a perspective that is completely at odds with the classical one, Machiavelli makes discord and internal disunion – the struggle in Rome between the senate and the plebs – the origin and wellspring of Roman liberty. "To me those who condemn the quarrels between the nobles and the plebs, seem to be cavilling at the very things that were the primary cause of Rome's retaining her freedom, and that they pay more attention to the noise and clamour resulting from such commotions than to what resulted from them, that is to the good effects which they produced."[3]

Marx also takes his distance from Montesquieu, that other Machiavellian who eulogized the divisions and the popular riots of Rome and who threw peace, that menacing figure of the One, into question by distinguishing between a union that rests on dissonance – the concert – and a union that is despotic, that brings together not citizens, but dead bodies. Thus the warning: "What is called union in a body politic is a very equivocal thing," which Marx apparently does not heed, since he sees unity simply as a positive good, and does not appear to suspect either a link between certain forms of unity and despotism, or inversely links between social division, the rise of conflict, and liberty.[4] But if Marx undeniably associates the truth of democracy with the disappearance of conflict, it is equally evident that this unity is not based on a model of organic totality, nor on the model of the body. The principle of adjunction Marx aims for, which at times he seems to construe starting from a nervous system or a system of circulation, is to be placed on the side of action. Even if this principle does not appear to leave the field of the system, it belongs no less to the mystery of a people's life, to its indetermination – all at once theoretical and practical energy – such that the unity of a people is nothing less than the infinitude, the opening, the plasticity or fluidity of willing.

The refusal of conflict, moreover, is not a sufficient basis for accusing Marx of thinking true democracy according to the model of the Greek city, and it is not a ground for rejecting him as thinking only the liberty of the Ancients either. Ascertaining the refusal of conflict is not the same thing as stating its origin. Marx – and in this sense Benjamin Constant's criticisms of Jacobinism cannot be wielded against him – does not refuse conflict because he intends to make objective liberty the dominant factor, as though he were playing the substantial element of the Greek city against the principle of subjective liberty. It is, on the contrary, at the heart of modernity, in the logic of the philosophy of subjectivity specific to the modern world, that Marx disjoins democracy from the division of the social and reunites democracy with the will for coincidence. It is because Marx brings political objectification back to a subject that he sets in a position of sovereignty – certainly a political sovereignty, but above all the metaphysical sovereignty of self-presence – that democracy is thought beyond conflict. In the speculative structure of Marx's thought, to make room for division would be tantamount to striking against the very status of the *whole demos* which, construed in terms of self-consciousness and self-knowledge, functions as the center and gauge of all things. To allow for division would be to introduce a hurtful deviation, to open a breach that would by the same stroke jeopardize the perpetual realignment and totalization of the *demos* that, yielding to the fascination of the Same, establishes itself in the perfect mastery of its action, in a full self-adequacy.[5] The 1843 Critique therefore raises the question of the *whole demos* (*ganzen demos*) which Marx, in his anti-Hegelian offensive, asserts as the effective unitary subject, the real people to which the constitution as political objectification is continually reconducted. To show that democracy forestalls any deviation between the objectification of one of its moments and its meaning – to show that democracy intercepts any moment that would "take flight" and make itself equivalent to the whole – this is essentially a way for Marx to grasp the *specific difference* of democracy. In short, true democracy may be defined as a state of appropriateness between the people and their objectifications that is perfect to the point of averting any risk of a turn from objectification to alienation. "In democracy none of the moments obtains a significance other than what befits it. Each is really only a moment of the *whole demos*."[6]

Marx, in a sense without his knowing it, and despite the care with which he denounced the ascendancy of logic in Hegel's thinking of the political realm, allows modern metaphysics to guide no less his own analysis of the political realm under the invocation of the *demos*. The people appear in the political realm as *subjectum*, as self-presence, without any passivity mediating the least lag or division, and this is particularly evident with respect to time. The people moreover manifest themselves as a system in action, as the mustering of a totalization that has found its true center. The effective life of this unitary subject is established, then, in the deployment of its moments in their totality. But can a conception of the people that owes so much to metaphysics still be genuinely political? Might not a better political analysis of the people be found in the work of such historian-philosophers as Jules

Michelet and Edgar Quinet? Far from engaging in a philosophy of a subject, Michelet and Quinet think of the people in light of their problematic – for always deferred – identity. Rather than embodying a self-presence, the people either are *above* themselves – the people in the heroic state that establish themselves in the very invention of liberty – or they are *below* themselves, when the experience of liberty threatens to revert into its opposite, namely servitude. In short, never coinciding with themselves, never equal to themselves, the people are simultaneously where they are manifest, and where they come to existence, confronted with the ordeal of an insurmountable self-discrepancy. A discrepancy that would wrongly be considered a shortcoming, for it is quite certainly by this deficiency, and by maintaining it, that the opportunities for an anti-authoritarian city are encountered.

To think the truth of democracy in terms of the advent of the *whole demos* – or as a totality – that would hold the key to the enigma of all the constitutions, does this imply forgetting the Aristotelian thesis according to which political affairs are characterized by an indetermination that invalidates the very idea of their resolution, and that renders the "idea of a face-to-face with the fulfilled *politeia*" – the modern idea of an *Eschaton* – inconceivable?[7] Besides positioning itself outside of conflict, the valorization of unity in the form of the *demos* also seems anti-political to the extent that, as François Chatelet has argued, it superimposes the *demos* as the figure of the one over the plurality of actors, the *polloï,* who define the scope of the political field. Does Marx leave a place for the plurality of singular individuals? Does he really reach the point of thinking the mass of men, a mass he nonetheless posits as the primary element of the family and civil society? Is it not here that Marx bypasses the epistemological question of the determining cause in order to rediscover the political question of the acting power? "The fact is that the State issues from the mass of men existing as members of families and of civil society."[8]

Marx's thought is sufficiently complex, even bordering on contradiction, to make us wary of an unequivocal answer to these questions. We may recall how, confronted with the Hegelian deduction of the power of the prince and the determination of the decisive moment of the whole in the person of the monarch, Marx threw this fusion of personality and the *monos* into question. "Clearly the one has truth only as many ones. The predicate, the essence, never exhausts the spheres of its existence in a single one but in many ones."[9] Does this protest against the Hegelian one hold good for the Marxian one of the people – does the *demos* experience this same breaking up?

Whatever the case may be, the presence of a speculative matrix shows well enough that the 1843 Critique exemplifies a modern conception of democracy.

If this conception calls for criticism, it is thus not for having confused – as Marx himself had formulated the reproach with respect to the Jacobins – the modern world with the world of antiquity. Marx did not ignore the modern demand of differentiation; he subordinated this demand – while nonetheless acknowledging it – to the will of reconciliation. It is in the logic of the metaphysics of subjectivity that Marx's thinking of democracy is left to culminate in a refusal of exteriority, in a rejection of alterity and a foreclosure of finitude.

Restoring in this way Marx's conception of democracy to the heart of modernity is not insignificant. Once absolved from the unfounded accusation of being an artifact of antiquity, the 1843 Critique may be qualified as a fundamental text of democratic modernity. Which is not to say that Marx's text should be given a foundational or exemplary status; what is offered in the very structure of the argument – beyond the theoretical orientations of the great book on the State that Marx projected and never wrote – is the ambiguities and difficulties of the modern idea of democracy itself. This tension is all the more evident given that Marx's text has the merit of introducing an opposition between democracy and the political State, between the democratic self-institution of society and the formalism of the modern State.

If we follow through with the irresolvable tension of this text, we can in fact see that Marx presents not so much the key to the enigma as the valiant effort to gauge another one, the enigma that, without being named, is no less present as the modern imperative of autonomy (which in this sense is still alive). Caught in the schema of self-foundation, this imperative is endangered by a dialectic of emancipation: it risks falling over into its opposite – heteronomy, self-destruction – by failing to grant alterity its rights, by not bringing its movement of non-limitation before the fragility and the contingency of human affairs. Perhaps it is in view of this danger that we may understand why Marx, the thinker of radical autonomy, in a rather surprising move returns to an idea of objective reason that would impose limits on the infinitude of the people's will. "The will of a people can no more exceed the laws of reason than can the will of an individual. In the case of an irrational people one cannot speak at all of a rational organization of the State."[10]

Marx, we have observed, on several occasions presents the people as at once principle, subject and end – or put differently, as subject which in relation to itself is its own end. By this is understood that true democracy, perpetually brought back to the activity of the people, is deployed as an ideality. An exclusively political conception of the people comes in view that corresponds to what Bernard Groethuysen, in "The Dialectics of Democracy," calls "the heroic phase of democracy." "The collectivity seeks its own political realization. As long as the collectivity is within this phase of self-organization, the general will seems to be its own subject and its own object: the citizen wants to become *citizen*."[11] There is no social existence of the people, no sociological reality that would precede the democratic institution and that true democracy would have as its goal to encompass and express politically. There is therefore an ideality of the people in the sense that the very being of the people is will to liberty itself. The democratic institution of the social realm and the birth, the "invention" of the people, constitute one and the same act, a single and identical acting. Experiencing the ordeal of its non-essentiality in the confrontation with the political moment, society has no choice but to acknowledge its problematic existence. This additional ambiguity, then, attenuates the criticisms made earlier, for this element of ideality specific to the democratic political element, and which is characterized by a collective will seeking its own identity, allows for a retrieval of a portion of the indetermination that the project of a total fulfillment of human sociality would obliterate.

Yet as soon as we turn to a text written immediately afterwards, the "Contribution to the Critique of Hegel's Philosophy of Right," published in the *Deutsch-Französische Jahrbücher* in 1844, a new question arises. By designating the proletariat as the new actor on the stage of history, did Marx seek to withdraw himself from the ideality and the indetermination that define the people so long as they remain within the political element? By going from the people to what Saint-Simon called "the greatest and poorest class," by raising this class to the rank of the subject holding the key to history – the universal class – did Marx seek to give a real face, a name, that of the proletariat, to that non-identifiable people and thus remove himself from the ordeal of indetermination? As Marx and Engels would put it in *The Holy Family*: "It is not a question of what this or that proletarian, or even the whole proletariat, at the moment *regards* as its aim. It is a question of *what the proletariat is*, and what, in accordance with this *being*, it will historically be compelled to do."[12]

Might we consider, then, that once Marx discovers "the being of the proletariat," he leaves the Machiavellian moment and turns away from the logic of political affairs?

To draw such a conclusion would be hasty, to say the least.

Without taking sides in a debate concerning the nature of the proletariat according to Marx, it is enough to recall that this class can all the less be shut in the social realm given that, in Marx's own estimation, its being is paradoxical: "a class in civil society that is not of civil society."[13] In other words, by virtue of its revolutionary situation and therefore the mission set down in its being, this class surpasses a localization as much as a sociological determination. As a new figure of the historical negativity that realizes the transformative method in the field of practice, the proletariat appears as the class for which the social – its social being – is inextricable from the political, its political being. "The working class is revolutionary or it is nothing," as Marx puts it in a letter to Johann Baptist Schweitzer in 1865.[14] Indeed, the last pages of *The Poverty of Philosophy* are organized around refuting equally the economists that enclose the workers in the existing society and the thinkers that view the proletariat as nothing more than a social movement. Marx, on the contrary, strives to retrace the path that leads from the class *in itself*, such as it results from big industry and economic conditions, to the class *for itself*, the class that transforms its position *in relation* to capital into a political struggle *against* capital, in view of a total revolution. Thus the reminder of some essential facts: "Do not say that social movement excludes political movement. There is never a political movement that is not at the same time social" – a reminder that Marx translates promptly by citing George Sand: "Struggle or death."[15]

Other paths out of the Machiavellian moment are easily foreseen. In an interval of a few years, identical metaphors and expressions reappear that address in a different context other regions of reality and reflect the progress and processes of Marx's thought. In the wake of Kant, Marx sees in the world of the press that which favors free communication between human beings; he refuses to dissociate the freedom to think from the freedom to publish. But by contrast to Kant, Marx does not believe that the freedom of thought and the freedom to communicate one's thoughts can constitute all the political activity of human beings. Marx thus sees the press as serving functions other than those of communication. As the objectification of the spirit of a people, the press allows for a people to gain self-knowledge. Formulating matters in a hermeneutical vein, Marx declares in the "Debates on Freedom of the Press" (May 1842): "The free press is the ubiquitous vigilant eye of a people's soul, the embodiment of a people's faith in itself, the eloquent link that connects the individual with the State and the world . . . It is a people's frank confession to itself, and the redeeming power of confession is well known. It is the spiritual mirror in which a people can see itself, and self-examination is the first condition of wisdom."[16] As a "spiritual mirror," the press is constitutive of the political place: it is what opens a path to this political place, this public space where, by the specular image they send back to themselves, a people constitute themselves, obtain their social identity and reach self-knowledge, the condition of liberty. By virtue of the press, on the occasion of the multiple conflicts which arise in society, the people daily practice recognition, or better, mutual knowledge.

The metaphor of the mirror surfaces again in the preliminary notes to the economic and philosophic manuscripts of 1844, only now it refers to production. Under the title of "Human Production," Marx writes:

> Let us suppose that we had produced as human beings. In that event each of us would have doubly affirmed himself and his neighbor in his production. (1) In my production I would have objectified the specific character of my individuality . . . (2) In your use or enjoyment of my product I would have the immediate satisfaction and knowledge that in my labor I had gratified a human need, that is that I had objectified human nature and hence had procured an object corresponding to the needs of another human being. (3) I would have acted for you as the mediator between you and the species, thus I would be acknowledged by you as the complement of your own being, as an essential part of yourself. I would thus know myself to be confirmed both in your thoughts and your love. (4) In the individual expression of my own life I would have brought about the immediate expression of your life, and so in my individual activity I would have directly confirmed and realized my authentic nature, my human, communal nature (*Gemeinwesen*). Our productions would be as many mirrors from which our natures would shine forth.[17]

The displacement Marx brings about in his resumption of the metaphor of the mirror may certainly be read as his leaving the Machiavellian moment behind. Faithful to his project of a monadology, interpreted through Feuerbach as intersubjectivity, Marx converts the determination of the focal-point from which communication between human beings may be played out, as if here again he intended to substitute the concretion of production for the immateriality of political life, to substitute a solid foundation for the celestial life of the political realm, thus giving priority to the link established through work between human beings as a species, and between the human species and nature.[18] In short, the press, the "eloquent link that connects the individual with the State and the world," is replaced by production. Mutual knowledge is no longer established starting from ethical nature, or from the linguistic nature of man as a political animal. Instead, communication, that is, harmony, is realized on the basis of the relation between monads defined as productive beings.

If *production* that comes to take the place of the political principle is chosen as the focal-point for the fulfillment of what Marx calls "human exchange," it simultaneously designates the focal-point of servitude, the womb of all forms of servitude. In the *1844 Manuscripts*, Marx posits an equivalency between the emancipation of society from private property and the emancipation of workers, since the workers' emancipation would be equal to universal emancipation. And universal emancipation indeed represents what is at stake, not only by virtue of the specific nature of the proletariat, but also because the relation of alienated work to private property is determined as a universal focal-point of servitude. "The whole of human servitude is involved in the relation of the worker to production . . . *all relations of servitude are but modifications and consequences of this relation.*"[19]

It seems, then, that we are entitled to conclude that Marx ends up obliterating the Machiavellian moment, and that he ultimately retreats from the milieu proper to politics. The whole movement of his thought suggests that the complexity of the political realm was suddenly undone, that he kept only the couple domination/servitude, and that he brought it back to the empirically localizable site of production. It is as if Marx transferred the shared life of human beings to another level, to another element, by replacing the *whole demos* with the collective worker, as if the solution to the enigma (for there does indeed exist a continuity regarding the goal of a solution) was displaced from democracy to communism. In 1843, democracy is welcomed as the solved enigma of all constitutions, as the resolution of the political principle itself; in 1844, Marx delivers the following verdict on communism: "This communism, as fully developed naturalism, equals humanism, and as fully developed humanism equals naturalism, it is the genuine resolution of the conflict between man and nature and man and man . . . it is the enigma of history solved, and it knows itself to be this solution."[20]

From the outset of the year 1844 Marx takes his leave from the Machiavellian moment, both in relation to its appearance in the first constellation (democracy) and with respect to the second (communism). The law of the State's gravitation is no longer seen as residing within the State itself. Marx's orientation shifts from an impassioned quest for the essence of the political realm – starting from the activity of the *demos*, from its comprehension in a philosophy of action or of acting – toward communism conceived in the horizon of being as production.

In this way our inquiry seems to reach its conclusion; at it were, we need only take note of the loss of the political element that never again would appear in Marx's writings, and admit that the meaning of the political realm and its specificity had vanished.

Yet such a position is not tenable. We may well recall that in 1845 Marx presented a German publisher with a projected work in two volumes that would have *Critique of Politics and of Political Economy* as its title. And if we consult certain of Marx's notes from the same period, written presumably as an outline for that project, we see that he intended to retrace the genesis of the modern State in relation to the French Revolution, to examine the question of human rights, the relations of the State to bourgeois society, the separation of powers, the different powers, the political parties, and planned to conclude by raising, against the backdrop of the right of suffrage, the question of "the fight for the *abolition* of the State and of bourgeois society."[21] By the looks of this title and this outline, the imposing multitude of Marx's often journalistic political writings (if only those that concern France) may appear legitimately as the life-long elaboration of the project of 1845.[22] Consequently, while we may easily agree with Maximilien Rubel that Marx's writings stem from a coexistence of the criticism of politics and the criticism of political economy, unlike Rubel we may nonetheless add that the first was rapidly conceived as dependent on the second by virtue of the so-called "intimate connection between politics and economy" itself, a connection that shows the materialist conception of the State determining the political as a secondary and derived element. If it is true that Marx never abandons the criticism of politics, it is nevertheless necessary to recognize that in his own eyes it no longer aims to describe the logic of political affairs, as was the case in the text from 1843. Why then place the author of *Capital* in the wake of Étienne de La Boétie? If there is an inconceivable phenomenon for Marx, it is certainly voluntary servitude. In relation to the interpretative alternative that we have described by proposing another reading hypothesis, starting with the years 1844–5 it is undoubtedly the "epistemological" version that triumphed. Thus the criticism of politics, instead of continuing on the path of political intelligence, oriented itself toward the economic substrate by the mediation of civil society.

And what then becomes of the enigma of true democracy? Should the impassioned questioning of the 1843 Critique be viewed as a kind of hapax legomenon, as if this inscription concerned only a single writing? Was it merely the breakthrough of an exceptional moment that, like a bolt of lightening, illuminated the early writings of Marx only to abandon them to obscurity, leaving the suddenly revealed scenery to pitch-darkness and oblivion? In this case, is there anything beyond an archeological interest that would incite the reader to engage with the 1843 Critique? Another choice is possible. Rather than posit the harmonious and well-mastered coexistence of the criticism of politics and the criticism of political economy – leading, in the last analysis, to the sublimation of "true democracy" in communism – we may consider instead that what surfaced in the 1843 Critique in the name of "true democracy" did not totally disappear, but persisted as a hidden and latent dimension of Marx's writings, ready to resurge, susceptible to awaken by the shock of the event. Thus, if we consult Marx's texts on the Paris Commune as a whole – the published version of *The Civil War in France*, and the two drafts of the address to the International Workingmen's Association of 30 May 1871 – we find, as it were, an awakening of the 1843 problematic, doubled by a return of the theme of the enigma. A new Oedipus of modern times, of the revolution recommenced without respite, Marx takes it upon himself to answer the question: "What is the Commune, that sphinx so tantalizing to the bourgeois mind?"[23] Certainly, compared to the 1843 Critique, a number of new themes appear in the 1871 analysis. The crux of the matter is understood as "the secret of the Commune," and Marx's analysis of this secret aims at bringing out its irreducible novelty, against the interpretations that pull the Commune down to previous and even bygone political forms in order to diminish its historical significance. The rupture of the Commune, that which makes it an unequalled event, is its very being as "a government of the working class," as the political form at last discovered of the workers' social emancipation.

Moreover, Marx's engagement is different in 1871. The issue is no longer to be on a par with the modern present (that of France) through the criticism of Hegel but, as the director of the International Workingmen's Association, to account for what he considers the greatest revolution of the nineteenth century. Marx aims at presenting the unprecedented character of the Commune, at showing how it is to be found precisely in the fate reserved for the State, in the revolution's determination to "smash the modern State power."[24]

But beyond these specifications, it would be difficult not to remark on how close the general schema of the two texts is, at least once the Feuerbachian language of 1843 and its three categories

– objectification, alienation, reduction – are translated into the language of the critical theory of society, which itself has the central opposition between civil society and the State at the heart of its offensive. This opposition was in truth already present in the 1843 Critique but, as I have here argued, it was not the primary opposition, since it was subordinated to a political problematic that had the life of the people as its reference point and the *whole demos* as its originary source.

This language is all the easier to translate when we consider how the concepts of 1843 give way to images in the 1871 writings. Thus, what had been the object of criticism in 1843, that is, the process by which a political objectification of the *demos* turns to alienation by having failed to submit the State to the practice of the reduction (and again, the presumptuousness of the State as a formalism that feigns equivalency to the whole, both to dominate and to determine it) is denounced in 1871 by staging the confrontation between a living body (civil society, at the center of which is the proletariat) and an apparatus that encloses it and oppresses it in the most material sense of the word. Boa constrictor, parasitical excrescence, deadening incubus, State vermin, artificial body – images that are as many attempts to put a finger on that formal "thing" which, like the robe of Nessus, paralyzes the spontaneity of social life and the free development of labor.

The couple objectification/alienation is not far; it transpires under the idea of an inversion of positions: the State apparatus has made itself the master of society when it should be the servant of society. And if the revolution goes beyond the reduction, this does not mean that the reduction is unknown to the revolution: revolution is an inversion of the inversion, "a resumption by the people for the people of its own social life."[25] It is true that the 1871 text, especially the first draft, considerably adds to the 1843 Critique, since Marx's analysis in 1871 is buttressed by a genesis of the modern State. We may note that, for Marx, the State established under absolute monarchy, in the struggle of modern society against feudalism, significantly increased in power through the developments in centralization and organization introduced by the French Revolution. An irony of history is that this reenforcement of the State appears to have been the constant result of the revolutionary phenomenon. "All revolutions thus only perfected the State machinery instead of throwing off this deadening incubus."[26] Marx locates the Second Empire – as it were, the zenith of the modern State – at the end of this trajectory, with the Commune as its perfect antithesis. Thus the Commune's unprecedented character:

as the absolute contradiction of the State, the Commune indicates a rupture in revolutionary history; for the first time ever, the question is not to take over existing powers in order to make them serve a new social group, but for the proletariat to "smash the modern State power." It is no longer such or such form of State – monarchy or republic – but the State-form itself that is rejected, and it is rejected with the implicit consciousness that this very form, irrespective of its name or political allegiance, contains within it a specific relation of domination that is hateful as such.

At this point in Marx's analysis, it is legitimate to see a contradiction between an instrumental conception of the State which he continues to profess – and which comes with the idea that the State apparatus is neutral, to the point that the nature of the State would depend on the class that takes it over – and the more fruitful and complex thesis that the State, far from being neutral, would engender as a specific formalism a relation of domination that batters down on society as a whole. For this reason, emancipation does not demand to take the State over but indeed to smash it in order to destroy by the same stroke the form of domination intrinsic to it.

Evidently, the problematic of 1843 has been considerably enriched. As if by analogy to the conception of the people in 1843, the Commune is presented as a subject that is its own end, as the collective will in search of its very own political expression – "the heroic phase of democracy," to borrow again Bernard Groethuysen's formulation. Marx's text offers a political and primarily political interpretation of the Commune. Reviewing the in truth still modest social measures of the Commune, Marx declares in his address to the General Council of the International: "The great social measure of the Commune was its own working existence. Its special measures could but betoken the tendency of a government of the people."[27] The greatness of the Commune is that it attained existence against all the forms of State that denied it the right to existence. Moreover, on close examination the interpretation Marx proposes is reinforced, for it holds a unique place in revolutionary literature:

- Neither Jacobin, since the question is no longer to gain control over the State and make it serve the people (Jacobinism does not escape from the irony of history; as a revolution by the State, it unknowingly contributes to the expansion and perfection of modern State power).
- Nor *immediately* social, in the sense that for Marx, contrary to certain schools of utopian thought well analyzed by Martin Buber

in his work on utopia, the point is not to remake the social fabric destroyed by capitalism and the State, nor to restructure and regenerate the social realm in view of rendering the State superfluous and null.

The lesson of the Commune, at least the one retained by Marx, is that the social emancipation of the workers – the emancipation of labor from the domination of capital – can only be realized by the mediation of a political form that Marx repeatedly calls "the Communal Constitution." We need hardly insist on the specificity of a political form that as such promises to escape from the autonomization of form – not only because the members of the Commune are revocable, but above all because this form establishes itself, reaches its particularity and reestablishes itself by deploying itself *against* State power, in a permanent insurrection against the State apparatus, with the foreknowledge that, as it were, any fall under the hold of State power – whatever the name or tendency – would immediately signify its death sentence. Such is the distinctive trait of the Communal Constitution *qua* political form. It is by positioning itself *against* the State that this constitution attains existence, manifests itself and perseveres in its being. Self-instituted in a principled hostility to the State and in a resistance to its spell, the Communal Constitution must not surrender this ongoing abolition lest it turn toward a resumption of State power. In this sense, the specificity of this political form distinct from formalism rests on its not being threatened by a turn off course, to the extent that it sets itself against that which would produce this turn: namely, the impudence of the State-form.

But just as there remains, in every translation, an irreducible residue resistant to the operation of translation, in this case a difference remains between the disappearance of the State and the action that consists in smashing modern State power.

In the first case – the 1843 Critique – Marx describes a process that arises from working out a particular device: true democracy that is translated by the disappearance of the political State *qua* form. At the end of the 1843 manuscript, Marx seems to envision this disappearance at the very most starting from a transformed practice of the right of suffrage, the right to vote and limitless eligibility. "Within the abstract political State the reform of voting advances the dissolution (*Auflösung*) of this political State, but also the dissolution of civil society."[28] In the 1871 texts, Marx brings to light a whole other operation; the advent of the Communal Constitution is associated with a political act, with an action in which the revolutionary negativity of a dominated class is deployed, enabling its effective social emancipation. This change in levels is all the more considerable given that the central element of this new situation is the position *against* and that which this *against* implies: the construction of this position with the determination of the field of open defiance, the choice of the adversary, the conjecture of the battle or the battles to be waged – in short, the putting to play on a political stage of an agonistic relation that aims to forestall the State's return, to institute a new political form against this formalism, thus mobilizing a critical knowledge and a *thumos* where desire for liberty and hate of servitude are mixed indistinctly.

Without returning to its philosophical modernity, true democracy indeed belongs to post-revolutionary political modernity, such as it arises from the French Revolution, the *Journées* of July 1830 in Paris, the 1831 Belgian Revolution and the Reform Bill.

Moreover, the association of true democracy with the disappearance of the State is not a momentary revolutionary rocket or a curiosity without a future in Marx's writings, even if the criticism of politics is closely related to the critique of political economy and ultimately subordinated to the latter. The 1843 manuscript and its interpretation of the formula of the French moderns almost has the import of an anti-statist matrix that persists in the form of a latent dimension in Marx's œuvre, always susceptible to rise again and produce new fruit. It resurfaces, then, in 1871, when Marx discerns in the Commune the invention of an emancipatory political form proper to the proletariat. Despite his divergence concerning the unity of the State, Marx opts for the Communalist tradition. He prefers to side with Communal autonomy – the beam capable of bringing down and smashing governmental power – than with the Saint-Simonian tradition and its slogan "from the government of people to the administration of things."[29] Despite eclipses, this latent dimension of Marx's writings has a relative constancy. We may thereby sum up this comparison of 1843 and 1871 with the juxtaposition of two formulas: for the French moderns, the political State would disappear in true democracy; for those other French moderns represented by the Communards, State power is smashed by the Communal Constitution. We may thus hypothesize an ambiguity that remains in Marx with regard to the Machiavellian moment: if he leaves this moment behind when he turns toward production in order to think through his monadology, does he not return to it when, in the Constitution of the Paris Commune, he revives the figure of true democracy?

CONCLUSION

Are we at a Machiavellian moment today? As announced at the outset, this inquiry is guided by questions concerning the present. A contemporary Machiavellian moment implies a transposition of Pocock's categories:

- To the revalorization by the Italian humanists of the *vita activa* and the *vivere civile* would correspond a rediscovery of politics and of political intelligence. I say rediscovery, since according to the philosophical interpretations of totalitarian domination elaborated by Hannah Arendt and Claude Lefort, totalitarianism is characterized by an obscuring of the political domain that is all the more disturbing as it aims to destroy or deny the political dimension of the human condition proper. In order to share this position completely, it would moreover be necessary to analyze totalitarian domination as a willed destruction of politics, and not as an excessive politicization; only by interpreting the problem in this way is it made clear that the criticism of totalitarian domination and the return to political affairs are interwoven inextricably.
- To Pocock's opposition Republic/Empire would respond the opposition democratic revolution/totalitarian domination, and it would here have to be specified immediately that the latter opposition does not, as some would have it, belong necessarily to a liberal problematic.
- Finally, to the fight against the Christian eschatology that cared little for the terrestrial city, there would correspond the criticism of the philosophies of history in view of their replacement by political philosophy, or rather, by political thought which alone is of a nature to orient us toward an alternative theory of historicity and the quest for a practical temporality.

In support of this transposition, I would like to propose a hypothesis: There is a sort of fate at the heart of modernity, at once a gift and a burden, that makes those who raise the question of the political realm inevitably encounter Machiavelli in the process. I have in mind a movement that brought several thinkers, starting from a critical distance between themselves and Marxism – with variations in the relation to Marx – to take two conjoining paths: the "return" from Marx to Machiavelli, doubled by the return from Machiavelli to us, as if what they had for a time sought in Marx, they discovered suddenly in the author of *The Prince*. The constellation of these trajectories, in which we encounter Maurice Merleau-Ponty and Claude Lefort as well as Hannah Arendt, reveals well enough the resurgence of a Machiavellian moment among us. Might the writings of the Florentine secretary be one of the sites from which a modern theory of the political realm may be worked out?

The main roads of this Machiavellian thematic are easily established. With Merleau-Ponty, we are invited to explore a politics that, under the name of Machiavelli, is neither of the understanding, nor of reason, but according to the last words of the Introduction to *Signs* (1960), "unremitting *virtù*." With Claude Lefort, the emphasis on originary social division at once encompasses and bypasses class conflict to reappear in every human city in the form of an irreducible opposition between the powerful and the people. Thus the desire to think the political realm afresh so as to make up for Marx's lacuna, and the definition of the political institution of society as a specific rendering in form of human coexistence that stages the question of its meaning. As such, a new basis for critique of totalitarian domination and, at the same time, a fresh look at the "democratic invention" – or better, a new description of shared democratic life under the banner of "savage democracy" – is offered. Finally, with Hannah Arendt, we encounter what Étienne Tassin has termed "a phenomenology of action," considered in its three dimensions – revealing, instituting, linking – and oriented toward the establishment of a public space as a space of appearance. Starting from a vigorous criticism of political philosophy, an unprecedented conception of political heroism is elaborated, in that it successfully outmaneuvers the pitfalls of heroism while maintaining politics' imperative connection with this singular disposition.

Exploring this constellation further is not my intention here. No doubt linking Marx to the Machiavellian moment would, with regard to the ambiguities I have fleshed out, clearly complicate the problem. What kind of relationship might the contemporary Machiavellian moment have with Marx's writings? Just as an account of this new Machiavellian constellation would be fruitful – whether we examine its orientations with the goal of locating their areas of divergence and conflict, or whether we aim to bring them together inventively – so too is it decisive not to neglect the movement of Marx's thought, notably in the 1843 Critique. For we have seen that Marx's impassioned questioning of "true democracy," and its ultimate product, the opposition that deserves to be thought between democracy and the State, turns out to be a subterranean dimension of his writings, rising to the surface according to the demands and solicitations of the event. And is it not this opposition, this revelation of the conflict between democracy and the State, that is up to a certain point the outcome of the contemporary Machiavellian moment itself, as exemplified in Arendt's republic of councils, or Lefort's libertarian conception of democracy? From this perspective, Marx brings to light a living power that, since the French Revolution, and in every revolutionary rupture, from Paris 1848 to Budapest 1956, reminds us how emancipation in its multiple flights, in its democratic manifestations, is also directed against the State and rises inexorably against it. If the democratic revolution is to keep pace with the modern idea of liberty, it cannot do otherwise than to take full measure of the problem of the State. Since the foundering of the purportedly socialist bureaucratic regimes, the question of liberty has become the primary question, the primordial question. The question of emancipation is to be maintained absolutely. But is it in truth necessary to work at maintaining it? Is it not the spontaneity "of the people inhabiting the earth" who maintain it themselves, despite all the words of disparagement that claim regularly to have liquidated it? To inspire greater modesty to the "liquidators," it may be recalled that in the 1830s, under the July Monarchy, the "eminent authorities" announced from the top of their pedestals that the era of revolution had come to an end. Does the demand of liberty come first? If the issue is to rediscover the political question in its integrality, as the inextricable link of justice and liberty, this also means that priority is given to liberty, to the institution of a free city; or rather, it means that we can and must attain justice through liberty, that in this way only the demands of justice can be met. The link of justice and liberty is thus of a nature to make the demand of justice in turn counteract the transformation of liberty into a conquering and predatory autonomy.

With this permanence of the problem of the State in mind, let us return to the thesis of Marx's 1843 manuscript. What should be retained from it? The device described by Marx is most valuable in two respects. First, by virtue of the link it establishes between the development of true democracy, its advent, and the disappearance of the State. The closer democracy comes to attaining its truth (but does a political community ever attain its truth?) the more the State dwindles, undergoes a process of disappearance – that is, it ceases to exert an efficacy, a domination of a part that feigns to be equivalent to the whole. This disappearance does not imply a fulfilled socialization, nor that the political would be effectively bypassed, but that the political realm would be maintained as a moment that coexists with the other realms of social life, with the other instances of objectification by the real subject, the people.

Second, it is worth emphasizing for a last time the great importance given to the reduction in Marx's 1843 Critique. The reduction constitutes the centerpiece of true democracy. It is by virtue of the reduction that the heterogeneity of democracy is asserted, that its rupture with the State is consummated, while the other political forms, even the republic, only reproduce and thereby reinforce the State. As seen, the reduction designates a double movement: as an act of interpretation, it needs to state the essence of the subject, to recognize the subject that manifests itself through political objectification; as an act of limitation – and once this recognition has been made – it needs to gauge political objectification correctly and to reduce it to its proper limits, to a moment and only a moment in the people's existence. It is by means of the reduction that the political principle can at once avoid the overweening conceit of the State – objectification drifting over to alienation – and as such permeate society as a whole in a way that brings all the realms of the social to a common ground. Indeed, it is by being brought back to what it is essentially that the political moment is able to spread out to the totality of the social realms and to permeate them by diffusing democratic action. Such is the paradox of the reduction: the block it brings about, that forestalls the transfiguration of the political element into the State-form, triggers the extension of what is at stake and exemplified in the political realm – an experience of universality, the negation of domination, the establishment of an isonomic public space – as if in being brought back to its roots in this way, democratic action could become apparent in public space *per se* and make itself part of the life of the people as a whole. Only this generalization of democratic action accounts for the unity of the universal and the particular by contrast to the application of a unifying form construed according to the model of reason.

Thus described, true democracy functions as a reprisal or counterattack to what Georg Simmel calls the tragedy of culture, at the heart of which the State as form plays an eminent role. From the perspective of a philosophy of life, Simmel points to an insurmountable aporia. Life can become manifest only by way of that which, as soon as the manifestation has been attained, acts as its contradiction; the manifestation of life depends on a force hostile to life. "Life is ineluctably condemned to become reality only in the guise of its opposite, that is as form."[1] This contradiction is insoluble, for on the one hand life becomes apparent and finds its specific existence only in form; on the other, and from the very moment of its appearance, the movement of form consists in leading its own life, in detaching itself from the vital force that created it in order to let its immanent logic unfold, gaining independence to the point of going well beyond its detachment and turning back against life. This conflict arises from the contrast between the qualities of life – dynamism, the continuous flux of experience, impulsion, overflowing spontaneity – and the characteristics of form as a crystallization that acts as a power of conservation in view of maintaining the cohesion of the whole. The condition of possibility for attaining existence, it is also the form specific to objective spirit that transforms itself into an imprisoning "thing" – Marx's "boa constrictor" – that encloses and suffocates. "They (the forms) are the vessels for the creative life . . . They have their own logic and laws, their own significance and resilience arising from a certain degree of detachment and independence vis-à-vis the spiritual dynamism that gave them life. At the moment of their establishment they are, perhaps, well-matched to life, but as life continues they tend to become inflexible and remote from life, indeed hostile to it."[2]

Translated into Simmel's terms, Marx's argument would therefore run as follows: the State-form makes itself independent, develops its specific logic (domination, totalization, appropriation of the name of the One) to the point of forgetting in its arrogance the source from which it stems – to the point of turning against the life of the people and crushing all manifestations that do not fit into its perspective. In short, there is a structural conflict between the logic of the State on the one hand, and the logic of democracy on the other. This juxtaposition of the two thinkers is all the more legitimate when we consider that Simmel had observed for himself the extent to which some of Marx's descriptions of economic life – notably commodity fetishism – correspond perfectly to the tragedy of culture, to the paradox of a relation in which the terms are at once opposed and inextricably linked.[3] For Marx, however, the tragedy of culture does not exist in the field of economy only; the 1843 Critique shows plainly enough that Marx was able to discover it in the political field as well. A single precaution should be taken when making this comparison: that which is thought by Simmel in the framework of a philosophy of life is thought by Marx from the standpoint of a philosophy of action. The tragedy Simmel attributes to the dynamism of life, to its spontaneous impulsion, resurfaces in Marx in the form of an action that does not exhaust itself in the act that is always exceeding itself, and is ready to take hold of itself in order to rebound and to carry itself further.

Returning to the question of democracy, this detour through Simmel makes it substantially more compelling to think democracy within the schema Marx resorted to in order to define the Paris Commune than in the one he turned to in 1843; in other words, Marx rightly comes to think democracy as a form of conflict rather than as a process. Democracy, then, is less the result of a process that brings about a disappearance of the State, in a largely smooth space devoid of bitterness, than the determined institution of a space of conflict, a space *against*, an agonistic stage on which the respective logics of two antagonistic powers pitilessly attack each other. A struggle without respite here develops between the becoming independent of the State as form, and the people's life as action. In this struggle democracy has everything to gain by knowing its permanent adversary is the State-form, the presumption of the State as an organizing form, and by recognizing that the reduction is its weapon in this struggle. In a first instance, it is necessary to force the State to avow that "democracy is enigma of all constitutions solved," to confess that whatever its form may be, its origin is the sovereignty of the people, the people as an acting power. Once the logic immanent to the State – autonomization, totalization, domination – is clearly denounced, the reduction must be put in play. At stake is giving "the constitution" its proper place, reducing it to a moment and only a moment in the life of the people, and opening, by way of the space regained, a path toward the democratic institution of society. If we attend to the confrontation of these two logics, we are far indeed from the idyllic dreams of the democratic State, whose theoreticians appear as salesmen of slumber, hawking illusions that are all the more deceptive given that, should we pause to consider the origins of democracy, we discover nothing less than an ongoing insurrection against the State.

As already remarked in relation to the Paris Commune, the position *against* is determinant in the constitution of this political space; it is the position *against* that makes it possible to institute the democratic city in its specificity, and to endow conflict with the creative power of liberty already recognized by Machiavelli and Montesquieu, who saw in the ongoing struggles of the Senate and the common people the chances for liberty in Rome. Only this conflict, this veritable mainspring of liberty, is here multiplied: at the heart of this political space where antagonistic poles are formed, where objects of dispute are stated, where struggles are organized, a new essential conflict between democracy and the State arises – not only because the powerful seize the State and because the people set themselves against the powerful but equally because, for democracy, the State represents a permanent danger of degeneration. Once democracy ceases to limit the State, the latter swells out to the point of feigning a unifying form. Far from representing a harmonious complement for democracy, a useful and appropriate framework, the State reveals itself as the organ of democracy's decline; by becoming immobilized in its independence, by considering itself as a whole, it endangers the whole. There is, as such, a reciprocal struggle between the two terms of the relation: if true democracy aims at the disappearance of the State, or rather, struggles against the State, inversely the unfettered expansion of the State signals that democracy is degenerating to the point of bordering on nothingness. With its newly won territory the State-form replaces the life of the people and presents itself as an organizing and totalizing form.

Democracy *against* the State: this formula covers a great variety of situations. We may point out the two most characteristic:

- Either the habitual matrix of modern history: the State is always already there, like a form of constraint that tends to make human society a second nature whose laws are to be obeyed; for example, democracy, inasmuch as it is democracy, is to a certain extent opposed to the historically specific form of this first crystallization and is inclined to limit the State by substituting for absolutism, an arbitrary use of power – the police State – what the French and German tradition calls the State of right (*État de droit*, *Rechtstaat*). In this case, a moderate and sober use of democracy is called for, with the idea that the potentially authoritarian tendencies of the State would thereby be averted.
- Or a revolutionary situation wherein the antagonism between democracy and the State appears in broad daylight; if the State is inextricably linked to submission, conversely the democratic revolution is inseparable from the destruction of State power, or from an attempt at its destruction. We here encounter a fundamental dimension of the great revolutionary crises of modernity, an essential confrontation of antagonistic revolutionary tendencies that, under various names, appears time and time again. On one side

of the confrontation, the Jacobin tradition aims, in the name of revolution, at a reinforcement of the State or at the constitution of a new form of State; on the other, the Communalist or Councilist tradition which, by contrast to the Jacobin tradition and against it, assigns revolution the task of smashing the power of the State so as to replace it with a new form of the political link that remains to be invented. The revolutionary moment is in this sense fascinating, for it presents a multifaceted arena of conflict at the heart of which the struggle for democracy is confronted by at least two adversaries; it rises against not only the State of the "Old Regime," but also against the one that is *in statu nascendi* during the course of the revolution itself. The question of the State, positioned at the center of the phenomenon of modern revolution, thereby presents us with a crucial choice. Either democracy is conceived as an initial moment, a beautiful sunrise that fills the hearts of actors and spectators alike with enthusiasm but that is destined to slowly die out and give way to a new, rationalized and perfected State. Or democracy is conceived and practiced as an ongoing institution of the social, developing and amplifying itself by struggling simultaneously on two fronts: against the State of the "Old Regime," and against the new State. In this case, democracy is permanently on its guard to prevent the moment when the revolution swerves, when the revolutionaries become in turn the powerful, the newly powerful, as desirous as their predecessors to dominate the people. From the standpoint of the revolutionary leader who for his part struggles simultaneously against the Old Regime and against "the world turned upside down" that threatens his supremacy, the question is indeed to seize power, and not to smash it.

Democracy against the State can signify for us an inclination toward a particular form of political experience that, unfolding in time and actuality, gives itself political institutions as a way for politics to be, to borrow Jacques Rancière's term. The constitution of the people's collective will – politics' way to be – becomes manifest without its unity harming the condition of plurality. In order to preserve its institutions, in order to maintain its democratic institution of the social, this way for politics to be rises up incessantly against the State; it affirms *in actu* the possibility of annihilating the division between governors and governed, or of reducing it to almost nothing, inventing a public space and a political space under the banner of isonomy. In short, this way for politics to be is a transformation of the power in potential to act in concert: it signifies the passage from power *over* human beings to power *with* and *between* human beings, the *between* being the place where the possibility of a common world is won.

I have argued that there is a reciprocal struggle between democracy and the State, that democracy must struggle all the more against State power since this power is a menace to democracy or even tends toward its destruction. This is to say that the quasi-automatic association between democracy and the State of right is in need of criticism. According to the discourse established by public opinion, democracy represents the fulfillment of the State of right. Jacques Rancière, in *Disagreement*, denounces this identification that moreover depends on a definition of democracy exclusively in terms of a political regime.[4] But a step beyond this refusal of identification may be taken, for it is a genuine opposition that establishes itself between the State of right and the democratic institution of society. In fact, if we consider the course of the State of right in modernity, it provides a perfect illustration of the arrogance of the State and a political example of the "tragedy of culture." First conceived in order to limit the arbitrariness of power and to protect the rights of individuals, establishing in advance the options that must be taken by the State in the pursuit of its ends, the State of right – the substitution of the government of people by the norm – has experienced in the course of its development a series of inner contradictions that have destroyed it in a sense from the inside, or at least emptied it of its initial meaning.

In the rank of the most injurious contradictions, we may include one of the effects of the perfectionism of the State of right that compels it to subject to a norm the exceptions to its own principles. While the State of right was conceived in order to tie the hands of power, it ends up untying them to the extent that it acts normatively, out of respect for normativity. The result of these inner contradictions consists in producing a veritable inversion of the initial institution: the rule of norms, originally conceived in order to limit power, feeds the illusion of a juridical perfectionism, to the point of absolutizing rule itself and giving way to a power without gaps. In a remarkable work of political criticism, Walter Leisner writes: "The State of right tends essentially toward a normative perfectionism . . . And if the *Rechstaat* wants to be perfect, it must be everywhere . . . Lawfulness is an absolute if not totalitarian notion; the person who is not for it is against it. The *Rechstaat* is not only expansive, it could not exist except as an absolute value."[5] Instead of being envisioned and practiced as a regulative ideal, the State of right transforms itself into a closed system that mobilizes the verticality of juridical norms (their pyramidic organization) in order to generate a new concentration of power, a unitary hierarchical power that holds all forms of independence in contempt. Thus Leisner's conclusion: "As soon as the *Rechstaat* becomes a system, there are forms of an absolute character in the organization of the community that will be perfected incessantly until the very grounds of liberty are destroyed."[6] In this characteristic situation we find again the mechanism denounced previously: the autonomization of form, the moment that expands into an organizing form and that circumscribes the field of confrontation between democracy and the State. As a formula of compromise between absolutism and nascent democracy, the State of right has in turn transformed itself into a new absolutism against democracy. It has thrown the door wide open to what Anne-Marie Roviello calls so aptly the *hubris* of form, that is, form that takes itself for the whole of right.[7] Confronted with this "despotic" degeneration which threatens democracy in the name of the protection of individuals, there is nothing for democracy to do but denounce the contradiction of this State, to operate a reduction, to put the State back "in its place," to return it to its proper boundaries. Submitted to the question of the reduction-resolution, the State of right admits to its initial imperfection and appears as what it is, a mechanism that aims at withdrawing the individual from the arbitrariness of power, that therefore places itself at first from the perspective of the juridical safeguard of the individual, rather than having in view the invention of a *vivere civile*, that is, political action oriented toward the creation of a public space and the establishment of a citizenry. The State of right thus admits that it belongs more to the paradigm of juridical liberalism than to civic republicanism. Yet the point is less to make democracy deformalize itself – or to refuse all form – since democracy experiences forms, than to open the forms of democracy to a new future and break from forms that lead to autonomization and absolutization. Or again, at issue is recognizing the inherent limits of the rendering to form of democracy and maintaining an unsurpassable gap between formal and material justice.

As this investigation nears its end, we come before a stunning paradox, and it is dazzling to the point of withdrawing from our attention at the very moment it appears.

The paradox is that of democracy itself, and as most poignantly revealed by the "savage" qualifier attributed to it by Claude Lefort.[8] As seen, democracy, so often banalized and domesticated, is a particular form of experience that institutes politically the social and that simultaneously rises against the State, as if in this opposition and in its effervescence, it aims not at attaining the end of politics – its disappearance – but to open, in the most fruitful way, a breach that would allow for an incessant reinvention of politics beyond the State, and even against it. In order to explore this paradox, we may turn our attention to the specificity of this institution of society and inquire as to what is to be found there.

First, a resurgence of the question of the political that, in its realization, brings the enigma of the social – the enigma of the human link – to light in order to reformulate it.[9] Next, the reinvention of the political link in the very struggle against the State, as if a circular relation brought these two moments together. From this perspective, the French Revolution is exemplary, for it presents a political stage on which a people's struggle is waged on two fronts: against the monarchy of the Old Regime, but no less ardently against the new State that is always ready to reemerge. Indeed, does not this struggle allow for a fresh interpretation of the Revolution? Rather than keep the standard ascending curve that ends, depending on the interpretations, either in December 1793 or February–March 1794, with the descending curve starting from those dates and extending through to the *coup d'État* of the *18 Brumaire*, we could instead, once we bear in mind the struggle against the State, distinguish a series of successive waves, a series of repeated assaults against the makers of the State, against the legislators who followed one after another but who held in common the ambition to declare the revolution fulfilled – the king, the Monarchists, Lafayette, Mirabeau, the Girondins, Danton, Robespierre, the Directors. It is as if an immense wave from the depths, the unknown revolution beneath the official one, swelled and attempted to carry away the always re-erected "Bastilles," until a tired reason and an exhausted will made way for a general who arrived at the end of the last revolutionary assault – the revolutionary assault of Babeuf – to close ten years of revolution and to open soon the era of imperial wars.

Bitter or secretly satisfied, did not Hegel predict at the beginning of the 1830s, shortly before his death, "What began on 14 July 1789 is not about to be extinguished"?

This interpretation is not inconsequential. Should we accept it, we may read in it one of the principles of the democratic institution of society. If the commencement of the democratic revolution is defined in this way, this means that the struggle against the State is an ongoing presence in democratic existence. This moreover signifies that democracy, as Machiavelli held in relation to religions and republics, must not, if it wishes to keep its original vivacity, lose sight of its principle and must know how to return to it in order to resist the wear of time and the constancy of State control.

In order to understand properly this peculiarity of democracy, it is essential not only to reject the ideologies of consensus – notably that of a consensus between democracy and the State – but moreover to revitalize the idea of conflict, to be wary of making democracy tilt toward the banality of compromise, and to grant it instead a maximum of power. Which is to say that democracy is the always possible emergence of human struggle, the surge of the originary division that brings with it the menace of dissolution, of social explosion. If the State, as Hegel taught, is as a system of mediation, the integration and reconciliation of civil society beyond all conflict – the specific function of the Statist order is to integrate the plebes who carry savage demands that are alien to society: "no moment in it [the State] should appear as an unorganized crowd"[10] – is not the democratic revolution, insofar as it is a revolution, necessarily a movement against the State, against this deceptive reconciliation and this fallacious integration? As paradoxical as this may seem, democracy is the form of society that institutes a human link across human struggles and that, by this very institution, renews its link with the origin of liberty that is always in need of rediscovery.

Are we at a Machiavellian moment? If such is the case, would it not have to take shape starting from the encounter between the "political principle" and a libertarian spirit, each taking steps toward the other?

On one side, by having examined the seism of totalitarian domination, we have witnessed a slight sunray, a renewal of libertarian thought, or rather a reorientation of this thought that has not ceased to influence modern politics. It is as though the test of totalitarianism, the accumulated ruins, the radicality of the destruction, revealed as a consequence new demands for thinking liberty: how liberty can be thought not against law, but in tandem with it, in unison with the desire for liberty from which it stems; how liberty can no longer be thought against power, but with power understood otherwise, as the power to act in concert. And above all, how liberty can no longer rise against the political realm, as if it were necessary for liberty to rid itself of politics, but how the political realm is henceforth the very object of the desire for liberty. Invigorated by this reorientation, politics is thought and desired apart from any idea of a solution; it is practiced as an endless questioning of the world and the fate of human beings.

On the other, besides having to question the recourse to principle itself – the *arche* – the political principle points to the idea of *anarchy* detached from its purely political conception, and lets itself be affected by the turmoil this idea causes, thereby outlining a negative dialectic. Far from the State enclosing democracy as if it could be contained and determined from without, democracy severed from all *arche* reveals the limits of the State, and in so doing contests – and more, destroys – the totalizing movement of this authority that claims itself sovereign. Might the thinker of politics be moved by *anarchy*? Might political thought let itself be affected by its reappearance in contemporary philosophy, as an echo of the philosophical rupture, bereft of guarantees and determined limits – "without principle" – and as enigmatically expressed in the thought of Emmanuel Levinas? "It [anarchy] can only cause turmoil – but in a radical way, making possible moments of negation without any affirmation. The State then cannot set itself up as a Whole."[11]

A disorder that is not destined to be another order, democracy has an irreducible meaning as a refusal of synthesis, a refusal of order – an invention in time of the political relation that overflows and overtakes the State. For if democracy sets itself in opposition to the State, it is because politics comes up ceaselessly against it.

APPENDIX: "SAVAGE DEMOCRACY" AND THE "PRINCIPLE OF ANARCHY"

I would like to begin by insisting on the programmatic character of this essay: it offers only a broad description of a possible comparison between "savage democracy" in the terms of Claude Lefort and the "principle of anarchy" according to Reiner Schürmann.[1] This is a paradoxical undertaking, for one must remain at the threshold of the confrontation while at the same time reaching a conclusion about it. When interpreting Lefort's writings, the necessary outcome is indeed savage democracy, insofar as one does not reduce it to a "befuddled" anti-establishment variant of liberal democracy. It is as if the critic stumbled on this notion that, far from offering a key to his writings, returns to them their full enigmatic power.

The term "savage democracy" appears explicitly in Lefort's work several times. But the qualifier, rather than determining democracy – and inscribing its relationship consubstantial with indetermination, within limits that might serve as guiding posts – instead raises the whole question over again; the adjective rebounds on the noun and draws it toward an even greater indetermination under the banner of turmoil, the uncontrollable, and most specifically, of the untamable. Moreover, when one reads Schürmann's book devoted to Heidegger and the question of action one seems to glimpse certain points of overlap between savage democracy and what this critic of Heidegger calls, in a perfectly contradictory fashion, "the principle of anarchy." If we attempt the comparison, this detour via a "Left Heideggerian" perspective offers us – even if the reference to Heidegger is problematic – the possibility of thinking about savage democracy in its specificity and in its complexity.

The proposed path will be simple:

– First, I try to define savage democracy. This task is in my view all the more necessary since Lefort's highly specific notion of democracy seems to orient in an essential way all his writings, one that is often passed over in silence or toned down, reduced to the sole value of permanent contestation.

- Then, in a second move, after having clarified Schürmann's principle of anarchy, I outline the terms for a possible confrontation of their respective views. The point here is to show the extent to which the contextualization of democracy with anarchy, considered as principle, is of a nature to bring out democracy's most "savage" characteristics – but without for all that concealing the difficulties that this perspective provokes or reveals. For it is precisely by returning to and excavating the gap between anarchy and principle that we approach most closely democracy's "savage essence."

Savage democracy: A first attempt at definition

One may summarize the trajectory of Lefort as a continuous questioning – though never achieved because always unachievable – of what is new in our century, in other words of that unprecedented form of domination known as totalitarianism. At the heart of this uninterrupted questioning, we may essentially distinguish two periods of analysis:

- A first interpretation which corresponds to the *Socialisme ou Barbarie* period (from 1947 to 1958 in the case of Lefort) and that one finds most developed in his great article from 1956, "*Le Totalitarisme sans Staline.*"[2] Totalitarianism is here denounced as a historically specific mode of completing the project of socialization: the bureaucratic implementation of socialization, the summary appropriation of socialization by the party-State for the benefit of a new dominant social class, the bureaucracy. This first critique of totalitarianism is therefore conducted from the perspective of communism as the reappropriation of human community, that is, critique operates in light of a fully achieved socialization that provides criteria for judgment. Totalitarianism is condemned without appeal as a travesty of socialization, as a parody of communism, with the dynamic and the effects that this implies. More than "the great lie" that befalls the dominated from without, totalitarianism is viewed as the reign of illusion in which, to a certain extent, the dominated themselves participate.

- Later, during a second interpretive moment that starts from the beginning of the 1960s, it is no longer the mode of implementation of the project that is condemned, but *the very project of socialization* that is rejected; the communist idea itself becomes the object of his criticism. The issue is no longer to distinguish between an authentic socialization and its simulacrum, but to question the very aim of abolishing the separations proper to modern society. Thus the definitive break with the illusion of the social realm's fulfillment in the form of indivision: "As to the idea of an achieved socialization (. . .) I acknowledged that it upheld the myth of social indivision, of social homogenization, of society's self-transparency; moreover, I came to see that the disastrous consequences of this myth were indeed revealed by the totalitarian attempt to inscribe it in reality," wrote Lefort in 1979.[3]

In this second phase, one observes a complete change of course in the interpretation; the political horizon turns out to be radically different. Critique is no longer formulated from the standpoint of communism but of democracy; more specifically, it is by rethinking the democratic revolution that Lefort takes on the task of denouncing and unveiling in all of its dimensions, even the most hidden ones, this new form of domination that public opinion and various analysts tend to reduce to a simple resurgence of despotism or tyranny. Moreover, the opposition between democratic revolution and totalitarian domination, an opposition that must ceaselessly be worked out, is inscribed in a more vast movement of thought, according to which the coming out from Marxism in its singularity is accompanied by a rediscovery of the political realm. Far from thinking the political as something necessarily derivative – reducible to the economic, if only in "the last instance" and with the sophisticated alibi of its "overdetermination" – the point is to open a new field of reflection in which the political is henceforth grasped in relation to the originary division of society.

In the wake of his reinterpretation of Machiavelli (*Le Travail de l'œuvre,* 1971), Lefort posits that all human cities order and construct themselves from a originary division expressed best by the division of desire: the desire of the powerful to command and oppress, and that of the people not to be commanded or oppressed – the desire for liberty. In this context, every social manifestation is in the same movement a threat of dissolution, an exposure to division and to the loss of self, as if every manifestation were inhabited, indeed haunted, by the threat of its own dissolution. Thus a new intelligibility of the political realm emerges: all systems of power are considered a response to the question opened by the advent of the social and its exposure to dissolution. The political is the taking of a position or a positioning in relation to division; it is in the analysis of the relation society establishes to the fact of its existence – to the ordeal of division – that its political structure becomes intelligible.[4]

The previous proposition – that, starting in the 1960s, totalitarianism is judged according to the democratic revolution – now takes on its full meaning. It is on the basis of the originary division of the social realm and its political institution that Lefort distinguishes between democracy and totalitarian domination. Totalitarianism is defined as the mode of socialization based on a fantastic denial of division and, as a consequence, on a refusal of conflict, either because it pretends to have already abolished the split, or because it seeks to put an end to a division that, far from being considered as primary, is thought of as historical, and therefore as reducible. Inversely, democracy is seen as constituting itself through the acceptance, or better, the elaboration of the originary division of the social; democracy is the form of society that, unsatisfied with merely recognizing the legitimacy of internal conflict, comprehends conflict instead as the originary source of an ever renewed invention of liberty. To introduce the idea of savage democracy, I would add: democracy is the form of society that, through the play of division, leaves the field open for the question the social asks of itself ceaselessly, a question in perpetual want of resolution but that is here recognized as interminable. In a word, democratic society proper is necessarily shot through by a continuous self-questioning. The conceptual horizon according to which the idea of savage democracy is to be approached is thus that of the originary and irreducible division of the social, its enigmatic identity – the ordeal of the uncontrollable that allows the indetermination of the social realm, and its necessary inner opposition, to unfold freely.

Before going any further it is necessary to distinguish "savage democracy" from some possible misinterpretations.

- The connection of the term *savage* to that of democracy does not imply any relation to the "savage" societies described by ethnology: these societies' rejection of a separate power obeys a logic other than that of democracy.[5]
- "Savage democracy" has even less to do with Hobbes's state of nature, the absence of society, a chaos that calls for the establishment of a State to put an end to the real or imagined war of all against all.

– "Savage democracy" evokes, rather, the idea of the wildcat strike (*grève sauvage*), that is, a strike that arises spontaneously, that begins with itself and unfolds in an "anarchic" fashion, independent of any principle (*arche*), of any authority – as well as of any established rules and institutions – and that strikes in such a way that it cannot be mastered. It is as if "savage" connotes the inexhaustible reserve of turmoil that soars above democracy. In a word: to forge a "libertarian idea" of democracy is to think it as savage. The libertarian reference, as specified in *Un homme en trop,* escapes from ideological categories and designates instead an attitude that cannot be codified or solidified into doctrine. Libertarian is he who dares to talk when everyone is silent, she who does not shy from contradicting the public, unafraid to break the wall of silence so as to make the unexpected voice of liberty be heard. The link between the libertarian and savage modalities clarifies the specificity of modern democracy *qua* form, and allows one to apprehend and to describe a mode of political functioning that has an immediate philosophical meaning. As a refusal to submit to the established order, as the "dissolution of the bearings of certitude," democracy "inaugurates a history in which people experience an ultimate indeterminacy as to the foundations of Power, Law and Knowledge, and as to the foundations of the relations between *self* and *other* at every level of social life."[6]

This indeterminacy in relation to foundations is the veritable knot where the libertarian and the savage are intertwined. Even before attempting to define savage democracy starting from a collection of traits, we need to emphasize the aporetic character of this task. How is one to define what goes beyond all definition, what defies the very operation of defining? We could say that we are before a positive aporia, for if "savage democracy" is the term that Lefort chooses on several occasions, it is because he intends to dismiss the definitions that claim to reduce democracy to an institutional formula, to a political regime or to a set of procedures or rules:

> It is true that, in a certain sense, no one holds the formula for democracy and that it is most profoundly itself by being savage democracy. Perhaps this is what constitutes its essence; as soon as there is no ultimate reference on the basis of which the social order might be conceived and determined, this order is constantly on a quest for foundations, in search of its own legitimacy, and it is precisely the opposition and the demands of those who are excluded from the benefits of democracy that constitute its most effective wellspring.[7]

This means that democracy is not domestic or capable of being domesticated to the very extent that it remains faithful to its "savage essence": the resistance to domestication. Democracy, like an impetuous river that incessantly overflows its bed, cannot "go back home" and submit to the established order. But can one speak of a "savage essence"? No more, in a sense, than one can speak of a "principle of anarchy."

In both cases the contradictory character of these expressions, even as it indicates the inventive aporia of a novel situation, also reveals in its own way the loss of foundations. In Montesquieu's terms, it would no longer so much be a question of describing a nature as one of apprehending a principle. To which must immediately be added that, in the case of savage democracy, principle would win over nature to the extent that its effect would be the transformation of nature into an uninterrupted movement, or into a nature of a new kind whose peculiarity would be never to coincide with itself, to go perpetually beyond itself.

As a resistance to domestication, "savage democracy" points to the totality of struggles for the defense of rights to which one is already entitled and for the recognition of rights denied or not yet recognized. Borrowing here a thesis of the eminent English historian, E. P. Thompson, author of *The Making of the English Working Class,* Lefort focuses our attention on the permanent contestation that the demand for rights opens up at the very heart of the democratic revolution. He who formerly invited us to think the "proletarian experience" as a whole, calls upon us once again to conceive political struggle – in this case, a democratic struggle – as a total social phenomenon. Just as the demand for law bears within itself the demand for new social relations, the aspiration for another form of community cannot be disassociated from the struggle for rights: "Let it once again be said, it is not only the protection of individual liberties that is at issue, but also the nature of our social ties; where there is spreading feeling for rights, democracy is necessarily savage and not domesticated."[8]

Without engaging in detail Lefort's political reading of human rights, a reading that is neither ethical nor individualistic, one may nonetheless show briefly that it is in and through the articulation of law – law no longer thought of as an instrument of social conservation but as a revolutionary instance of authority, that is, as the source, in the strongest sense of the word, of a society that constitutes itself in its quest for itself – that the idea of democracy takes on its fully libertarian meaning.

Democracy is savage first by virtue of the essential relationship that this form maintains with human rights. From Rousseau to Fichte man-as-subject has been conceived as non-determined, as the absence of determinations. It is through the connection between savage democracy and human rights that democracy spontaneously becomes a movement of indetermination, since from this reference no preceding determination will *a priori* hinder its rise. Haunted by its recognition of a being that is indeterminate *par excellence,* democracy is that form of society in which law, by its external relationship to power, proves to be always in excess of what is established, as if the instituting instance, once posited, reemerges in order to reaffirm the existing rights and to create new ones. A political stage opens according to which there is a struggle between the domestication of rights and its permanent destabilization-recreation via the integration of new rights, new demands that are henceforth considered as legitimate. According to Lefort, it is the existence of this incessantly reborn protest, this whirlwind of rights, that brings democracy beyond the traditional limits of the "State of right" [*État de droit*, *Rechstaat*].

Savage democracy is where the symbolic dimension of human rights is most manifest. Lefort – unlike the young Marx who, in his critique of human rights in *The Jewish Question,* confused the symbolic with the ideological, or rather reduced the symbolic to the ideological by not having bothered to truly think the symbolic – posits that human rights form an essential piece of the symbolic constitution of modern democracy. This means among other things that it is through human rights that the citizens of a modern democracy can apprehend what presents itself to them as real, just as they discover the same and the other.

Through the principle of internalization to which they give rise, human rights engender a new sense of our relation to law, a new consciousness of law. For democracy also designates a society that is animated by an incessant conflict between the symbolic and the ideological. Whereas the savage essence of democracy forces democracy as a symbolic form to leave the field open for an experience of indetermination – for an experience of the loss of foundations – ideology will continually attempt to seize the symbolic, to appropriate it so as to better domesticate it, to impart in the name of a group or a person a determined content to that which resists and evades all determination.

Democracy is savage, finally, because given the disappearance of the body of the king and the disembodiment of the social realm that follows from it, society detaches itself, disentangles itself from the

State and thereby attains, through its self-questioning, a pluralistic and burgeoning experience of itself. With the constitution of what Lefort calls "the social power," new forms of struggle appear which become intelligible when brought back to the logic of democracy. The demands that emerge from the struggles "in the name of the law" are sufficiently heterogeneous to avert the illusion of a global solution. The peculiarity of modern democracy, thus understood, is that it opens the stage for an indefinitely continued raising of demands that move from one focal-point to another, transversally, as if the antagonism between the effervescent plurality that refers to a multiplicity of poles, and the Statist constraint re-enforced by organization, were in constant play. These movements are non-totalizable. They are born of multiple centers of socialization that feed upon the specificity they adopt, and even demand. They turn their backs to every form of a unifying subject that would supposedly concentrate and condense their struggles or that would attempt to encompass them.

Savage democracy, then, is meant to highlight the model that emerges from the anti-totalitarian revolution, a pluralist revolution that knows, moreover, to distinguish between the poles of collective institution and social differentiation and is not fooled by the illusion of a disappearance of division. This is in effect the paradox of democratic society: it does not aim so much at erasing the instance of power, the better to gather itself up and succumb to the attraction of the One, as at letting the turmoil that runs through it to unfold. Here the pole of power – a place that is for the first time empty – functions as a symbolic mediation through which society is brought back to itself at the same time that it experiences a split between its *inside* and its *outside*.

Savage: this qualifier is all the more appropriate since it would be illusory to claim that the invention of democracy can only be grasped in the empirical realm, in this or that set of positive institutions. Democracy, inasmuch as it is a symbolic matrix of social relations, is and remains in excess of the institutions through which it manifests itself. In response to his laudatory proponents as much as to his detractors, Lefort states: "It is to dream to think that we possess democracy. . .. Democracy is but a play of possibilities, one inaugurated in a still recent past, and about which we still have everything to explore."[9]

Savage? In the last analysis, what is the purpose of this conceptual adventure? Or rather, in the structure of this thought and in its link with Merleau-Ponty, what is the point of this quest that animates our democratic "living-together," this "flesh of the social," if not "*raw being* . . . vertical being . . . not the 'flattened' being offered to the dreams of a sovereign consciousness, it is the *savage spirit,* the spirit that makes its own law, not because it has submitted everything to its will, but because submitted to being, it ever awakens at the contact of the event to contest the legitimacy of established knowledge."[10]

This relationship between "raw being" and savage spirit indicates well enough that the struggle around law is caught in a much larger movement that overflows it: the democratic revolution, the invention without respite of a world and the work of a spirit which is equally without respite. In the last analysis, the democratic revolution, "a game of the possible" according to Lefort, is also in its very dynamic an experience of being, of its opening, the in principle non-fulfillment of all things.[11]

"The principle of anarchy"

Before detailing the terms of the comparison, some preliminary precautions are in order. The recourse to Schürmann's book does not mean that I endorse his interpretation of Heidegger, but neither does it mean that I am opposed to it. Judging his thesis as such is not my task. Nor do I want to introduce in an oblique way a relation between Lefort's thought and that of Heidegger. Without insisting, we may bear in mind a few points of rupture between these two thinkers that are obvious and important enough to undercut those efforts that are satisfied with comparing overall philosophies on a purely formal level. There are divergences on the question of humanism, and on the issue of technology and the interpretation of modernity as the epoch of technology; but above all the status and the determinacy of technology in Heidegger's philosophy could only arouse the opposition and the criticism of someone like Lefort, who returns to a political understanding of modern society and perceives in the democratic revolution a focal-point of primordial intelligibility that cannot be ignored in the name of "the enframing" or described as an effect derived from a non-political process.

My only concern is to bring to the fore by this detour the ontological dimension of savage democracy, a dimension that one cannot pass over in silence, and whose importance largely overrides the power of contestation intrinsic to this form of democracy; or more exactly, this power of contestation only takes on its real meaning if it is understood as caught within the ontological dimension. My recourse to Schürmann's book may also be judged rather peculiar. Undoubtedly,

I will not do justice to this work, since my aim is to derive a model from it that may be compared to savage democracy. Yet there are two ways of making a comparison: either one proceeds to lighten the peculiarities of the opposing phenomena, or, on the contrary, one accentuates them in the hope that by such a mode of comparison one may gain a new clarity that helps bring out the singularities at hand.

In a certain fashion Schürmann's thesis – which, via the surprising term "principle of anarchy," aims at situating in a new way the originality of the Heideggerian enterprise – is curiously connected to the question of democracy. In fact, one of its aims is to account for Heidegger's famous statement about democracy in an interview recorded posthumously: "It is a decisive question for me today how a political system, and what kind of one, can at all be thought as adequate in relation to the technological age. I do not know the answer to this question. I am not convinced that it is democracy."

It is this "I do not know," this admission of ignorance, that Schürmann attempts to account for by proposing a reading that is not biographical nor psychological nor immediately political, but fully philosophical : "But perhaps this avowal is not accidental. Perhaps it directly concerns the single question that never ceased to preoccupy Heidegger"(p. 2).[12]

In brief, the question is to relate this admission to the unthought in Heidegger and to to perceive in it an effect of the principle of anarchy that invalidates as such the very idea of deriving a political system.

To simplify, one can consider that under this term "principle of anarchy," Schürmann's work consists of opposing the classical metaphysical project to Heidegger's thought, which sides with this new principle, or more exactly, which is a new thought of what a principle is.

If one of the essential questions of the philosophical tradition, of our inherited thought, is that of the unity between theory and praxis, between thinking and action – the ground from which one can answer the question, What should I do? – then what is the effect of the Heideggerian deconstruction in this domain? Defined in relation to this question, deconstruction is: "the obsolescence of any such speculative base upon which life is to find its steadiness, its legitimation, and its peace"(p. 1), or again, deconstruction is that which "interrupts, throws out of gear, the derivation of practical philosophy from first philosophy. . .. As one of its consequences, deconstruction leaves the discourse on action suspended in a void . . . action itself, and not only its theory, loses its foundation or its *arche*"(p. 1).

Contrary to what some wrongly think, action is not overshadowed by the question of being; in truth Heidegger's position is entirely different: "He does not disjoin the ancient unity between theory and practice, but he does much worse: he raises the question of presencing in such a way that the question of acting is already answered; he raises it in such a way that action can no longer become a separate issue" (p. 4). This implies that the structure of traditional philosophy – a structure that may be called "archic" – is characterized by the reference to an *arche* for the question of action. Thus traditional theories of action answer the question, "What should I do?" by referring to what was considered the ultimate source of knowledge in their respective periods. The set of attempts to determine a referent for action designates metaphysics, or metaphysics is that device "where action requires a principle to which words, things, and deeds may be related"(p. 6) – a principle that simultaneously functions as foundation, as beginning, and as commandment: "The *arche* always functions in relation to action as substance functions in relation to its accidents, imparting to them meaning and *telos*"(p. 5). The metaphysical derivation of action from a first philosophy – or from a First – therefore leads to the unitary imposition of this first instance on the multiple. Moreover, these philosophies furnish power with its formal structure.

It is against the backdrop of this metaphysical and archic structure that one may understand the unprecedented meaning that Schürmann attributes to anarchy and, by the same token, to Heidegger's writings. In the epoch of the closure of metaphysics – the thesis of the principle of anarchy is strictly dependent on the hypothesis of this closure – the rule according to which the world is intelligible and controllable on the basis of a "First" (a first foundation) loses its hold. The derivation of a practical philosophy from a first philosophy is declining and the archic model is fading when "the epochal principles (metaphysical 'stamps', *Pragüngen)* that have ordered thoughts and actions in each age of history are *withering away*"(p. 5).

Whence the statement of this instructive and "stunning" paradox of the principle of anarchy. The two terms that make it up designate two aspects that are oriented in opposite directions: one that points to the hither side of metaphysics' closure, the other that points beyond it. At the same time that one refers to a principle, that reference is negated – or, this reference to a principle is enunciated, but in order to negate itself. This means that through its critique of metaphysics, the twentieth century appears to be the epoch in which one can no longer derive praxis from theory. Action will manifest itself as anarchic, that is, as devoid of *arche,* of foundation, of beginning, of commandment.

It is the epoch of "the principle without-principle," or of the principle that commands not to have one. This paradox shows how Heidegger's thinking is a work in transition: still implanted in the classic problematic of the "What is being?," but already tearing it away from the attributive or participative schema : "Still a principle, but a principle of anarchy. It is instructive to think this contradiction. The principle of reference then appears to be counteracted, both in its history and in its essence, by a force of dislocation, of pluralization.. . . The deconstruction is a discourse of transition"(p. 6).

For this reason Schürmann's concept of anarchy is essentially distinct from the political philosophy of modern anarchism. Anarchism remains entirely caught in the field of metaphysics to the extent that it continues to derive action from a referent. It does not attack the schema of reference, but instead remains within this schema by substituting reason for the principle of authority. In short, it maintains the traditional procedures of legitimation, only it chooses a new criterion of legitimacy. With Heidegger, however, any rational production of this metaphysical grounding now becomes impossible:

> Anarchy . . . is the name of a history that has struck the foundation stone of action, a history in which the bedrock yields and in which it becomes obvious that the principle of cohesion, be it authoritarian or 'rational,' is no longer anything more than a blank space devoid of legislative or normative power. Anarchy expresses the destiny that obliterates the principles to which Westerners since Plato have related their acts and deeds in order to shield them from change and doubt. (pp. 6–7)

The principle of anarchy – the withering away of the foundations that has affected action – is therefore what allows for a philosophical explanation of Heidegger's confessed ignorance and his doubt concerning democracy. For Schürmann, Heidegger's apparent ignorance or his expression of doubt can thus be viewed as a refusal to respond, if not as a ruse. Indeed, does not the decline of the schema of reference compel us to formulate the question of politics in terms other than those of first principles and of derivation? But, one could retort – without for the moment examining the legitimacy of such a philosophical interpretation of Heidegger's remark on democracy – would not the hypothesis of savage democracy lead to another conclusion, or at least render the proposed conclusion less self-assured and less rash? In its very movement, in its dynamic, does not savage democracy have something in common with anarchy, understood in the sense of a liberation of action from the hold of foundations – from an *arche* – in the sense of a manifestation of an "action without why"?

One can certainly grant that the political question must be posited outside the schema of reference. But can democracy be considered a political system among others? Or, on the contrary, does the savage essence of democracy imply from the outset a political relation distinct from the principle-derivation model of traditional systems? And in this case what relation does it have or is it capable of having with the principle of anarchy?

Such a question is all the more legitimate given that Schürmann implicitly seeks a political "illustration" of the principle of anarchy. This is clear enough in the chapter "Deconstruction of the Political," but it is also suggested by the attention given – albeit briefly – to Hannah Arendt. What Schürmann admires in Arendt is her deconstruction of the political field, the success with which she shows the origin of political forms as otherwise than *arche* and principle. Arendt is again mentioned when Schürmann investigates those moments when action is liberated, "the time that an ontic origin succumbs to another." At such moments there is a caesura between two forms of politics: "each of these modern efforts to free the public domain from coercive force (analyzed by Arendt in reference to the American model) marks the end of an epoch. At these moments the princeps (governance) and the principium (the system governance imposes and on which it reposes) are suspended for a time. In such caesurae, the political realm appears as the revealer of what the origin that connects words, things, and deeds truly is: not an entity . . . but the simple event in which all that happens to be present comes to presence"(p. 91). As such Schürmann views Arendt as the veritable thinker of action, she who thought action – praxis – as liberated from the theoretical hold, in its difference from *poiesis* or fabrication.

Thus, while I will juxtapose the principle of anarchy as defined above with savage democracy, I am not for all that viewing the latter as a political translation of the principle, which would be contradictory. Rather, the question is to discern the political invention that is worthy of comparison. We should bear four characteristics in mind:

1. The end of metaphysics and the crisis of foundations throws the traditional unity of theory and practice into question and breaks down the schema of reference according to which action is legitimized, whatever this first instance of legitimization may be (God, Nature, the Order of the world, Progress, etc.). In brief, at the same time that it hinders the possibility for derivation, the breaking down of the metaphysical schema liberates action from all

submission to principles and allows for the emergence of an anarchic form of action, devoid of any *arche*.

2. The disappearance of the schema of reference and of the submission of action to principle goes hand-in-hand with the "subversion of teleocratic representations." This is a complex process: it implies the discovery that the history of imperative principles has come to an end, but it also means that the very moment when the opposition to principle is possible, the turn toward the closure of metaphysics has been realized. This opposition, moreover, is causally related to a radical change in the way we think the political realm: "With the turning, a certain way of understanding the political realm becomes impossible, and a new one inevitable"(p. 38).

   This modification in political thinking can only be understood by an alternative way of thinking presence, presence becomes historical as opposed to mechanical or constant, which is to say that presence is now thought as event: "If presence is manifest as event, it is hostile to the domination of ends" (p. 255). By the same stroke the liberation of action is gauged; not only does it escape from any reference, but it no longer obeys any of the finalities attributed to it. Action rediscovers its real nature as an end in itself and thereby refuses an abusively transposed schema of finality that has more to do with fabrication than with action proper. Heidegger's "anarchic" displacement did not negate finality, but limited it to its specific domain, that of fabrication: "Action, too, must free itself from the domination of finality, which is a category specific to production"(p. 256). By virtue of being rethought as event, action is withdrawn from the forms of domination embodied by the One, and finds again its own element: what Arendt calls the ontological condition of plurality.

3. This modification in political thought means that as soon as the reference to an *arche* – to a First – decays, the political realm can no longer be thought in the framework of foundationalism. According to Schürmann's analysis, there here arises a conception of the political realm that is at once more modest and more independent: far from founding, or implementing a first principle that has the value of foundation, the political realm is limited to situating.

   "The political realm is the site where things, action, and speech may be adequate to each other" (p. 40), in other words it is the arena where these elements can come together. Just as for Heidegger the site is "the place where a phenomenon unfolds its essence" (p. 41), the political site is the place that manifests the force of cohesion of the principle in a given period. By manifestation is meant two things: a coming to presence or a disclosure, but also an exposure, since the political realm renders public and exposes this very principle. The turn – "the break in the modalities of presence" – undoubtedly modifies the political realm again: rather than revealing an epochal principle, the political is the site of the event or of presence as history. Significantly, this new conception implies carrying the ontologies of the political body over to the topology of the political site in order to delegitimize them. Whereas the ontologies of the political tradition subordinate practice to an ideality and function as discourses justifying subjection to the State, the new topological conception, inasmuch as it is a deconstruction of the metaphysics of the political body, returns action to itself and thus clears the way for a free adventure.

4. The attempt to elaborate an alternative political philosophy starts with the deconstruction of foundations and the refusal of the metaphysical project, that is, the emancipation of political thinking from any reference to an ideal and normative instance. This implies another way of thinking the origin such that inaugural moments no longer dominate and command action but to the contrary set it free from epochal principles.

I began by warning that it would be illegitimate to present savage democracy simply as the political translation of the principle of anarchy. It would be contradictory, indeed, to attribute a function to a principle that has as its dominant trait the absence of any application, the absence of an archic function. Action in this constellation ceases to be a derivation of theory and reveals itself as anarchic. And one cannot take the question from the other end. For how can one reduce savage democracy to the realization of a principle, even if it is a principle of anarchy? Instead of wrongly enclosing anew savage democracy in a schema of reference, it is more appropriate to apprehend a double paradox, one that in each case is both dazzling and instructive. For is not the "savage essence" of democracy no less surprising than a principle that is a "principle of anarchy"? Just as anarchy destroys the idea of principle, the savage unsettles the idea of essence, the definition of quiddity. But it is the link in the paradox that catches our attention and that pushes us to consider a new question: In what way does savage democracy, understood as the manifestation of an experience of liberty, present a structure that answers or corresponds to the inner organization of the principle of anarchy?

Without here confronting the hypothesis of the end of metaphysics, specific affinities between savage democracy and the principle of anarchy may be discerned. With the help of this comparative framework, and in light of the above mentioned characteristics, I will outline various forms of action that respond to what, confronted with the historical constellation of modernity, Merleau-Ponty called "a certain modern obscurity."[13]

- To the decline of the metaphysical project of derivation, savage democracy responds by an indetermination with regard to the foundations of Power, Law, Knowledge, and the basis of their inner connection in the social realm as a whole.
- To the fall of the teleocratic domination that liberates action from its finalist schema, savage democracy responds by the dissolution of the references of certitude and by an indetermination opposed to all forms of ultimate finality, whatever they may be. Faced with an enigmatic present and embarked on a journey for which "the way cannot be known in advance," savage democracy grounds itself in a permanent questioning of the social and political realms of existence.[14]
- To the disappearance of the ontologies of the political order that functioned as discourses of legitimization and subjection, savage democracy responds by the disembodiment of the social realm and a concomitant disembodiment of power – that is, the form of power that Lefort relates, at least in Europe, to the historical experience of regicide.
- Finally, in relation to Schürmann's suggestion of a political philosophy inspired by the deconstruction of foundations, one finds a revealing "hesitation" in Lefort's writings, or rather a coexistence between the call to "restore political philosophy" and the emphasis on thinking the political realm as such. By this I mean a way of thinking that understands from the outset that the rediscovery of the properly political is an endless adventure, since it can no longer function in the context of traditional narratives. Political thought thus breaks with the conceptual framework of classical political philosophy and renders obsolete the foundational categories that have been the ground for legitimizing political orders in the past. This relation to the origin is all the more problematic given that the question is not for democracy to constitute itself according to the authority of an inaugural moment but to welcome the emergence of the originary division of the social realm and to encourage in this way a renewed experience of liberty. It is here that the break

> with the foundation stone of traditional ontology – Aristotle's – becomes most obvious. In *Le Travail de l'Œuvre,* Lefort credits Machiavelli with having outlined a new ontology. For Lefort, the author of *The Prince* is unsatisfied with judging tyranny unjust in relation to the model of the just State by applying the Aristotelian categories of essence and accident. Instead, Machiavellli welcomes the diversity of situations. Society is seen as in principle open to the event by virtue of the originary division that inhabits it. As a result of this "break" – at once unavoidable and irreparable – the conception of being as constant and stable presence is undone. The very idea of degradation vanishes in favor of a new conception of being characterized by the upsurge of the unprecedented: "But being can only be apprehended in relation to what happens, in the articulation of appearances, in the movement that forbids them finality, in the incessant recasting of what is established."[15]

It is in the context of this new ontology discovered in Machiavelli that savage democracy may be understood. The permanent contestation that characterizes it in the fields of law and politics is but the effect of this experience of being, of this conception of being as that which happens, as event. In other words, permanent contestation, if one consents to think its true dimension, is not an empirical trait of a democratic regime but is the perennial unveiling of the experience of being in time, at the center of which there is a human struggle that takes on "historical creation as a whole," or the complex and endless play of exchange and human struggle.[16]

As interesting as the parallels in Schürmann and Lefort's thought may be, they are not for all that exclusive of dissonances. First of all, there is the question of humanism, and Schürmann's emphasis on the threefold break with humanism implemented by Marx, Nietzsche and Heidegger that implies a structure of anarchic presence. Without presently developing this apparent dissonance, one need only recall that if Lefort's notion of savage democracy explicitly refers to human rights, humanity is not for all that established as a pedestal of determinations but is on the contrary conceived as a focal-point of indetermination. Lefort's thought is all the more removed from an anthropocentrism given the incompatibility of his thought with a philosophy of the subject, or of a metaphysics of subjectivity. At the heart of history Lefort posits the originary division of the social that is always already there – in truth a redoubled division, since the desire for liberty is permanently measured by its inversion into servitude (lured by "the charm of the name of One") – a division that brings the indetermination specific to the human being before the endless ordeal of being.

And this difference from a philosophy of the subject is all the greater if one considers that the people to which democracy refers are, as Michelet and Quinet have argued, affected by an identity which is at the least problematic; either the people are *above themselves* – the people in the heroic state that constitute themselves in the very invention of liberty – or they are *below themselves,* when the experience of liberty threatens to revert into its opposite, servitude. In short, never coinciding with themselves, never equal to themselves, the people at the moment they are manifest, that they come to existence, experience the ordeal of an insurmountable self-discrepancy. To this may be added that democracy opens – or opens itself to – an unexplored reserve of indetermination by the relation it maintains with what Lefort calls, without further description, the human element, taking advantage of the enigma that surrounds it to discredit and condemn the historical projects, such as totalitarianism, that claim to create the human element or that attempt to organize it as if it were a material that could be shaped by the will: "Suppressing the human element, or rather believing that it can as such be treated as matter, this is how we can recognize the reign of organization . . . What is at stake in the new State is precisely this . . . to obtain finally abstract human beings, without links that unite them, without property, without family, without attachment to a professional milieu, without an established space, without history – uprooted people."[17]

What defines democracy proper is the immersion in this immaterial element and the fusion with its texture in all its complexity, the opening to the contours of this element in its diversity and plurality, the tendency to accompany its movement in its unpredictability, unlike totalitarian domination which negates the specificity of the human element by identifying it with matter, doing it violence to the point of risking its utter destruction. Seeking through its will for omnipotence to pass as a power for constructing or organizing the human element, totalitarian domination subordinates the properly human to a rule or to a homogeneous norm, in contempt of the non-identical. Is this not what Adorno has in mind when he declares "the political form of democracy is infinitely closer to humanity"?

But it is not enough for democracy to respect the human element; better yet, it is sure enough within it, in this center of complications caused by the proliferation of links (those that unite as well as those that separate) – and amid the possible figures and combinations of turmoil (encroachment, entanglement, but also antagonism) – that democracy finds the source of its untamable power. It is by bathing ceaselessly in this reserve of indetermination that democracy becomes uncontrollable, savage, a destruction of established rule – not in order to establish itself as a sovereign power, but so as to welcome without compromise the ordeal of an instituting form that recognizes this human element that is itself savage (endowed with the "savage barbarism of otherness" according to Levinas). Democracy is predisposed, then, to engender new forms of relations, to let the heterogeneous happen, to be a "new disorder" that excavates a non-place (to borrow a beautiful phrase from Lefort), that is to say a new space or series of spaces of invention and evasion that, as it were, puncture the massiveness of the real: "Here the possible is reborn, an undetermined possible, a possible that will be renewed and redefined with each event . . ."[18]

Here the places of conflict and division are increased according to the multiplicity of human ties and their interlacement, so that the desire for liberty emerges as a form of resistance to the constant threat of domination. A chain of living paradoxes, the human element realizes in what happens, in the course of the event, the ontological play of exchange and human struggle, of friendship and servitude. Democracy, to the extent that one allows for its savage manifestation, is that form of society where the "flesh of the social" is in harmony with the style of being of the human element, with its unpredictability and resistance.

This proximity, this affinity even, brings about another question that I will merely mention given the difficulties it implies: must we only think the human as the ontological play that animates it, or should we instead interpret it with Levinas as an interruption of being, as a break with the effort of being, as a rupture with the perseverance in being – and in its wake the rise of the one-for-the-other, the responsibility for the other with all the disunity that this implies. In other words, should we not see the human element as otherwise than being, as if the metapolitical should be apprehended in the relationship between democracy and the event of the ethical? Can we consider that democracy – given its necessary relation to justice, to the responsibility of the democratic person, and given its non-indifference to those it does not know – would fail to heed the "otherness" of the human? Once the question is reformulated in this way, we may begin to think the relations between democracy, the originary division of the social realm, and the human element.

Moreover, can we be satisfied with this comparison between a new conception of the political realm and the principle of anarchy? If it is true that thinking the political as a site implies a deconstruction of the metaphysics of political order, the generality intrinsic to Heidegger's conception of the site caries dangerous ambiguities. In fact, the definition of the site – and therefore of the political realm – as that which brings together, seems to privilege mistakenly the unitary, and in this way covers over the division of the human city in two antagonistic desires. If the topological conception of the site is maintained, would not the political realm rather be the place where the originary fissure of the social, the division of all human societies, is first elaborated and instituted? For how could the principle of anarchy not take into consideration two of the essential characteristics of modern democracy, the separation of Power, Law, and Knowledge, and with regards to the question of place, the fact that the place of power is empty?

In the last analysis, can one accept this philosophically founded indifference and this doubt in relation to democracy? Is it in the name of a principle of anarchy that one can ignore the difference between a free political regime and a despotism? Should one see in this distinction a return of a finalist schema? If the becoming anarchic of action is action given back to itself – action becoming its own end – could action be engaged in a direction other than that of a free regime? A free regime implies the liberty of action, especially since democracy in its savage form, far from trying to be equivalent to a political solution, instead dismisses its very idea. In the quest for its identity, in the grip of indetermination, by virtue of its excess, democracy sides with the infinite movement of liberty that, according to Kant, "oversteps all assigned limits."[19]

An essential difficulty exceeds the weight of such correspondences and dissonances: can we consider savage democracy anarchic? Certainly the comparison helps us discern in permanent contestation, in the turmoil constitutive of a democratic society, an experience of being in time, "raw being," "vertical being." In the wake of the ordeal of being, savage democracy lodges itself in time, renews human struggles without the buttresses of tradition, awakens the instituting force that is always in excess of instituted forms, and is thus ready permanently to throw back into question that which presents itself as an established order. Nevertheless, what is its relation to law? Or more specifically, would not the relation of savage democracy to law make the comparison with anarchy problematic? In the case of traditional anarchism, the answer is clear: in its opposition to all forms of authority anarchism is exclusive, if not of right – the theory of social right can be developed in the anarchist framework – at least of law that, as an act of authoritarian sovereignty, would harm the spontaneity and harmony of the social realm. Is it the same for anarchy defined as the destruction of the foundations that have determined action? When reading Lefort's analyses, and more specifically his interpretation of Machiavelli, one quickly discovers how a certain conception of law can cohere with a libertarian idea of democracy and in this way belong to an anarchic constellation, particularly considering that the laws in favor of liberty are not laws like others. The Machiavellian innovation on this point consists of subverting the classic representation of law that assigns to law the task of containing and moderating the desires of the multitude through wisdom. In relation to free people, Machiavelli on the contrary considers the desires of the multitude to be productive. Far from being associated with moderation, this reformulation of law understands the excess of the desire for liberty as its condition of existence. Yet if the origin of law is to be found in the cravings of the oppressed, it is not for all that limited to it. Law in a sense takes off from these cravings and metamorphosizes into a desire to be, a desire that has no object, a pure negativity, a refusal of oppression. Linked back to the excess of the desire for liberty and disassociated from the traditional shackles of moderation, law becomes an integral part of the affinity between savage democracy and anarchy. We could even say it is the key to understanding their relation, since the only end pursued is liberty. "Thus in what appears at first sight like an outburst of popular passion, like an aggression against the State, '*modi straordinarii e quasi efferati*' (savage) one should read another excess, that of desire over the cravings, the only of a nature to found the excess of law over the established order of the City."[20]

Might we go so far as maintaining that law is "anarchic," devoid of an *arche* in the sense of having no origin or beginning? Once we relinquish the question of the origin of law (Machiavelli, for example, does not believe that law as such is a human product), might we think law beyond the autonomy/heteronomy opposition? Could not law, instead of being defined as the fruit of human will, be welcomed as the political relation always already present in human society, as the always debated stake of political institution, that is, as the stake of division and the confrontation of antagonistic desires?

At the end of the questions that have arisen along our path, we come before a paradox even more stunning than the principle of anarchy, and it is dazzling to the point of withdrawing from our attention at the very moment that it appears. The paradox is that of democracy itself, revealed by the "savage" qualifier. Democracy, so often trivialized and domesticated in order to be better trained, is a particular form of political experience that gives itself political institutions, so that it may endure with efficiency. Yet it simultaneously never ceases to rise against the State, and in such a way that its effervescent opposition has less to do with negating the political realm than with embodying, in a most powerful and paradoxical fashion, an incessant "new disorder" that reinvents the political realm beyond the State, and even against it. This disorder "is the work of a desire that maintains the question of the Unity of the State as unresolved, thereby forcing the leaders of the State to rethink its destiny."[21]

In order to open a path to this peculiarity of democracy, it is not enough to reject the ideologies of consensus; the very idea of conflict must be reborn, granted a maximum of power, so that democracy is redefined as the always possible emergence of human struggle – the surge of the originary division that brings with it the menace of dissolution, of social explosion. If the State, as Hegel taught, is as a system of mediation, integration and reconciliation – the Statist order has precisely as its function to integrate the plebes whose savage demands are foreign to society: "no moment within it [the State] should appear as an unorganized crowd" – the democratic revolution, by contrast, and to the extent that it is a revolution, is necessarily a movement against the State, a disorder against the State, against this deceptive reconciliation and this fallacious integration.[22] As paradoxical as this may seem, democracy is the form of society that institutes a human link across political struggles and that, by this very institution, renews its tie with the origin of liberty that is always in need of rediscovery.

Yet perhaps it is not so much with the principle of anarchy – to follow Schürmann's transitional thought – that one should compare democracy, but rather, without silencing the contradiction contained in the construction, to Levinas' analysis of the insurmountable opposition between anarchy and principle.[23] To think democracy in the framework of the principle of anarchy, is this not a way to tuck it in the bed of Procustus, to apprehend it mistakenly by the detour of that which remains an ideality? By forcing democracy into the corset of the principle of anarchy, rather than clarifying things, we actually deprive it of the power of adventure it carries, a power that outstrips all principle, all *arche*. In the logic of the opposition that he establishes between principle and anarchy, Levinas also refuses a purely political conception of anarchy. For him, anarchy proper is situated beyond the alternative of order and disorder: "The notion of anarchy we are introducing here has a meaning prior to the political (or anti-political) meaning currently attributed to it."[24] Indeed, a political conception of anarchy is no more than the imposition of a principle on anarchy.

For Levinas, anarchy reaches a realm that is much more profound, one that is pre-political, or rather one that is beyond the political and the ontological. Severed from the *arche*, the sudden emergence of the human as ethical event interrupts the play of being: "Anarchy troubles being over and beyond these alternatives. It brings to a halt the ontological play which, precisely *qua* play, is consciousness, where being is lost and found again, and thus illuminated."[25] As a disjunction of anarchy and the political, it is a disjunction of anarchy and any principle (anarchism, as we saw, is simply the substitution of a principle of reason to the principle of authority): "It would be self-contradictory to set it [anarchy] up as a principle (in the sense that the anarchists understand it). Anarchy cannot be sovereign, like an *arche*."[26]

A point that is again suggestive of savage democracy and its opposition to the State. For even if Levinas distinguishes anarchy from its purely political meaning, because otherwise it would pass through the ideality of a principle and contradict itself, anarchy does not imply any less turmoil, and outlines in this way a negative dialectic. Far from the State being able to enclose democracy as if it could be contained and determined from without, savage democracy, severed from any *arche,* reveals the limits of the State, and in so doing contests – and more, destroys – the totalizing movement of this authority that claims itself sovereign: "It [anarchy] can only cause turmoil – but in a radical way, making possible moments of negation *without any affirmation*. The State then cannot set itself up as a Whole."[27]

Such is the disorder that, as Levinas maintains against Bergson, is not destined to be another order, for savage democracy has an irreducible meaning inasmuch as it is a refusal of synthesis, a refusal of order – an invention in time of the political relation that overflows and overtakes the State.

NOTES

Translator's Introduction

1 "Postscript: 1976" in E. P. Thompson, *William Morris: Romantic to Revolutionary*, NY: Pantheon Books, 1977, p. 800.
2 The study in question is Abensour's 1973 doctoral dissertation, "Les Formes de l'Utopie Socialistes-Communistes." Portions of this work were published in two parts: "L'Histoire de l'Utopie et le Destin de sa Critique I," *Textures* 6–7 (1973), pp. 3–26, and "L'Histoire de l'Utopie et le Destin de sa Critique II," *Textures* 8–9 (1974), pp. 55–81. For Abensour's most recent thinking on Morris, see his "William Morris: The Politics of Romance," in Max Blechman, ed., *Revolutionary Romanticism*, San Francisco: City Lights Books, 1999, pp. 125–61.
3 E. P. Thompson, *William Morris: Romantic to Revolutionary*, p. 788.
4 M. Abensour, "Utopie et Démocratie," *Raison Présente* 121 (1997), p. 31. See also M. Abensour, *Le Procès des Maîtres Rêveurs,* Paris: Sulliver, 2000; M. Abensour, *L'Utopie de Thomas More à Walter Benjamin*, Paris: Sens & Tonka, 1997. For Levinas, see M. Abensour, "To Think Utopia Otherwise," *Graduate Faculty Journal* 20/21, 1/2 (1998), pp. 251–79, and M. Abensour, "l'Extravagante Hypothèse," *Rue Descartes* 19 (1998), pp. 55–84.
5 M. Abensour, "L'Histoire de l'Utopie et le Destin de sa Critique II," p. 70.
6 When all is said and done, the politics of *Democracy Against the State* are strikingly consistent with the project of the "Critique de la Politique" series Abensour founded with the Paris-based Payot publishing house in 1973. The series filled an evident gap in French political letters, introducing the French reading public to the major works of the Frankfurt School, while offering original critique in political thought: texts on and/or by Machiavelli, Hobbes, Étienne de la Boétie, Rousseau, the Kant-to-Hegel circuit, Marx, Leroux, Simmel, Hannah Arendt, Ernst Bloch, Giorgio Agamben, and so on. The statement of the series begins with a clear taking of sides: "The critique of political economy does not and cannot enclose the criticism of politics that was an integral and distinct project of the young Marx in the great texts of 1843 and 1844 [. . .] Beyond the object proper to it – the specific historical structure of the domination-servitude relationship – the criticism of politics

is defined: (1) by the refusal of political sociology as a process of driving back the critical questions raised by political philosophy: just as it feigns to erect a science of the political realm, it tends to make a science of politics; (2) by the choice of a point of view: to write on the political realm from the side of the dominated, from those on bottom for whom the state of exception is the rule; (3) by the questioning brilliantly expressed by La Boétie: Why is it that the great majority of the dominated do not rebel?"

7 J. G. A. Pocock, *The Machiavellian Moment: Florentine Political Thought and the Atlantic Republican Tradition*, Princeton: Princeton University Press, 1975. This approach is quite different from the one suggested by Althusser, who wants to oppose Machiavelli's "realism" to "all the political theories of antiquity" and "even the radical humanists" (Louis Althusser, *Machiavelli and Us*, ed. François Metheron, trans. Gregory Elliott, London: Verso 1999, p. 7). Althusser follows Gramsci in interpreting *The Prince* as a revolutionary manifesto for establishing Italian unity from the standpoint of the people, and accordingly for interpreting the modern Prince as the Marxist-Leninist proletarian party itself. For an overview of the issues involved in such a reading, it is helpful to consult Lefort's essay, "Réflexions Sociologiques sur Machiavel et Marx: La Politique et le Réel," (*Les Formes de l'Histoire,* Paris: Gallimard, Folio-Essais, 2000, pp. 286–382. Lefort here outlines the critical approach toward political reality common to Machiavelli and Marx as follows: (1) the rupture with idealist political philosophy, be it of a Platonic or Hegelian tendency; (2) a primacy of empirical history for knowledge, and the rejection of finalist rationalism; (3) the examination of real dispositions and interests in the determination of the political field, as opposed to the reference to a rational human essence; (4) a general critique of moral humanism as an illusory cover for violence; (5) the denunciation of Christianity as an anti-political force that distracts from the historical reality of a people's oppression; and finally, (6) contempt for the main body of the political leaders of their respective times. Like Althusser, Lefort takes Gramsci's "Notes on Machiavelli" as a point of departure for reflecting on the relation between Machiavelli and Marx. But he evaluates Gramsci's Marx-Machiavelli device in a way Althusser does not: "By feigning to carry the truth of the proletariat, by establishing itself as an institution analogous to those engendered by bourgeois society, by moreover imitating in its very structure that of an army, the party gives rise to an unforeseen alienation of the revolutionary class" (*Les Formes de l'Histoire*, p. 330). For Lefort, the implications are not slight, as the very determination of reality in the being of the proletariat is thrown in question once the subject of totality is historically dislocated, and the correspondence between theory and practice consequently dissolved. At the end of the day, Lefort leaves us with the following verdict: "Marx and Machiavelli are at the heart of our thinking because they destroyed the artifices of idealism to face a society without natural hierarchy, a power without legitimacy, a history without finality" (*Les Formes de l'Histoire*, p. 331). Though Lefort has bones to pick with the category of civic humanism (see his essay, "Machiavelli and the Verità Effetuale," in Claude Lefort, *Writing: The Political Test*, trans. David Ames Curtis, Durham: Duke University Press, 2000, pp. 107–41), this is now quite close to the "Machiavellian moment" put in play by Abensour, and to the political temporality of the civic humanism Abensour sees it as covering.

8 Maurice Merleau-Ponty, "A Note on Machiavelli" in *Signs*, trans. Richard McCleary, Evanston: Northwestern University Press, 1964, p. 223.
9 Hannah Arendt, *The Human Condition*, Chicago: University of Chicago Press, 1958, p. 222.
10 Karl Marx, "Critique of the Gotha Programme" in Karl Marx, *Selected Writings*, ed. David McLellan, Oxford: Oxford University Press, 1977, p. 564.
11 Hannah Arendt, *The Human Condition*, p. 33. Arendt is quite likely referring to what Aristotle outlined as the democratic ideal of "not being ruled, not by anyone at all if possible, or at least only in alternation" (which, far from suggesting representation per se, Aristotle famously understands as "ruling and being ruled in turn"). See *The Politics*, VI, ii 1317a–b.
12 Maximilien Rubel, "The Commune versus the State: An Agelong Dream" in *Rubel on Karl Marx: Five Essays*, ed. Joseph O'Malley and Keith Algozin, Cambridge: Cambridge University Press, 1981, p. 283.
13 Abensour evidently shares Maximilien Rubel's strategy of reading Marx against Marxism (Abensour in fact published Rubel's *Marx Critique du Marxisme* in his "Critique de la Politique" series at the Payot publishing house), but he simultaneously wants to avoid the limitations of thinking Marx simply as a "theoretician of anarchism" (as Rubel does in *Marx Critique du Marxisme*, Paris: Payot, 19 pp. 81–103). For a dialogue with Rubel from the standpoint of a "synthesis to be found today between anarchism and Marxism," see Daniel Guérin, "Un Marx Libertaire?," in Guérin, *Pour un Marxisme Libertaire*, Paris: Robert Laffont, 1969, pp. 93–9. A historically based critique of Rubel's attempt to make an anarchist of Marx is offered by Eric Vilain in "Rubel, Marx et Bakounine," in *I.R.L.* 64, October/November 1985.
14 G. W. F. Hegel, *Phenomenology of Spirit*, trans. A. V. Miller, Oxford: Oxford University Press, 1977, p. 387.
15 Karl Marx, *Critique of Hegel's Philosophy of Right*, ed. Joseph O'Malley, Cambridge: Cambridge University Press, 1970, p. 30.
16 Ibid., pp. 47 and 119.
17 Karl Marx, *Selected Writings*, ed. David McLellan, Oxford: Oxford University Press, 1977, p. 237.
18 Ibid., p. 238.
19 Karl Marx, *Critique of Hegel's Philosophy of Right*, p. 47.
20 Antonio Negri likewise takes constituent power in Marx as "the motor or cardinal expression of democratic revolution" (Negri, *Constituent Power and the Modern State*, trans. Maurizia Boscagli, Minneapolis: University of Minnesota Press, p. 10). Given Negri's own use of a Machiavellian paradigm to rethink democracy against the State, a certain overlap between the concerns of Negri and Abensour is well worth exploring. In particular, Negri similarly attributes the creative strength of the Marxian concept of constituent power to "the reduction" of the political moment "to a conscious, innovative, free, and egalitarian social activity" (*Constituent Power and the Modern State*, pp. 264–5).
21 Randolph Bourne, "Fragment on the State" in *Untimely Paper*, New York: B. W. Huebsch, 1919, p. 209.
22 Ibid.
23 François Émile Babeuf, *Tribun du Peuple* (13 April 1796), cited in Daniel

Guerin, *Pour un Marxisme Libertaire*, Paris: Robert Laffont, 1969, p. 59.

24 Alexander Berkman, *The Bolshevik Myth* (1925), London: Pluto Press, 1989, p. 341.

25 Niccolò Machiavelli, *The Discourses*, trans. Leslie J. Walker, London: Penguin, 1970, p. 113.

26 Stathis Kouvelakis, *Philosophy and Revolution from Kant to Marx,* trans. G. M. Goshgarian, London: Verso, 2003, p. 313. In his illuminating reading of Marx's political writings, Kouvelakis hesitates on this crucial question. In all fairness, a similar hesitation may at times be glimpsed in Abensour. See Michael Löwy's review of the French edition of *Democracy Against the State* in *Actuel Marx* (22, 1997), pp. 202–4.

27 See for instance Michel Henry's analysis of the 1843 Critique in *Marx: Une Philosophie de la Réalité*, Paris: Gallimard, vol. I, 1976, p. 56: "It is in this way that democracy differs from other forms of State. It differs precisely in that it is no longer a form." By form, then, is meant the "separation " of "organizing form" – form that asserts itself over and against content as it takes itself for the whole of that content. Democracy, in other words, resists political form in the same sense that it resists what Guy Debord would name "that oldest of all social divisions of labor, the specialization of power" (Guy Debord, *The Society of the Spectacle*, trans. Donald Nicholson-Smith, New York: Zone Books, 1995, p. 19). Poignantly enough, when Debord speaks of "realized democracy" as a form, it is rigorously qualified as a "disalienating form . . . that surveys its own action" (*Society of the Spectacle*, p. 154). This idea of a form that actively challenges the specialization of power is helpful to keep in mind when Abensour considers Marx's texts on the 1871 Paris Commune or when he compares "true democracy" to the revolutionary councils of Budapest in 1956.

28 Karl Marx, *Critique of Hegel's Philosophy of Right*, p. 121.

29 V. I. Lenin, *The State and Revolution*, trans. Robert Service, London: Penguin Books, 1992, p. 55.

30 Maurice Merleau-Ponty, *Adventures of the Dialectic*, trans. Joseph Bien, Evanston: Northwestern University Press, p. 207.

31 Hannah Arendt, *Crises of the Republic*, New York: Harvest/HBJ, 1972, p. 233.

32 Karl Marx, *Selected Writings*, p. 556.

33 Ibid., p. 559.

34 Claude Lefort, "Dialogue with Pierre Clastres" in *Writing: The Political Test*, trans. David A. Curtis, Durham: Duke University Press, 2000, p. 217. Abensour worked quite closely with Pierre Clastres in the 1970s, as well as with Claude Lefort, Cornelius Castoriadis and Marcel Gauchet for ten issues of the review *Libre*, which the four founded collectively in 1977. Pierre Clastres, who tragically died later that year, had a decisive influence on all of them through his work in ethnology. He famously distinguished between the modality of political power exercised within primitive tribal societies (directed against the emergence of the State) and the statist modality of political power wrongly identified with political power per se. See Pierre Clastres, *Society Against the State*, trans. Robert Hurley and Abe Stein, New York: Zone Books, 1987, and his *Archeology of Violence*, trans. Jeanine Herman, New York: Semiotext(e), 1994.

35 Karl Marx, *Selected Writings*, pp. 556–7.

36 Miguel Abensour, Preface to *L'Esprit des Lois Sauvages: Pierre Clastres ou une Nouvelle Anthropologie Politique*, Paris: Seuil, 1987, p. 15.
37 Karl Marx, *Selected Writings*, p. 554.
38 Ibid., p. 553.
39 Ibid., p. 555.
40 Ibid.
41 Miguel Abensour, "Les Leçons de la Servitude et leur Destin," Preface to Étienne de la Boétie, *Le Discours de la Servitude Volontaire*, Paris: Payot, 1976, p. XIV.
42 Miguel Abensour, "Les Leçons de la Servitude et leur Destin," p. XV.
43 Alain Badiou, *La Commune de Paris: Une Déclaration Politique sur la Politique*, Paris: Les Conférences du Rouge-Gorge, 2003, p. 20.
44 See, for instance, J. G. A. Pocock, *The Machiavellian Moment: Florentine Political Thought and the Atlantic Republican Tradition*, p. 292: "It is clear that arms and a full equipment of civic rights are inseparable: on the one hand, to deny men arms which are allowed to others is an intolerable denial of freedom; on the other, those who bear arms in the militia become morally capable of a citizenship which it would be equally impossible to deny them."
45 Karl Marx, *Selected Writings*, p. 544.
46 Ibid., p. 545.
47 Ibid., p. 548.
48 Étienne Tassin, "L'Action Politique: Une Réflexion Arendtienne," in *Les Choses Politiques*, ed. Miguel Abensour, special issue of *Les Cahiers de Philosophie*, Winter 1994–5, p. 168. The Arendtian conception of political action as presented by Tassin appears to radicalize Cornelius Castoriadis's concern for the social-historical, "the union *and* the tension of instituting society and instituted society." (C. Castoriadis, *L'Institution Imaginaire de la Société*, Paris: Seuil, 1975, p. 148).
49 Jacques Derrida revealingly speaks of "the coming democracy" as a "paradigm anti-paradigm" of permanent critique against all forms of extant ("democratic" or otherwise) political sovereignty. The "coming democracy" is thus not an injunction that lingers on the horizon but "the legacy of a promise" that solicits my action, beyond and against the boundaries of the State-form, "here and now" (J. Derrida, *Voyous*, Paris: Galilée, 2003, pp. 118–27). Jacques Rancière states quite simply that democracy should henceforth be thought of as the division of the egalitarian argument whose privileged, modern form is the form of class struggle itself (J. Rancière, *On the Shores of Politics*, trans. Liz Heron, London: Verso, 1995, p. 33).
50 See Miguel Abensour, "De L'Intraitable" in Dolorès Lyotard and Gerald Sfez eds, *Jean-François Lyotard: L'exercise du Différend*, Paris: Presses Universitaires de France, 2001, pp. 241–60.

Preface to the Italian Edition (2008)

1 "Les citoyens et les citoyennes de toutes les sections indistinctement partiront de tout point dans un désordre fraternel, et sans attendre le mouvement des sections voisines, qu'elles feront marcher avec elles, afin que le gouvernement astucieux et perfide ne puisse plus enmuseler le peuple comme à son ordinaire, et le faire conduire, comme un troupeau, par des chefs qui lui sont vendus et

qui nous trompent," K. D. Tonnesson, *La Défaite des Sans-Culottes*, Presses Universitaires D'Oslo, Clavreuil, 1959, p. 251. Our translation.

2 "Une loi contraire aux institutions est tyrannique . . . Obéir aux lois, cela n'est pas clair; car la loi n'est souvent autre chose que la volonté de celui qui l'impose. On a le droit de résister aux lois oppressives," Saint-Just, *Œuvres complètes*. Édition établie et présentée par Anne Kupiec et Miguel Abensour, Paris: Gallimard, 2004, p. 1136.

3 Karl Marx, *Les Luttes de classes en France. 1848–1850*. Présentation par Pierre Nora, Paris: Jean-Jacques Pauvert (Libertés 14), 1965, pp. 85–6.

4 "[C]elle-ci est une limitation des actions, celle-là un modèle positif d'action," Gilles Deleuze, *Instincts et Institutions,* Paris: Hachette, 1953, p. IX.

5 Maurice Merleau-Ponty, *Résumés de cours. Collège de France 1952–1960*, Paris: Gallimard, 1968, p. 61.

6 "L'institution est, à tous les égards, la catégorie du mouvement," quoted by Georges Gurvitch, *L'Idée du droit social*, Paris: Recueil Sirey, 1932, p. 664.

7 William Godwin, *Enquiry Concerning Political Justice,* edited by Isaac Kramnick, Penguin Books, 1976, pp. 252–3.

Foreword to the Second French Edition (2004)

1 Reiner Shürmann, *Le Principe d'anarchie. Heidegger et la question de l'agir*, Paris: Éditions du Seuil, 1982, p.107.

2 See my "Savage Democracy" and "the anarchy principle published in the Appendix of this volume."

3 Jacques Rancière, *La Mésentente, Politique et Philosophie*, Paris: Galilée, 1995, p. 51.

4 Ibid., p. 139. Or also: "Politics has no *arkhe*. It is, strictly speaking, anarchic. It is what the very name of democracy indicates. As Plato noted, democracy has no *arkhe*, no measure" (Jacques Rancière, *Aux bords du politique,* Paris: La Fabrique, 1998, p. 84).

5 J. Rancière, *La Mésentente*, p. 141.

6 Even if it concerns a problem of a different order, one must refer back to the text of Nicole Loraux, "Repolitiser la cité," *in La Cité divisée,* Paris: Payot, 1997, pp. 41–58.

7 G. W. F. Hegel, *La Société civile bourgeoise*, Presentation and translation by J.-P. Lefebvre, Paris: François Maspero, 1975, n. 3, pp. 54–6.

8 G. W. F. Hegel, *Principes de la philosophie du droit*, text presented, translated and annotated by Robert Derathé, Paris: Librairie philosophique, J. Vrin, 1975, p. 250–1.

9 Pierre Clastres, *La Société contre l'État*, ed. De Minuit, 1974, ch. I, "Copernic et les sauvages."

Preface

1 Michel Henry, *Marx*, I: *Une Philosophie de la Réalité*, Paris: Gallimard, 1976, p. 9.

2 Maximilien Rubel, *Marx Critique du Marxisme*, Paris: Payot, 1974.

3 Jacques Derrida, *Specters of Marx: The State of the Debt, the Work of Mourning, and the New International*, trans. Peggy Kamuf, NY: Routledge, 1994, pp. 31–32.
4 T. W. Adorno, *Negative Dialectics*, trans. E. B. Ashton, NY: Continuum, 1973, pp. 321–2 (translation modified).
5 "Das Räthsel des 19. Jahrhunderts" (The Enigma of the 19th Century) in Moses Hess, *Philosophische und sozialistische Schriften*, 1837–1850, eds. Auguste Cornu and Wolfgang Mönke, Berlin: Akademie Verlag, 1961, p. 175.

INTRODUCTION

1 Alexis de Tocqueville, *Democracy in America*, trans. Harvey C. Mansfield and Delba Winthrop, Chicago: University of Chicago Press, 2000, p. 6.
2 Ibid.
3 *Democracy in America*, p. 37.
4 Ibid., p. 7.
5 Tocqueville, Letter of 21 February 1835 to E. Stoffels, cited by J. P. Mayer in *Alexis de Tocqueville*, Paris: Gallimard, 1948, pp. 48–9.
6 *Democracy in America*, p. 663.
7 Karl Marx, *Critique of Hegel's Philosophy of Right,* trans. Annette Jolin and Joseph O'Malley, Cambridge: Cambridge University Press, 1970, p. 31.
8 The texts here analyzed consist essentially in the following: The articles published by Marx as a journalist writing for the *Rheinische Zeitung* from May 1842 to March 1843; the *Critique of Hegel's Philosophy of Right*, writtten presumably from March to August 1843; of secondary interest, the *Contribution to the Critique of Hegel's Philosophy of Right* and *On the Jewish Question*. These two essays were written in Germany and published in the *Deutsch-Französische Jahrbücher* (Paris, February 1844).
9 For example, John Maguire, *Marx's Theory of Politics*, Cambridge: Cambridge University Press, 1978.
10 Eric Weil, "Machiavel aujourd'hui," in *Essais et Conférences*, Paris: Librairie Vrin, 1991, t. II, p. 190.
11 Leo Strauss, "The three waves of modernity," in *Political Philosophy: Six Essays by Leo Strauss*, ed. Hilail Gildin, Indianapolis: Pegasus, 1975. Regarding the relationship with Marx, see also the article "N. Machiavelli" in Leo Strauss and Joseph Cropsey, *History of Political Philosophy*, Chicago: University of Chicago Press, 1972, p. 273.
12 Karl Marx and Friedrich Engels, *Collected Works*, III, trans. Clemens Dutt et al., New York: International Publishers, 1976, p. 201.
13 The exception is presented by Michel-Pierre Edmond (*Philosophie Politique*, Paris: Masson, 1972) who, precisely in order to avoid the Straussian framework of successive periods, is careful to distinguish between the "Machiavalizing of political philosophy" (chs. 7–9) and the "naturalizing" of the political realm which begins with Hobbes.
14 J. G. A. Pocock, *The Machiavellian Moment: Florentine Political Thought and the Atlantic Republican Tradition*, Princeton: Princeton University Press, 1975. In relation to this work, see also the remarkable essay by Jean-Fabien Spitz, "La Face Cachée de la Philosophie Politique Moderne," *Critique 504* (Paris), May 1989, pp. 307–34.

15 *The Machiavellian Moment*, p. 550.
16 It should be noted that, without pushing the point, Pocock relates the Marxian ideal of non-alienated humanity to the civic ideal of virtue, in the political sense of the term (pp. 502 and 551). His French critic, however, is much more explicit. With regard to the struggle between civic humanism and market ideology, he writes: "There is therefore no hiatus, and the proletarian and Marxist critique is the direct inheritor of the idea that the specialization of functions makes people lose their civic capacities and their virtue at the same time as it impoverishes their legal status by ceasing to define them as political animals; this moreover allows us to resituate Marx in the tradition of European humanism, instead of presenting him as a solitary genius without predecessors." See Jean-Fabien Spitz, "La Face Cachée . . .", pp. 333–4. See also Ernest Grassi, *Humanisme et Marxisme*, Lausanne: L'Âge d'homme, 1978.
17 Karl Marx and Friedrich Engels, *Collected Works*, I, pp. 397–8.
18 Karl Marx, *Critique of Political Economy*, trans. S. W. Ryazanskaya, New York: International Publishers, 1970, pp. 20–1.
19 Nonetheless, a few exceptions may be noted: the German edition, *Kritik der Hegelschen Staatsphilosophie*, in Marx, *Die Frühschriften*, edit. S. Landshut, Stuttgart: A. Kröner Verlag, 1953, pp. 20–149; the remarkable English edition, Karl Marx, *Critique of Hegel's Philosophy of Right*, ed. Joseph O'Malley, Cambridge: Cambridge University Press, 1970; Maximilien Rubel takes into consideration Joseph O'Malley's interpretation in K. Marx, *Œuvres*, III: *Philosophie*, Paris: Gallimard, "Bibliothèque de la Pléiade," 1982, pp. 863–1018; Kostas Papaioannou's edition with his introduction, *Critique de l'État Hégélien*, Paris: "10/18", 1976, and finally Albert Baraquin's edition, K. Marx, *Critique du Droit Politique Hégélien*, Paris: Éditions Sociales, 1975. For more general considerations of this text see Jean Hyppolite, "Le Concept Hégélien de l'État et sa Critique par K. Marx," in *Études Sur Marx et Hegel*, Paris: Marcel Rivière, 1955, pp.120–41; Shlomo Avineri, "Marx, Critique of Hegel's Philosophy of Right in its Systematic Setting," in *Cahiers de l'ISEA*, S. 10, n. 176, August 1966, pp. 45–81; Michel Henry, *Marx, I: Une Philosophie de la Réalité*, Paris: Gallimard, 1976, pp. 35–83.

1 The Utopia of the Rational State

1 These writings are not for all that limited to expressing a "phase" in Marx's career – as it were, his liberal-democratic initiation to politics – for Marx himself decided to include some of these articles in a volume of his selected writings published in Cologne in 1851, and notably the articles on Prussian censorship, the freedom of the press, and the theft of wood.
2 Lawrence Stepelevich, ed., *The Young Hegelians*, Cambridge: Cambridge University Press, 1983, p. 211.
3 *The Young Hegelians*, p. 220.
4 Max Stirner, *The Ego and Its Own*, trans. Steven T. Byington, Cambridge: Cambridge University Press, 1995, p. 91.
5 Karl Marx and Friedrich Engels, *Collected Works*, I, pp. 382–3.
6 Ibid., III, p. 133.

7 Claude Lefort, "La Naissance de l'Idéologie et de l'Humanisme," in *Les Formes de l'Histoire*, Paris: Gallimard, 1978, p. 236.
8 Ibid.
9 Ludwig Feuerbach, "Necessity for a Reform of Philosophy," in *The Fiery Brook: Selected Writings of Ludwig Feuerbach*, ed. Zawar Hanfi, NY: Anchor, 1972, p. 220.
10 Ludwig Feuerbach, *The Fiery Brook*, p. 150.
11 Ibid.
12 Jacques Taminiaux, "Modernité et Finitude," in *Recoupements*, Brussels: Ousia, 1982, pp. 74–90. A shorter version of the following analysis of Marx was originally published in an anthology of essays in honor of Jacques Taminiaux, under the title *Phénoménologie et Politique*, Brussels: Ousia, 1989.
13 Ludwig Feuerbach, *The Fiery Brook*, p. 151.
14 Maximilien Rubel, "Marx à la Rencontre de Spinoza," in *Cahiers Spinoza*, No. 1, Summer 1977, pp. 7–28.
15 Karl Marx and Friedrich Engels, *Collected Works*, I, p. 191.
16 Ibid., I, p. 197.
17 Ibid., I, p. 198.
18 Ibid., I, p. 200.
19 Ibid., I, p. 201 (emphasis added).
20 Ibid.
21 Ibid., I, p. 202.
22 Ibid.

2 Political Intelligence

1 Karl Marx and Friedrich Engels, *Collected Works,* I, p. 295.
2 Ibid., I, pp. 304–5.
3 Ibid., I, p. 305.
4 Ibid., I, p. 241.
5 Ibid., I, p. 257.
6 Ibid.
7 Ibid., I, pp. 245–6.
8 Ibid., I, p. 306.
9 Ibid., I, p. 135.
10 Ibid., I, pp. 296–7.
11 Alain Renaut, "Système et Histoire de l'Être," in *Les Études philosophiques*, 1974, n. 22, pp. 254–64.
12 August von Cieszkowski, *Prolégomène à l'Historiosophie* (1838), Paris: Éd. Champ Libre, 1973.
13 Robert Legros, *Le Jeune Hegel et la Naissance de la Pensée Romantique*, Brussels: Ousia, 1980, p. 9.

3 From the 1843 Crisis to the Criticism of Politics

1 "A Contribution to the Critique of Hegel's Philosophy of Right" in Karl Marx, *Critique of Hegel's Philosophy of Right*, trans. Annette Jolin and Joseph O'Malley, Cambridge: Cambridge University Press, 1970, p. 139.

The Kreuznach crisis is multifaceted: in a first instance it is subjective, in the sense that it occurs during a moment of retreat after the prohibition of the *Rheinsche Zeitung* (March 1843) and before Marx's move to Paris (October 1843). At this time, Marx attempts to resolve the doubts that tormented him by writing a critical review of Hegel's political philosophy, an indirect way for Marx to tackle the problems of the present. Besides Hegel, Marx studies the history of the French Revolution and authors susceptible of informing political criticism: Machiavelli, Montesquieu, Rousseau, Hamilton. Yet the crisis is simultaneously objective, since the Kreuznach period marks the discovery of a specific crisis shaping the modern world: "The relation of industry, of the world of wealth generally, to the political world is one of the major problems of modern times" (*Collected Works*, III, p. 179). Crisis and criticism cohere, then, in that criticism attempts to address the practical interest that would resolve the crisis. On this point, see Maximilien Rubel, *Karl Marx: Essai de Biographie Intellectuelle*, Paris: M. Rivière, 1971, pp. 43–50; M. Rubel, "Chronologie de Marx" in Karl Marx,, *Œuvres* I, Économie, Paris: Gallimard, Collection La Pléiade, 1982, pp. lxii-lxv; Jurgen Habermas, "Between Philosophy and Science: Marxism as Critique" in *Theory and Practice*, trans. John Viertel, Boston: Beacon Press, 1973, pp. 220–1.

2 Karl Marx and Friedrich Engels, *Collected Works*, III, p. 176.

3 Karl Marx, *Early Writings*, trans. Rodney Livingstone and Gregor Benton, New York and London: Penguin Books, 1992, p. 201. The use of the term "democratic State" should be noted. Is it a neutral usage, borrowed from the vocabulary of the period, or does it signal that Marx had not yet conceived the opposition, discovered by the French moderns, between democracy and the State?

4 Ibid.

5 Ibid., p. 208.

6 Ibid., p. 209.

7 Ibid., p. 208.

8 Ibid.

9 Emmanuel Levinas, *Discovering Existence with Husserl and Heidegger*, trans. Richard A. Cohen and Michael B. Smith, Evanston: Northwestern University Press, 1998, p.116.

10 Karl Marx, *Selected Writings*, p. 37.

11 Ibid.

12 Ibid.

13 In his introduction to the *Critique de l'État Hégélien. Manuscrit de 1843* (Paris: "10/18", 1978), Kostas Papaiannou rightly evokes Victor Considérant in relation to the "French of the modern period" who interpret true democracy as the disappearance of the political State (Victor Considérant, Papaioannou, pp. 51 and 312). Yet Marx's allusion may very certainly be specified further. Instead of referring to the *Destinée sociale* (1834–1838), as Papaioannou suggests, Marx had in mind Considérant's *Manifeste de la démocratie au XIXe siècle*, which dates, significantly enough, from 1843. Without taking up V. Tcherkezov's theses – who concludes that Marx's text is "very scientific plagiarism" – we can only appreciate the game Marx plays with Considérant's text in the 1843 Critique. Indeed, we encounter in the *Manifeste* of 1843 the opposition false democracy/true democracy, connected to the theme of the political and social enigma. Moreover, this theme

is articulated in terms of appropriating, in the name of the people, the word of democracy, identified not with a class but with totality. Finally, we should note that "true democracy" for Considérant does not signify the disappearance of the political realm (Cf. "Manifeste de la démocratie au XIVe siècle," *Cahiers du Futur*, no. 1, Paris: Champ libre, n.d.).

14 Karl Marx, *Early Writings*, p. 209.

4 A Reading Hypothesis

1 Leo Strauss, *The Political Philosophy of Hobbes: Its Basis and Its Genesis*, trans. Elsa M. Sinclair, Chicago: University of Chicago Press, 1963.
2 Ludwig Feuerbach, *The Fiery Brook*, p. 154.
3 See Henri Arvon, *Ludwig Feuerbach*, Paris: PUF, 1957, *The Social and Political Thought of Karl Marx*, New York: Columbia University Press, 1968, and Joseph O'Malley's introduction to K. Marx, *Critique of Hegel's Philosophy of Right*, Cambridge: Cambridge University Press, 1970, p. xxviii and following.
4 Ludwig Feuerbach, *The Fiery Brook*, p. 172.
5 Karl Marx, *Critique of Hegel's Philosophy of Right*, p. 8.
6 Ibid., p. 9.
7 Ibid., pp. 48–9.
8 Karl Marx and Friedrich Engels, *Collected Works*, III, p. 130. Written presumably in August 1843, this passage from the Kreuznach notebooks goes on to emphasize the eminently political character of the 1843 Critique. "Owing to the fact, therefore, that Hegel makes the elements of the State idea the subject, and the old forms of existence of the State the predicate, whereas in historical reality the reverse is the case, the State idea being instead the predicate of those forms of existence, he expresses only the general character of the period, its *political teleology*. It is the same thing as with his philosophical-religious pantheism . . . This metaphysics is the metaphysical expression of reaction, of the old world as the truth of the new world outlook."
9 Karl Marx, *Critique of Hegel's Philosophy of Right*, p. 9.
10 Ibid., p. 24.
11 Ibid., p. 30.
12 Ibid., p. 12.
13 Ibid., pp. 14–15.
14 Ibid., p. 19.
15 Ibid., p. 59.
16 Ernest Grassi, *Humanisme et Marxisme*, Lausanne: L'Age d'Homme, 1978, p. 50 and following. This original book on civic humanism and Marx also offers an excellent selection of texts by the Italian humanists.
17 Maurice Merleau-Ponty, "Note on Machiavelli" in *Signs*, trans. Richard McCleary, Evanston: Northwestern University Press, 1964, p. 214.

5 The Four Characteristics of True Democracy

1 Karl Marx, *Critique of Hegel's Philosophy of Right*, p. 31. In the German original the phrase runs as follows: "Die neueren Franzosen haben dies so

aufgefaßt, daß in der wahren Demokratie der politische Staat untergehe," Karl Marx, *Die Frühschriften*, Tübingen: A. Kröner, 1953, p. 48.

2 Karl Marx, *Selected Writings*, ed. David McLellan, Oxford: Oxford University Press, 1977, p. 215.

3 Ibid., pp. 564–5.

4 Emilienne Naert, *La Pensée Politique de Leibniz*, Paris: PUF, 1964, p. 21.

5 Karl Marx, *Critique of Hegel's Philosophy of Right*, pp. 28–9.

6 G. W. F. Hegel, *Elements of the Philosophy of Right*, ed. Allen Wood, Cambridge: Cambridge University Press, 1991, p. 308.

7 "La Juridiction du Monarque Hégélien," in Jean-Luc Nancy, *Rejouer le Politique*, Paris: Galilée, 1981, p. 55.

8 "Philosophie der Tat" in Moses Hess, *Philosophische und Sozialistische Schriften* (1837–1850), ed. Auguste Cornu and Wolfgang Monke, Berlin: Akademie-Verlag, 1961, p. 217.

9 "Socialismus und Communismus," in Moses Hess, *Philosophische und Sozialistische Schriften*, p. 198.

10 Moses Hess, "Socialismus und Communismus," p. 199.

11 Moses Hess, "Philosophie der Tat," p. 218

12 Ibid., p. 220. For an analysis of Hess's political criticism see Gérard Bensussan, *Moses Hess: La Philosophie, le Socialisme,* Paris: Presses Universitaires de France, 1985, pp. 99–105.

13 Spinoza, *Theological-Political Treatise*, trans. Samuel Shirley, Indianapolis and Cambridge: Hackett, 1998, ch. XVI, pp. 183, 185.

14 Ibid.

15 Lucien Mugnier-Polliet, *La Philosophie Politique de Spinoza*, Paris: Vrin, 1976, p. 250.

16 Karl Marx, *Critique of Hegel's Philosophy of Right*, p. 30.

17 Hannah Arendt, *The Human Condition*, Chicago: University of Chicago Press: 1973, pp. 22–3, 28 ff.

18 Karl Marx, *Critique of Hegel's Philosophy of Right*, p. 81.

19 Ibid.

20 Ibid., p. 112.

21 Ibid., p. 81.

22 Ibid., p. 77.

23 Ibid.

24 Ibid., p. 29.

25 Ibid.

26 Ibid.

27 Ibid.

28 Ibid.

29 Ibid.

30 William Godwin, *Enquiry Concerning Political Justice*, Middlesex: Penguin Books, 1976: p. 252.

31 Karl Marx, *Critique of Hegel's Philosophy of Right*, p. 58.

32 Jean-Jacques Rousseau, *Politics and the Arts: Letter to M. D'Alembert on the Theater*, trans. Allan Bloom, Ithaca: Cornell University Press, p. 126.

33 Moses Hess, "Philosophie der Tat," p. 219.

34 Ibid.

35 Ludwig Feuerbach, "Preliminary Theses on the Reform of Philosophy" in *The Fiery Brook*, p. 162.

36 Jacques Taminiaux, *Recoupements*, Brussels: Oussia, 1982, p. 9.
37 Karl Marx, *Critique of Hegel's Philosophy of Right*, p. 30.
38 Ibid.
39 Ibid., p. 58.
40 Ibid., p. 31.
41 Ibid.
42 Ibid.
43 Ibid., p. 30.
44 Ludwig Feuerbach, *The Essence of Christianity*, trans. George Eliot, Amherst: Prometheus Books, 1989, p. 31.
45 While I agree with Shlomo Avineri when he invites us not to confuse "true democracy" with a radical democracy of a Jacobin kind (one that conceives the State as a unifying form), I cannot agree with his analysis once he identifies and thereby confuses "true democracy" with communism, (with the upheaval of community in the site and place of the State). Marx's thought is in this way simplified: the disappearance of the political State in the sense meant by Marx is presented by Avineri as a pure and simple disappearance of the State, since he fails to make the distinction between an organizing form and a particular moment. See Shlomo Avineri, "Marx's Critique of Hegel's *Philosophy of Right* in its Systematic Setting," in *Cahiers de l'ISEA*, S. 10, n. 176, August 1966, pp. 74–7. See also Avineri's *The Social and Political Thought of Karl Marx*, Cambridge: Cambridge University Press, 1968, pp. 34–5.
46 For a criticism of the constitutional State as formalist see Karl Marx, *Critique of Hegel's Philosophy of Right*, pp. 32–3 and p. 65; for a criticism of formalism in relation to bureaucracy see p. 46 and pp. 62–4.
47 For the 1844 project of a study on the State, see Maximilien Rubel's Introduction in Karl Marx, *Œuvres, II: Économie*, Paris: Gallimard, "Bibliothèque de la Pléiade," 1968, pp. lxviii-lxix.
48 Karl Marx, *Critique of Hegel's Philosophy of Right*, p. 31.
49 Ibid., p. 80.
50 Ibid., pp. 31–2.
51 Ibid., p. 114. (Translator's note: I have modified the translation of Marx's phrase "wiedergefundenen Staatsgesinnung" according to the meaning in this context. See Marx, "Kritik der Hegelschen Staatsphilosophie," in *Die Frühschriften*, Tübingen: A. Kröner, 1953, p. 134.)
52 In this sense the critique of political emancipation that constitutes the object of *The Jewish Question* is already addressed by the 1843 Critique and we may thus see "true democracy" as a figure of human emancipation.
53 Ludwig Feuerbach, "Principles of the Philosophy of the Future" (1843) in *The Fiery Brook*, p. 240.
54 Claude Lefort, "Entretien avec François Roustang" in *Psychanalystes: Revue du Collège de Psychanalystes*, no. 9, October 1983, p. 42.
55 Claude Lefort describes "this model of a new division of power . . . between organs that we could call politico-political and politico-economic" in his essay, "Une Autre Révolution," in *Libre*, no. 1, 1977, pp. 102–7.

6 True Democracy and Modernity

1 Claude Lefort, *L'invention démocratique*, Paris: Fayard, 1981; see also "The Question of Democracy" in Claude Lefort, *Democracy and Political Theory*, trans. David Macey, Minneapolis: University of Minnesota Press, pp. 9–21.
2 Claude Lefort, *Machiavel, le Travail de l'Œuvre*, Paris: Gallimard, 1972, p. 480.
3 Niccolò Machiavelli, *The Discourses*, ed. Bernard Crick, London: Penguin Books, 1970, Book I, ch. IV, p. 113.
4 Montesquieu, *Consideration on the Causes of the Greatness of the Romans and their Decline*, trans. David Lowenthal, Indianapolis: Hackett, p. 93.
5 True democracy in this respect is placed in the tradition of modern subjectivity. Despite a change in perspective, Taminiaux's analysis of the continuity between the Marx of 1844–1845 and modern philosophy also holds for Marx's 1843 Critique. See Jacques Taminiaux, "L'art et la vérité," in *Le Regard et l'Excédent*, La Haye: Nijhoff, 1977, pp. 60–1.
6 Karl Marx, *Critique of Hegel's Philosophy of Right*, p. 29.
7 Jacques Taminiaux, "Modernité et finitude," in *Recoupements*, pp. 78 and 82.
8 Karl Marx, *Critique of Hegel's Philosophy of Right*, p. 9.
9 Ibid., p. 27.
10 Ibid., p. 58.
11 Bernard Groethuysen, "Dialectique de la Démocratie," in *Philosophie et Histoire*, Paris: Albin Michel, 1995, p. 185.
12 Karl Marx and Friedrich Engels, *Collected Works*, IV, p. 37.
13 "A Contribution to the Critique of Hegel's 'Philosophy of Right'" in Karl Marx, *Critique of Hegel's Philosophy of Right*, p. 141.
14 Karl Marx, *Selected Writings*, p. 586.
15 Ibid., p. 215.
16 Karl Marx and Friedrich Engels, Collected Works, I, pp. 164–5.
17 Karl Marx, *Early Writings*, pp. 277–8.
18 See Alexis Philonenko, "Étude Leibnizienne: Feuerbach et la Monadologie," in *Revue de Métaphysique et de Morale*, January–March 1970, no 1, pp. 27–8, and especially the following citations from Feuerbach: "The idea that matter is the general link between monads – one of the most sublime and profound intuitions of the Leibnizian philosophy . . ." Feuerbach specifies that matter is the source of all distress and joy and that this is what makes it the universal link between souls – "for distress as much as joy links beings between themselves."
19 Karl Marx and Friedrich Engels, *Collected Works*, III, p. 280. Emphasis mine.
20 Ibid., III, pp. 296–7.
21 Ibid., IV, p. 666. These notes appear under the title of "Draft Plan for a Work on the Modern State." Regarding this 1845 project, see Maximilien Rubel's Introduction in Karl Marx, *Œuvres*, vol. IV, *Politique*, I, Paris: Gallimard, 1994, p. xciv.
22 According to Maximilien Rubel (Introduction, *Politique*, I, pp. xlvii-xlviii): "The multitude of articles written for several English and American journals, in continuation with those published in the German periodicals . . . constitute in their totality at once a rich material basis and a doctrinal exposé of

the criticism of politics in gestation. Together with the *Critique of Political Economy*, it may even be considered as Marx's real work, as writings in which the science of the real and the conception of the possible are reunited."

23 Karl Marx, *Selected Writings*, p. 539.
24 Ibid., p. 543 (translation modified).
25 Ibid., p. 552.
26 Ibid.
27 Ibid., p. 548.
28 Karl Marx, *Critique of Hegel's Philosophy of Right,* p. 121.
29 For the communalist tradition, see Gustave Lefrançais, *Étude sur le Mouvement Communaliste à Paris en 1871*, Neuchâtel: G. Guillaume et Fils, 1871.

Conclusion

1 Georg Simmel, "The Conflict of Modern Culture," in *Simmel on Culture*, eds. David Frisby and Mike Featherstone, London: Sage Publications, pp. 89–90.
2 *Simmel on Culture,* p. 76.
3 Georg Simmel, *Sociologie et Epistémologie*, introduction by Julien Freund, Paris: PUF, 1981, p. 43.
4 Jacques Rancière, *Disagreement: Philosophy and Politics*, trans. Julie Rose, Minneapolis and London: University of Minnesota Press, 1999, pp. 101–2.
5 Walter Leisner, "L'État de droit, une contradiction?," in *Recueil d'Études en Hommage à Charles Eisenmann*, Paris: Éditions Cujas, 1977, p. 67.
6 W. Leisner, "L'État de droit, une contradiction?", p. 79.
7 Anne-Marie Roviello, "L'État de droit et la question du formalisme," in Les Choses Politiques, ed. M. Abensour, special issue of *Les Cahiers de Philosophie,* Winter 1994–5, pp. 103–23, and notably p. 112 and following.
8 See my essay, "'Savage Democracy' and the 'Principle of Anarchy,'" published in the appendix of this volume.
9 See Marc Richir, *Du Sublime en Politique*, Paris: Payot, 1991.
10 G. W. F. Hegel, *Elements of the Philosophy of Right*, trans. H. B. Nisbet, Cambridge: Cambridge University Press, 1993, § 303, p. 344.
11 Emmanuel Levinas, *Otherwise than Being or Beyond Essence*, trans. Alphonso Lingis, Boston: M. Nijhoff, 1991, p. 194.

"Savage Democracy" and the "Principle of Anarchy"

1 Reiner Shürmann, *Heidegger on Being and Acting: from Principles to Anarchy*, trans. Christine-Marie Gros, Bloomington: Indiana University Press, 1987.
2 Claude Lefort, "Totalitarianism without Stalin," in *The Political Forms of Modern Society: Bureaucracy, Democracy, Totalitarianism*, ed. John B. Thompson, Cambridge: MIT Press, 1986, p. 52.
3 Claude Lefort, *Éléments d'une Critique de la Bureaucratie*, Paris: Gallimard, 1979, pp. 10–11.

4 See Claude Lefort and M. Gauchet, «Sur la Démocratie: Le Politique et l'Institution du Social,» in *Textures*, 2–3, 1971, pp. 8–9.
5 See Pierre Clastres, *Society Against the State*, trans. Robert Hurley and Abe Stein, NY: Zone Books, 1989.
6 Claude Lefort, "The Question of Democracy", in *Democracy and Political Theory*, trans. David Macey, Minneapolis: University of Minnesota Press, 1988, p. 19. Translation modified.
7 Claude Lefort and P. Thibaud, «La Communication Démocratique,» in *Esprit*, 9–10, Sept.–Oct. 1979, p. 34.
8 Claude Lefort, *Éléments d'une critique de la bureaucratie*, p. 23.
9 Ibid., p. 28.
10 Claude Lefort, «L'Idée d'Être Brut et d'Esprit Sauvage», in *Sur une colonne absente: Écrits autour de Merleau-Ponty*, Paris: Gallimard, 1978, p. 44.
11 See Marc Richir, «Le Sens de la Phénoménologie dans Le Visible et L'Invisible» in *Maurice Merleau-Ponty*, *Esprit*, 6, June 1982, p. 132.
12 Translator's note: although the page numbers refer to the English edition (see note no. 1), I have modified for reasons of content or clarity some of the citations using the original (*Le Principe d'Anarchie: Heidegger et la Question d'Agir*, Paris: Éditions du Seuil, 1982).
13 Maurice Merleau-Ponty, *Résumés de Cours*, Paris: Gallimard, 1968, p. 144.
14 Claude Lefort, *Democracy and Political Theory*, p. 1. Translation modified.
15 Claude Lefort, *Le Travail de l'Œuvre: Machiavel*, Paris: Gallimard, 1972, p. 426.
16 Ibid., p. 725.
17 Claude Lefort, *Un Homme en Trop. Reflexions sur l'Archipel du Goulag*, Paris: Éditions du Seuil, 1976. No doubt one should understand "element" in relation to the meaning attributed it by Merleau-Ponty, such that "it was used to speak of water, of air, of earth, of fire, that is, in the sense of a general thing, in midway between the spatio-temporal individual and the idea, a sort of incarnate principle that brings a style of being wherever there is a fragment of being," *The Visible and the Invisible*, trans. Alphonso Lingis, Evanston: Northwestern University Press, 1968, p. 139.
18 "Le Désordre nouveau" in Edgar Morin, Jean-Marc Coudray [a.k.a. Cornelius Castoriadis], Claude Lefort, *Mai 1968: la Brèche*, Paris: Fayard, 1968, p. 49.
19 I. Kant, *Critique of Pure Reason*, trans. J. M. D. Meiklejohn, Buffalo: Prometheus Books, 1990, "Transcendental Dialectic," Book I, Sec. I, p. 200.
20 Claude Lefort, *Le Travail de l'Œuvre*, p. 477.
21 Ibid.
22 G. W. F. Hegel, *Elements of the Philosophy of Right,* ed. Allen W. Wood, Cambridge: Cambridge University Press, 1991, § 303, p. 344.
23 See in particular the enlightening note no. 3, p. 194, of Emmanuel Levinas, *Otherwise than Being or Beyond Essence*, trans. Alphonso Lingis, Boston: Nijhoff, 1981.
24 Ibid.
25 Ibid.
26 Ibid.
27 Ibid.

INDEX

www.ingramcontent.com/pod-product-compliance
Ingram Content Group UK Ltd.
Pitfield, Milton Keynes, MK11 3LW, UK
UKHW020142250726
13967UKWH00002B/816

9 780745 650104